CAMBRIDGE NATIONAL
LEVEL 1/2

Creative iMedia

Kevin Wells
Victoria Allen
Sarah McAtominey
Tony Stephens

DYNAMIC LEARNING

HODDER EDUCATION
AN HACHETTE UK COMPANY

Although every effort has been made to ensure that website addresses are correct at time of going to press, Hodder Education cannot be held responsible for the content of any website mentioned in this book. It is sometimes possible to find a relocated web page by typing in the address of the home page for a website in the URL window of your browser.

Hachette UK's policy is to use papers that are natural, renewable and recyclable products and made from wood grown in well-managed forests and other controlled sources. The logging and manufacturing processes are expected to conform to the environmental regulations of the country of origin.

Orders: please contact Bookpoint Ltd, 130 Park Drive, Milton Park, Abingdon, Oxon OX14 4SE. Telephone: +44 (0)1235 827827. Fax: +44 (0)1235 400401. Email education@bookpoint.co.uk Lines are open from 9 a.m. to 5 p.m., Monday to Saturday, with a 24-hour message answering service. You can also order through our website: www.hoddereducation.co.uk

ISBN: 978 1 5104 5720 1

© Kevin Wells, Victoria Allen, Sarah McAtominey, Tony Stephens 2019

First published in 2019 by

Hodder Education,
An Hachette UK Company
Carmelite House
50 Victoria Embankment
London EC4Y 0DZ

www.hoddereducation.co.uk

Impression number 10 9 8 7 6 5 4 3 2 1

Year 2023 2022 2021 2020 2019

Cover photo © only4denn - stock.adobe.com

Typeset in India by Aptara Inc

Printed by Bell & Bain Ltd, Glasgow

A catalogue record for this title is available from the British Library.

Contents

Introduction

This book will help you develop the knowledge, understanding and practical skills you need to complete your Level 1/2 Cambridge National Creative iMedia course.

Each unit follows the required topics in the course specification. Content and detail is brief in the less popular units, but key points are still covered.

Mandatory and optional units

The Cambridge Nationals in Creative iMedia qualification comprises 12 different subject units. Each unit requires 30 hours of study time, including study time for the final assignment. All students need to complete the mandatory units R081 and R082.

Award in Creative iMedia: Complete two units, including the examined unit R081 (pre-production) and the mandatory unit R082 (digital graphics).

Certificate in Creative iMedia: Complete four units, including the examined unit R081, the mandatory unit R082 and two additional units from R083 to R092.

Assessment: Examined unit and final set assignments

- **Unit R081** is an examined unit where you will sit a 1 hour 15 minute examination paper, which is set and marked by OCR.
- **Units R082** to **R092** are assessed through a series of tasks for a set assignment that you will be given. The assignments are set by OCR, marked by your tutor and then moderated by OCR.

All examination questions and set assignment tasks contain 'command' words. These tell you what you have to do to answer a question or complete the task. Definitions of the command words are in the OCR Marking criteria glossary of terms at the end of this introduction. Always check the command word before starting a task or answering a question. If you describe something when an explanation is required, for example, you will not gain full marks; this is because an explanation requires more detail than a description.

Once you have learned the required parts of the unit, you will complete an assignment to assess your knowledge and skills of the subject. It will be set in a vocational context, which means that it will simulate what it would be like to be given a project by a client or employer in a work situation. You will use the OCR set assignment for the assessment. This assignment will include a series of tasks that follow the same process and sequence of the unit, to explore, plan, create and review a creative media product.

Plagiarism and referencing

Your work for the OCR set assignments in units R082–R092 *must be in your own words*. You must not plagiarise. Plagiarism is the submission of another's work as one's own and/or failure to acknowledge the source correctly. Sometimes you might need to use a diagram or include a quotation from someone else or a website. If you do this, it is important that you provide a reference. Quotation marks should be placed around any quoted text. You should put the source reference next to the information used. In addition to referencing the picture, diagram, table or quotation, you should explain in your own words why you have used it, what it tells you, how it relates to your work or summarise what it means.

When producing your work for the assessment, you can use templates provided by OCR or others you find yourself. However, you must always decide for yourself how to present your information.

OCR Marking criteria glossary of terms

Accurately	Acting or performing within care and precision; within acceptable limit from a standard
Advanced	Being at a high level; progressive
All	All relevant as described in the unit content for a specified area
Appropriate	Relevant to the purpose/task
Basic	The work comprises the minimum required and provides the base or starting point from which to develop. Responses are simple and not complicated; the simplest and most important facts are included
Brief	Accurate and to the point but lacking detail/contextualisation/examples
Clear	Focussed and accurately expressed, without ambiguity
Comment	Present an informed opinion
Communicate	Make known, transfer information
Complex	Consists of several interwoven parts, all of which relate together
Comprehensive	The work is complete and includes everything that is necessary to evidence understanding in terms of both breadth and depth
Confident	Exhibiting certainty; having command over one's information/argument etc.
Consider	Review and respond to given information
Considered	Reached after or carried out with careful thought
Consistently	A level of performance which does not vary greatly in quality over time
Create	To originate (e.g. to produce a solution to a problem)
Critical	Incisive – exposing/recognising flaws
Describe	Set out characteristics
Design	Work out creatively/systematically
Detail	To describe something item by item, giving all the facts
Detailed	Point-by-point consideration of (e.g. analysis, argument)
Discuss	Present, explain and evaluate salient points (e.g. for/against an argument)
Effective	Applies skills appropriately to a task and achieves the desired outcome; successful in producing a desired or intended result
Efficient	Performing or functioning in the best possible manner with the least waste of time and effort; having and using requisite knowledge, skill and effort
Note on effective versus efficient: both express approval of the way in which someone or something works but their meanings are different. Effective describes something which successfully produces an intended result, without reference to morality, economy or effort, or efficient use of resources. Efficient applies to someone or something able to produce results with the minimum expense or effort, as a result of good organisation or good design and making the best use of available resources	
Evaluate	Make a qualitative judgement taking into account different factors and using available knowledge/experience
Explain	Set out the purposes or reasons
Extensive	Large in range or scope

Few	A small number or amount, not many but more than one
Fully	Completely or entirely; to the fullest extent
High	Advanced in complexity or development
Independent	Without reliance on others
Limited	The work produced is small in range or scope and includes only a part of the information required; it evidences partial, rather than full, understanding
List	Document a series of outcomes or events or information
Little	A very small amount of evidence, or low number of examples, compared to what was expected, is included in the work
Many	A large number of (less than 'most' see below)
Most	Greatest in amount; the majority of; nearly all of; at least 75% of the content which is expected has been included
Occasionally	Occurring, appearing or done infrequently and irregularly
Outline	Set out main characteristics
Partly	To some extent, but not completely
Plan	Consider, set out and communicate what is to be done
Present	1. Produce an exposition/résumé for an audience (e.g. at the conclusion of the project to demonstrate what has been done and the outcome) 2. Set out (project) aims, content, outcomes and conclusions clearly/ logically for the use/ benefit of others
Range	The evidence presented is sufficiently varied to give confidence that the knowledge and principles are understood in application as well as in fact
Reasoned	Justified, to understand and to make judgements based on practical facts
Relevant	Correctly focused on the activity
Simple	The work is composed of one part only, either in terms of its demands or in relation to how a more complex task has been interpreted by the learner
Some	About 50% of the content which would have been expected is included
Sound	Valid, logical, shows the learner has secured relevant knowledge/ understanding
Support	Teacher gives training, instruction, guidance and advice as appropriate and monitors activities to assist learners in tackling/completing their projects, ensuring authenticity and a fair and accurate assessment
Thorough	Extremely attentive to accuracy and detail
Wholly	Entirely; fully
Wide	The learner has included many relevant details, examples or contexts thus avoiding a narrow or superficial approach, broad approach taken to scope/scale; comprehensive list of examples given

How to use this book

Key features of the book

About this unit

Pre-production is about planning the production of your media product. If done well, it makes the production process quicker and easier, and creates a better product.

Introduction to the topic covered in the unit and the resources you will need.

Learning outcomes

LO1 Understand the purpose and content of pre-production

LO2 Be able to plan pre-production

Prepare for what you are going to cover in the unit.

How will I be assessed?

You will be assessed through a 1 hour 15 minute written exam, which is set and marked by OCR.

● There will typically be three sections, at least one of which will be based around a scenario.

A brief explanation of the assessment requirements of the qualification to help you understand what you have to do.

Getting started

What is a pre-production document and where is it used?

In small groups, discuss the production of a new movie.

Short activity to introduce you to the topic.

Links to other units

You can find further information on how to categorise a target audience in **unit R081**.

Relevant links to other units and learning outcomes.

Key terms

Assets: the content collected or created for the final product, such as images, sound and video.

Graphic: a combination of multiple assets and text that forms the final product.

Understand important terms.

Classroom discussion

Think of your favourite website. What features make it your favourite? What makes you like it?

Discuss topics and answer questions with others in your class to test your understanding.

Stretch activity

You are required to create a comic that can be emailed to readers and printed in large scale A3 for a sample poster. What file types would you use for each requirement and why?

Activities designed to test your understanding of the topic and take your knowledge a step further.

Group activity

In small groups, share ideas about settings and compositions. Use a digital camera to take digital photographs using:

1 different camera settings (shutter speed, aperture, ISO and WB)

2 different compositions and rules of photography.

Work in groups to discuss and reflect on topics, and share ideas.

Know it!

1 Explain the difference between *copyright free* and *royalty free*.

2 You have an outdoor project to complete at a public place. What planning documents and considerations do you need to think about?

Test your understanding with this end of unit task.

Assessment preparation

As part of this unit you will have learned about the importance of planning.

Some general guidelines on things you will need to consider when revising or working towards assessment.

Read about it

My Revision Notes: OCR Cambridge Nationals in Creative iMedia L1/2: Pre-production skills and creating digital graphics, by Kevin Wells (Hodder Education, 2017).

Includes references to books, websites and other various sources for further reading and research.

Acknowledgements

Every effort has been made to trace all copyright holders, but if any have been inadvertently overlooked, the Publishers will be pleased to make the necessary arrangements at the first opportunity.

The Publishers would like to thank the following for permission to reproduce copyright material.

Adobe product screenshot(s) reprinted with permission from Adobe.

Microsoft product screenshot(s) used with permission from Microsoft.

Screenshots of GIMP software reprinted with permission from Gimp.

Screenshots of Serif software used by permission of Serif (Europe) Ldt.

Audacity product screenshot(s) reprinted with permission from Audacity.

Slashdot Media product screenshot(s) reprinted with permission from Slashdot Media.

Blender product screenshot(s) reprinted with permission from Blender.

Apple product screenshot(s) reprinted with permission from Apples.

Screenshot(s) from the National Archives website reprinted with permission from the National Archive.

The images in Figure 9.6 are from learnaboutfilm.com, reprinted with permission.

Screenshot(s) of GameMaker software reprinted with permission from YoYo Games.

Photo credits

Page 1 © gustavofrazao/stock.adobe.com; **Figure 1.2** © Petr Vaclavek/stock.adobe.com; **Figure 1.4** © skmp/stock.adobe.com; **Figure 1.7** © Yakobchuk Olena/stock.adobe.com; **Figure 1.8** © leungchopan/ stock.adobe.com; **Figure 1.12** © Dmitry/stock.adobe.com; **Figure 1.13** © trinetuzun/stock.adobe. com; **Figure 1.19** © ojtisi/stock.adobe.com; **Page 24** © Rawpixel.com/stock.adobe.com; **Figure 2.2** © sakurra/stock.adobe.com; **Figure 2.6** © bramgino/stock.adobe.com; **Page 48** © hutangach/stock. adobe.com; **Page 56** © irina_levitskaya/stock.adobe.com; **Figure 4.1** © Alexei Sysoev/stock.adobe.com; **Figure 4.4** © Gstudio Group/stock.adobe.com; **Figure 4.6** © Lucky1984/stock.adobe.com; **Figure 4.7** © Gstudio Group/stock.adobe.com; **Page 72** © Julien Eichinger/stock.adobe.com; **Page 94** © Miceking/ stock.adobe.com; **Figure 6.1** © The Ray and Diana Harryhausen Foundation; **Page 115** © sdecoret/ stock.adobe.com; **Figure 7.2** © scharfsinn86/stock.adobe.com; **Figure 7.3** © aey/stock.adobe.com; **Figure 7.4** © Anthony Kay/Loop Images Ltd/Alamy Stock Photo; **Figure 7.7** © dehweh/stock.adobe.com; **Page 135** © James Steidl/stock.adobe.com; **Page 148** © PicturenetCorp/stock.adobe.com; **Figure 9.3** © Patryk Kosmider/stock.adobe.com; **Figure 9.5** © skmp/stock.adobe.com; **Figure 9.9** © turbodesign/ stock.adobe.com; **Figure 10.2** © undrey/stock.adobe.com; **Figure 10.9** © LIGHTFIELD STUDIOS/stock. adobe.com; **Page 192** © Rawpixel.com/stock.adobe.com; **Page 202** © Africa Studio/stock.adobe.com

R081 Pre-production skills

About this unit

Pre-production is about planning the production of your media product. If done well, it makes the production process quicker and easier, and creates a better product. You will learn about pre-production documents including mood boards, mind maps, visualisation diagrams, storyboards and scripts. If these are detailed and created to a good standard, you will know exactly what you need to do and when in the production stages. This is a core unit that creates a foundation for every other unit in the qualification; the skills you learn will be used many times over.

Resources for this unit

This is the examined unit, so there is little opportunity to use computers and software applications in the final assessment (a written exam paper). However, you may use a range of these in your learning about pre-production documents prior to taking the exam, which may help you in your answers to the questions.

Learning outcomes

LO1 Understand the purpose and content of pre-production

LO2 Be able to plan pre-production

LO3 Be able to produce pre-production documents

LO4 Be able to review pre-production documents

How will I be assessed?

You will be assessed through a 1 hour 15 minute written exam, which is set and marked by OCR. It will be marked out of 60 and worth 25% of the total when working towards a Certificate in Creative iMedia.

● There will typically be three sections, at least one of which will be based around a scenario.

This provides a context for the paper – your answers should relate closely to it.

● The last section is often an extended response question that tests your knowledge **and** your written communication (use of spelling, punctuation and grammar).

Links to other units

Unit R082: The mandatory unit on digital graphics will use pre-production techniques in LO2, including the creation of a visualisation diagram. You will also apply concepts of using assets and any legal issues in an applied context.

All units (LO2): Concepts of planning, interpreting client requirements, the target audience, use of assets, use of resources, what the product will look like and relevant legislation.

All units (LO4): The need to review the product that has been created and identify areas for further improvement.

Preparing for the exam

You should think and learn about exam technique. This means answering the specific question and not just writing about something that you know. Marks are only given where your response correctly answers the question. Some questions will have an applied context. Your answer must relate to this – so include a reference or connection to the scenario as part of your answer. An applied context means it is similar to what it would be like in a real-world scenario when creating creative media. Bear in mind that it is only your first answer(s) that will support any marks – multiple attempts won't be given marks even if the right answer is at the end.

Exam command verbs

Identify: your answer just states what it is.

Describe: your answer must include some characteristics in addition to stating what it is. You could use words to express an overall concept, idea or need so that it is clear for the reader/listener.

Explain: your answer must include comments on the purposes and reasons for your statement; state *what* and *why*.

Discuss: your answer must give both sides of the argument.

Evaluate: you must apply your knowledge and understanding in order to arrive at an overall judgement that takes into account a number of different factors.

Justify: you must give reasons to support your choice or statement.

LO1 Understand the purpose and content of pre-production

Getting started

What is a pre-production document and where is it used?

In small groups, discuss the production of a new movie. Think about planning the hundreds or thousands of scenes, who says what, where they stand, what they do and what the camera shot will look like. Then think about a film poster for the movie – what do they put on it, where and what could it look like? A production crew won't make it up as they go along!

The purpose, uses and content of different pre-production documents

Mood boards

A mood board is a collection of sample materials, existing products and related **items** that represents the style of a new product that could be **created**. It can be a physical mood board with randomly placed pictures, samples and ideas, or a digital mood board with electronic images, documents, sounds and video.

A mood board does **not** show what a new product could look like – that would most likely be a visualisation diagram or storyboard, which are covered later in this unit.

Purpose of a mood board
- To assist the generation of ideas by collecting a wide range of material that will give a 'feel' for what is needed.
- To stimulate creativity and innovative approaches.

> ### 🔑 Key terms
>
> **Purpose:** what is it used for; the reason.
> **Items:** objects that are on a document.
> **Create:** you need to actually draw the answer.

Figure 1.1 Example of a mood board

Where mood boards are used
- As a starting point for any creative media project.
- A place to collect samples, materials and relevant content.
- As a constant reminder of possible styles.
- To share thoughts, ideas and styles among a creative team.

Content of a mood board

Images: from anything that is relevant or related, such as existing similar products, photographs, logos, screenshots from films, website pages, advertisements and posters.

Colours: especially those that fit the brief and audience or have been successfully used before in a similar product.

Text: with key words, fonts and styles.

Other materials: such as textures and fabrics.

Sound and video: on a digital mood board.

Mind maps/spider diagrams

A mind map or spider diagram is a way of recording and organising thoughts and ideas in a structured format. It is based around a central theme (or node) and has branches off for the different aspects using sub-nodes. There should be a logical flow and process when following any of the branches that are based on related aspects of the project.

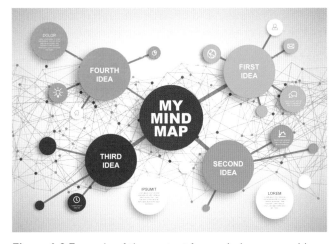

Figure 1.2 Example of the content for a mind map or spider diagram

Purpose of mind maps/spider diagrams
- To quickly record thoughts and ideas in a structured way.
- To develop and show links between different thoughts, aspects and processes of a project.
- To help the generation of ideas.

Where mind maps/spider diagrams are used
- With any project to show the range of ideas.
- To show the connections and links between different parts of the project.
- To illustrate all aspects of a project so that the range of activities needed for a work plan can be included.

Content of mind maps/spider diagrams

Central node: with the main theme.

Sub-nodes: with interconnecting lines or branches for the different parts.

Text: at each sub-node for key points, ideas, activities, requirements, and so on.

Images: can also be used on sub-nodes.

Visualisation diagrams

Visualisation diagrams provide a draft layout to show what the final static image media product is intended to look like. Examples of a static image would be a magazine advert, DVD or Blu-ray cover, CD insert, poster or website page. These are often hand drawn but good art skills are not essential – it is the concept, layout and content that is being illustrated. A good visualisation diagram is one that could be given to somebody else, such as a graphic designer, and provide enough information for them to create what you have in mind.

Purpose of a visualisation diagram
- To plan the layout of a static media product.
- To show how a finished media product might look.
- To provide a graphic designer with enough information to create what you have in mind.

Where a visualisation diagram is used
- For any static media image project, such as:
  - CD/DVD/Blu-ray cover
  - poster, e.g. for film, event or advertisement
  - game scene or display screen (for example, for the game environment or game menus)
  - comic book page layout

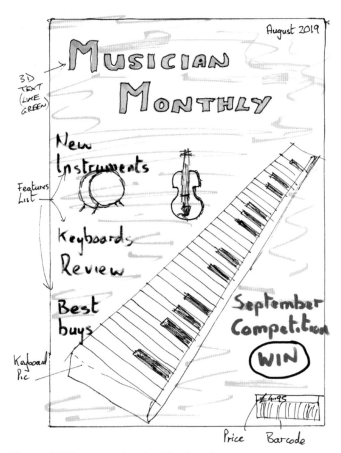

Figure 1.3 Example of a visualisation diagram

  - webpage/multimedia page layout
  - magazine front cover
  - print based advertisement (for example, magazine, newspaper or poster).
- In a proposal to a client.
- Within a production team to show what the intended product will look like.

Note that a wider interpretation of visualisations – such as charts for projected growth or predictions of where something is going – are not related to creative media. The context for the visualisation diagram should always be a draft layout for a media product that is to be created.

Content of a visualisation diagram

Images/graphics: showing their size and position.

Logos: of the client or organisation that it relates to.

Colours: (and colour schemes) to make it more eye catching.

Text: showing position and style e.g. the name of the product or service being promoted.

Fonts: to be used, which can enhance the appeal and interest.

Annotations: to provide more detail where needed.

Storyboards

A storyboard is used to show the sequence and flow of scenes in a moving image product such as a video or animation.

A visualisation diagram is for a single static scene but a storyboard will have multiple scenes that flow from one to another along a timeline.

Purpose of a storyboard

- To provide a viewer with a visual representation of how a media product will look along a timeline (such as a digital video or comic that tells a story).
- To provide a graphical illustration of what a sequence of movement will look like (such as an animated 3D character).
- To provide guidance on what scenes to film or create (for production crew).
- To provide guidance on how to edit the scenes into a story (for the editor).

Uses of a storyboard

- Any media product with movement or a sequence of scenes, especially along a timeline, such as:

  ○ video projects
  ○ digital animation
  ○ comic books
  ○ computer games (to illustrate the game flow or game narrative)
  ○ multimedia products (to illustrate the sequence between scenes).

Contents of a storyboard

Number of scenes: such as 12, 24 – in a numbered sequence.

Scene content/action: what is seen by the viewer in each scene so the storyboard will be made up of images, pictures and title/chapter text.

Timings: duration of the shot or scene.

Camera shot types: such as long, mid, close up (CU), extreme close up (XCU).

Camera angles: such as high angle (looking down), low angle (looking up), aerial (from a place high up such as a rooftop), over the shoulder (to show what somebody is doing).

Camera movement: such as panning left to right, tilting the camera slowly up or down, zooming in or out, moving with the camera such as walking or placing the camera on a track and dolly.

Figure 1.4 Example of a storyboard

Lighting: such as natural light, studio light and special effects. As an example, a narrow spot light could be used to highlight a person's face in a dark room; it may be that bright sunlight is wanted to stream through a window for a particular effect but if a cloudy day, it may have to be created artificially with bright studio lights.

Sound: such as background music, dialogue, sound effects (footsteps, car engine, telephone ring, and so on), ambient sound (wind, heavy rain, and so on).

Locations: such as inside (identifying type of room and layout), outside places and environments (street, park, forest, beach, and so on).

Camera type: this will depend on the type of product that is being made. If a video or short film, then a video camera would be used. If creating an animation using stop motion, then a still camera could be used to take the separate frames. If a digital animation or 3D model is being produced then it might be a virtual camera, which is a software tool to simulate what the view would be like. Many computer games use this simulated view as if it was a camera in the game world, especially first person shooter (FPS) games.

Scripts

A script is a piece of written work for a movie, audio, audio-visual product or screenplay. The format and layout will follow some conventions for it to be a script, otherwise it is more of a story outline.

A script is often the starting point for a media product before a storyboard is produced and any production work begins. A client or director will read a script before deciding whether it will be put into production.

When moving into the production stage, a script will be used by a number of different people. Each of these people will do their own script breakdown and annotate it with the information they need. Some examples would be to identify camera shots, cast/character lists, costume needs and sound effects.

Purpose of a script
- To identify the location where the action takes place (such as indoor room, outside street).
- To identify who will be in the scene (such as actors and narrators).

```
          SCRIPT - THE 42nd FLOOR

EXT. STREET LEVEL - LS LOOKING UP AT THE
SKYSCRAPER

Harry walks into the building

INT. CLOSE UP - HARRY AT RECEPTION

              HARRY
           (Confidently)
        I'm here for an interview.

              RECEPTIONIST
        If you take the elevator to the 42nd floor
        and somebody will meet you there.

              HARRY
           (Smiling)
        Thank you!

Harry walks across and takes the lift. MS of
him pressing the button for the 42nd floor.

LS of the lift door opening - Harry steps out
and is greeted by a lady.

              HARRY
        My name is Harry and I have an appointment
        at 10am.
```

Figure 1.5 Example of a script

- To provide stage directions for actors and production crew.
- To provide dialogue (speech) for actors and other characters.
- To support a pitch or proposal for an idea.
- To tell a story for a reader and generate interest.

Uses of a script
- Any moving image product with a cast/characters, dialogue (spoken words), actions and a timeline, including:
  - video products (advertisements, films, and so on)
  - audio products (advertisements, jingles, radio plays, and so on)
  - animation products (short films, web advertisements, and so on)
  - computer game with a short storytelling scene or interaction between game characters
  - screenplay.

Contents of a script
Cover: with title, description and author/scriptwriter.

Set/locations: where the action takes place; for example, INT. (interior) and EXT. (exterior).

Scene descriptions: for example, how the scene is set up, if actors are stood or sat.

Direction: or 'action' (what happens in the scene, any interaction between characters, what they do, and so on).

Names: of actors/characters (usually in capital letters, such as JOHN).

Dialogue: (speech) and how it is spoken (loudly, softly, for example).

Some scripts may have additional information:

Camera shot types: such as long, mid, close up (CU), extreme close up (XCU). A long shot is also sometimes called an establishing shot if at the start of a scene.

Camera movement: such as pan left/right, zoom in.

Sounds: (and sound effects) such as telephone ring, footsteps, Foley sounds.

Format of a script
The format and layout of a script should follow some standard conventions; for example:

- **Location:** Left hand margin.
- **Camera shot:** Left hand margin.

- **Direction:** Left hand margin.
- **Actor names:** indented ~2.0 inches from the left margin.
- **Dialogue:** indented ~1.0 inch from the left margin.

The use of standard conventions makes it easier and quicker to find the information you need, when you know what to look for. As an example, an actor can quickly scan a page to find their name which is in capital letters. Their speech lines will be shown underneath.

Know it!

There are five different types of pre-production document. Make sure you are clear about the purposes, use and content for each one.

Develop the skill of extracting relevant information from a script. Find some examples of scripts and list:

- the number of scenes
- the number of characters.

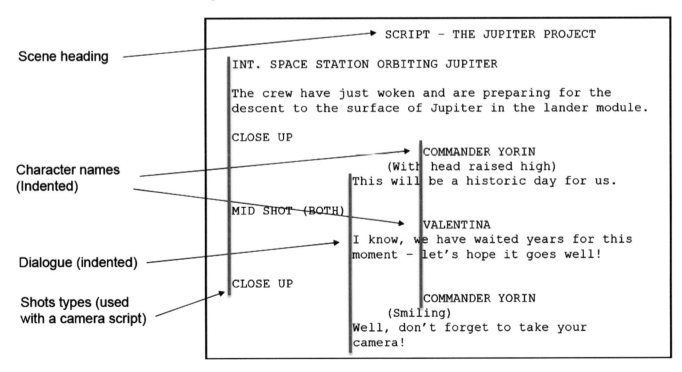

Figure 1.6 Script layout conventions

LO2 Be able to plan pre-production

Figure 1.7 Reviewing the client requirements

Interpreting client requirements and timescales

This vocational qualification aims to simulate the commercial world in how projects are commissioned. That means there will be a client brief and list of requirements that you will need to meet.

In a commercial project, it is important to meet client requirements and create something that is fit-for-purpose. Then, the client will be pleased with the outcome, happy to pay you, and keen to use you again. It's a bit like answering an exam question – you get no marks for what you know if it isn't relevant to what was asked.

Having said that, your *interpretation* of what they want allows you to use and apply your own individual ideas and creative thoughts on how to meet those client requirements. The first step is to summarise your thoughts and ideas, expanding on the content of the brief or specification.

Client requirements may be supplied in one of several formats:

Written brief: a (usually) short statement of what is needed; it is the most likely format of the assignments that you will complete in this qualification.

Script: a short film or animation might be defined using a script – your interpretation of this will be your script breakdown, which will extract a range of information; you could then begin to

sketch some ideas for the visual style before storyboarding the project.

Specification: a more comprehensive document that details all aspects of the required product. It is a more formal approach, possibly with signatures, dates and version numbers.

Client discussion: in addition to the brief, script or specification; it allows a better understanding of what is wanted, since you can ask questions to make sure you know exactly what the client wants.

Contents of the client requirements/brief or specification

Some or all of the following might be included.

Product: what type of media product is wanted, such as graphics, video, audio or game?

Purpose: such as to inform, entertain or advertise.

Content: depending on what type of product, the brief may require the use of logos, a particular image or story to be told.

Theme: depending on the purpose.

Style: this can be a house style to keep it consistent with the client's other products and services.

Genre: depending on the type of media product and its purpose; for example, a game might request a role player game or a video to be an action/adventure.

Target audience: perhaps an expected age range and gender, but without discriminating against any type of person or group.

Timescales: for when the product will be needed; this might be specified as a number of weeks or by a deadline date.

Constraints: can also include restrictions.

House style: to make sure the product is consistent with the organisation's own branding and recognised style.

Examples of genre in different media forms

Product type	Possible genre
Video	Action/adventure Comedy Thriller Science fiction Drama
Game	RPG Racing Puzzle Simulation
Music (audio)	Pop Rock Heavy metal Rap/hip-hop Classical

On some occasions, a client might approach a creative designer with a requirement to run an advertising campaign for a new product. The client might have some thoughts about what they want – a poster or video, for example – but, in these situations, your own ideas on how to reach and attract the target audience will be included in your interpretation.

Key terms

Primary sources: those where you obtain information 'first hand' from an original source and, therefore, typically more reliable.

Secondary sources: those where the information is obtained 'second hand', or where somebody else has already put their own interpretation on the original information. The accuracy of information might need to be checked.

Using research for a creative digital media product

Information about the product can be obtained via **primary** or **secondary sources**.

Primary sources	Secondary sources
Directly from the source (such as equipment manufacturer, audience)	*Indirectly sourced (such as forums, reviews and opinions from users)*
Autobiography	Biography
Original works	Commentaries
First-hand account	Second-hand account
Diary	History text book
Interview	Magazine article
Video footage	Encyclopaedias
Photo	Report
Relics	Other people's products
Official records	News broadcast

Producing work plans and production schedules

You will need to identify timescales for production, so that you know how long it will take to develop. This is an important piece of information for the client to know.

Work (or project) plans: structured lists of the tasks and associated activities – including timescales – that are needed to complete a project. A Gantt chart is often used to visualise these.

Production schedules: lists of what will be done on what day, date and time. For example, the recording of video for a film trailer might have a schedule that

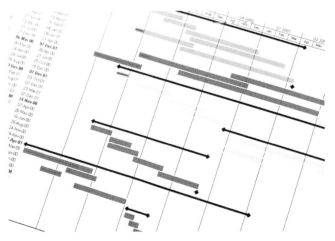

Figure 1.8 Formal work plan with Gantt chart

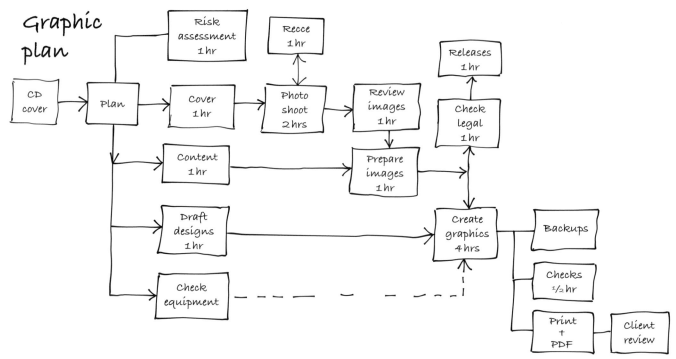

Figure 1.9 Informal work plans can still be detailed

defines what scenes are to be recorded on which days. All of the interior scenes might be recorded on one day and all the exterior shots on a different day when the weather is suitable. This is different to the work plan – which might have merely allocated a two-week period for all video footage to be recorded.

Content of work plans

Tasks: the different stages or main sections of the overall project. For any assignment work, these should include planning/pre-production, production and final review.

Activities: a series of things to do in order to complete a task. This is often the **workflow** for a task. If creating a digital graphic, it would cover the sourcing of assets, their preparation, construction of the main graphic, saving and exporting in the required formats. Testing can be another activity in some products such as websites and games.

Durations: the amount of time that a task or activity is expected to take. Each activity might be measured in hours or days.

Timescales: how long the different tasks or overall project is expected to take. A project timescale might be measured in weeks or months.

Milestones: key dates when a section is completed, especially for a first draft of the product or the delivery to the client.

 **Key term**

Workflow: this is the order that the activities will be completed in but can also be the sequence within a software application between importing assets and exporting the final output.

Deadlines: a date when something must be completed by. Try not to go past this date – there is usually a consequence for missing deadlines.

Resources: what is needed to complete the tasks and activities. Sometimes these can be included as an extra column in the work planning software. Alternatively, the resources can be identified in a separate list.

Contingencies: 'what if' scenarios, back up plans such as extra time or alternative ways to do things.

A work or project plan can be created for any media product, including:

- creating a comic book for R084
- interactive multimedia product (such as a website) for R085 or R087
- audio advertisement for R088
- video (such as a film trailer) for R089
- digital animation for R086
- photographic shoot for R090
- computer game for R092.

Classroom discussion

Imagine you have a client requirement to create an interactive multimedia product in the form of a website. As a class, use a mind map to identify what tasks and activities you will need to complete. Put the tasks in a logical sequence and estimate how long each will take.

Task	When	How long?
Pre-production		
- treatment	Monday	2 hours
- storyboard	Monday	2 hours
- shot list	Tuesday	1 hour
- check legal issues	Tuesday	1 hour
- recce & risk assessment	Wednesday	1 hour
Production		
- Record footage	Monday	3 hours
- Check footage	Monday	1/2 hour
- Save and store	Monday	1/2 hour
- Download	Monday	1/2 hour
Post production		
- edit sample	Tuesday	2 hours
- edit final video	Tuesday	3 hours
- reviews	Wednesday	1 hour

Figure 1.10 Draft work plan

For the purposes of this unit, you won't be using project software to create a work plan in the exam. However, the skills could be put to good use in other units, such as R082.

Here will we look at drafting a work plan on paper – this information could be transferred to a project planning software application.

Stretch activity

Imagine you have been asked to create a video advertisement for a racing computer game that costs £39.99. There will be a production crew to record the original video footage and sound effects, plus a post-production editor. People in the video will be spectators and two players competing in the computer game. Try putting together a production schedule for the recording and editing of the video advertisement over a two-day period.

The target audience

When deciding on the form and content of the media project, you should always keep in mind who it is for. It is easy to design something that *you* like, but the target audience might have very different expectations and needs. The first step is to identify who they are. The second step is to categorise them. Here are some of the categories that you should consider:

Age: be clear about the age group. This is usually a range, such as 6–12, 12–18, 18–40, or 40+. If you refer to the age group as 'everybody' it is likely to be considered too vague.

Gender: traditionally, this would be male and female, but also consider trans-gender and gender neutral approaches.

Ethnicity: we are a multi-cultural society, so ethnic groups are found on a local as well as national and international basis. Ethnic groups can be defined as a group of people that have a common background or culture, whether through race, religion or language.

Location: the main groups are local, national and international. The promotion of a media product might target one of these groups more than others, such as a small local music event compared with a national music festival.

Income: affects not just the type of product but also where the product is to be made available. Consider what might appeal to high income and low income people for a similar product – and where the media product will be found (is it somewhere that they normally look?).

Accessibility: refers to people with impaired abilities, such as sight or hearing. These are important to consider when choosing and designing your media product. As an example, a video advertisement with an audio description could be supported by text placed onto the scenes to explain what is being promoted. That way, anybody with impaired hearing can still see the information.

Beware of phrases and terms that could be seen as discrimination when discussing the target audience. It can be a sensitive area and social expectations continue to change; it is important to keep up-to-date.

Key terms

Resources: covers hardware, software and people.

Hardware: the equipment to be used, such as computer, display, tablet.

Software: what programs or applications can be used to create the pre-production documents, which is different to the software used for reports or web research.

Hardware, software and techniques for pre-production

Resources are defined as the **hardware**, **software** and equipment across the different units in this qualification. For the purposes of R081 Pre-production, the hardware and software are for use in creating pre-production documents and not the final media products such as a digital graphic, video or website.

To create pre-production documents you use the hardware and software resources to create the original pre-production document in a digital or electronic format. The work is then saved using a suitable file name and file format.

Sometimes the pre-production documents have not been created digitally, and you will have to produce a digital or electronic version from a hand-drawn or other paper-based document, such as a physical mood board with pictures. Digitising techniques include photographing or scanning the documents, which then allow you to distribute digital versions quickly and easily.

Hardware devices and equipment to create or digitise pre-production documents

- Computer systems such as desktops and laptops (PC or Mac), and tablets, such as iPads.
- Computer peripherals (keyboard, mouse, track pad, graphics tablet, display monitor, microphone, speakers, and so on).
- Imaging devices (digital camera, scanner, for example).
- Other equipment such as pens, pencils and paper.

Software applications to create pre-production documents

Image editing or desktop publishing: to create a digital mood board, visualisation diagram or storyboard. For example, Adobe® Photoshop®, Illustrator®, Fireworks®, Serif DrawPlus, Affinity, Pixelmator, Microsoft Publisher.

Word processor: to create a visualisation diagram, storyboard or edit a script. For example, Microsoft Word, Apple Pages.

Presentation software: to create a visualisation diagram or mood board. For example, Microsoft PowerPoint, Apple Keynote.

Web browser: to obtain content for a mood board, using online applications such as for mind maps. For example, Internet Explorer, Edge, Safari, Firefox, Chrome.

Dedicated software applications: examples include 'Freemind' for mind maps, 'Storyboard That', Toon Boom Storyboard Pro.

Spreadsheet applications: examples such as Microsoft Excel or Apple Numbers would not be used to create any of the main pre-production documents. However, they are used in more general planning, such as to create work plans or log the use of assets.

Health and safety considerations

Recces

Media projects typically use recces for outside locations for filming, sound recording or photography. Somebody will go on a recce (short for reconnaissance) to visit a location and gather information before production starts. They check what is there and note, for example, access, best positions, and environmental considerations. Within the media industry, a form is commonly used that has a series of questions and considerations.

Content of a recce
- Location (and how to get there)
- Access and car parking
- Lighting (natural, artificial, direction)
- Availability of power for lights or charging batteries

Location Recce

Completed By: _____ Date: _____

Location	Used for	Potential issues	Actions required

Figure 1.11 Example of a recce form

- Health and safety requirements (identify need for a risk assessment)
- Environmental considerations (background noise, people, flora and fauna, and so on)
- Any other potential issues that may arise
- A confirmation that it is suitable for what needs to be done

Risk assessments

A good approach would be to produce one of these for every media project and store it with the project files. The risks will vary depending on what activities you need to complete and whether any recording of material will be done outside. This would normally be completed at the same time as a location recce. The process of completing a risk assessment is as follows.

1 Identify the hazards and dangers.
2 Decide who might be harmed and how.

4 Steps of Risk Assessment

Figure 1.12 Risk assessment processes

3 Evaluate the risks and decide on precautions to be taken.
4 Record your findings and implement them.
5 Review your assessment and update, if necessary, through the project.

Risk assessments can be completed using a standard form or template. These must be stored to cover you and the organisation you work for. They will be your defence if things were to go wrong and somebody was injured.

Safe working practices

Safe working practices are closely related to risk assessments. Some basic ones cover the following.

Using computers
- Chair height
- Seating position
- Distance from screen to eyes
- Comfortable position for keyboard and mouse

Working at heights
- Filming
- Photography

Working with electricity
- Cable safety on the ground (trip hazards)
- Location

Working with heavy equipment
- Lifting
- Moving
- Setting up

Legislation in creative media production

There are several areas of legislation that you need to know about. These are:

- copyrighted material
- intellectual property
- certification and classification
- data protection
- privacy
- defamation.

Symbol	©	™	®
Meaning	Copyright	Trademark	Registered

Copyright, trademarks and intellectual property

Copyright is a legal right that allows the owner to distribute, license and profit from its use, which is typically for a limited period of time. In the UK, that usually means 70 years after the author's death. Once the copyright has expired, it changes its status to 'Public Domain', which means it can be freely used by anyone. Sometimes the internet is referred to as the public domain as in 'freely accessible to the public', but this is different to having a more formal 'Public Domain' status. The use of this phrase has two meanings and can easily be misunderstood. Note that the copyright owner is not always the original author or creator, since copyright can be transferred.

Trademarks are used to identify an organisation or product; their use is protected by law. The general rule is that these should not be displayed in a graphic without permission from the trademark holder. Logos are a typical example.

Intellectual property (IP) is a piece of work, idea or an invention, which may at some point be protected by copyright, trademark or patent. The concept of copyrighting an idea is becoming an increasingly big issue with the internet.

In short, inventions are usually protected by patent applications, ideas by intellectual property and materials by copyright.

Royalty free means that the work can be used without the need to pay royalties (a fee) each time. However, the work is most likely to be copyrighted. Note that royalty free is different to copyright free.

Regarding the use of assets, the best approach is to assume that any published content is protected by copyright. Some owners of that copyright might decide to make it free for use but that doesn't mean there is no copyright.

Published content includes:

- all content on the internet
- photographs
- images and graphics
- books and magazines
- music
- movies.

To use published content, you must:

- contact the owner
- ask for permission to use it
- be prepared to pay a fee.

You cannot get around copyright by creating your own version of somebody else's work (by tracing around it, photographing it or changing it beyond recognition, for example). Copyright protection is there to prevent other people from benefitting from someone's work.

Creative Commons (CC) is a licence agreement set by the creator; it allows you to use that person's copyrighted resources. There are different types of CC licence:

- **CC BY:** You can use, as long as you quote the source.
- **CC BY NC:** You can use, as long as you quote the source, and as long as it is for non-commercial purposes (in other words, you cannot profit from its use).

Other licences and considerations:

GFDL is a share-alike licence used by Wikipedia and others.

Certification and classification

Different countries have laws on what can be seen and shown.

Certification is the process of informing the audience broadly on the suitability of content. It is an important consideration when thinking about the target audience.

Censorship is when artists/filmmakers are not allowed to show their complete work.

Factors that affect the classification according to age ratings include:

- violence
- strong language
- scenes of a sexual nature.

Certification and classification are covered differently depending on the type of media product. The two types that you should know about are:

Films: BBFC (British Board of Film Classification). Ratings are U, PG, 12, 12A, 15 and 18.

Computer games: PEGI (Pan European Game Information). Ratings are 3, 7, 12, 16 and 18.

Data protection and GDPR

The principles of data protection have been around since the Data Protection Act (1998) with a number of amendments since then.

The original eight principles for data protection are:

1 fairly and lawfully processed
2 processed for limited purposes
3 adequate, relevant and not excessive
4 accurate
5 not kept for longer than is necessary
6 processed in line with your rights
7 secure
8 not transferred to other countries without adequate protection.

In May 2018, GDPR (the General Data Protection Regulations) came into force; it covers seven key principles:

1 lawfulness, fairness and transparency
2 purpose limitation
3 data minimisation
4 accuracy
5 storage limitation
6 integrity and confidentiality (security)
7 accountability.

The concept of data protection is covered in the new GDPR but adds accountability under principle 7. Note that GDPR is not explicitly mentioned in the specification but is included here to maintain up-to-date awareness of legislation in this area.

Other legal issues

One of the main issues in a media context is how people are presented to others.

Defamation: to damage the good reputation of someone such as by slander or libel. This is an offence under English Law.

Slander: to make a false verbal statement that damages a person's reputation.

Libel: to make a false statement in writing that damages a person's reputation.

Privacy: covered by the European Convention on Human Rights, which applies within the UK (there is no UK privacy law as such). This includes Article 8 which requires a 'right to respect for private and family life, your home and correspondence'.

Know it!

1 Explain the difference between *copyright free* and *royalty free*.
2 You have an outdoor project to complete at a public place. What planning documents and considerations do you need to think about?

LO3 Be able to produce pre-production documents

Getting started

You will have seen examples of pre-production documents earlier in this unit. Collect printed versions of these so you can make a mood board of the pre-production documents. Include a range if possible – some good and some very basic.

Creating pre-production documents

In this section, you will learn how to create each of the four types of pre-production document: mood board, mind map, visualisation diagram and storyboard. You will also learn how to analyse a short script to identify key information.

Note: In the exam, you will only be able to create the concept of a hand drawn mood board, or a hand drawn mind map, visualisation diagram or storyboard. However, you should know how to create them for real, whether in a physical or digital format.

Creating a mood board

Key points

- A mood board usually includes a wide range of image-based content.
- There is no set structure, so the content can be placed at random.
- The content does not have to be copyright free – the use of a mood board is there to show similar products and ideas which can help the generation of ideas. A mood board is not placed in the public domain – it is for personal or 'in-house' use only.
- The content should have some relevance or connection to your own project, brief or scenario – and follow a theme relevant to the client requirements.
- These can be placed on the mood board or re-drawn. Annotate the mood board with notes and comments to show your thinking.

Figure 1.13 A physical mood board

Figure 1.14 A digital mood board

Creating a mind map

Key points

The ideas and content must be linked by connections and have some sort of logical flow or breakdown between the nodes and sub-nodes. Mind maps are sometimes called spider diagrams.

Physical mind map

This can be drawn on a piece of paper.

- Start in the middle using a box or circle for the main theme.
- Draw lines in any direction for each different aspect of the idea. These are the branches.
- At the end of each line (branch), draw another box or circle with one aspect of the main idea. These are called nodes.

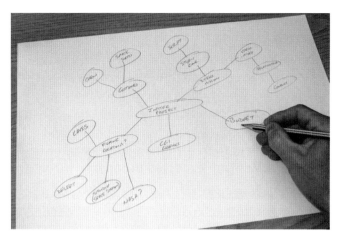

Figure 1.15 A hand-drawn mind map

● From each node, draw additional lines to expand on the ideas and aspects. These extra lines will connect the sub-nodes.

A simple mind map will have only a single level (in other words, nodes around a main theme).

A complex mind map will have multiple branches and levels with nodes and sub-nodes.

Digital mind map

These can be produced in different types of software application such as Word, PowerPoint and graphics editing packages. Dedicated software applications are available, such as Freemind, together with online mind mapping tools, such as bubbl.us.

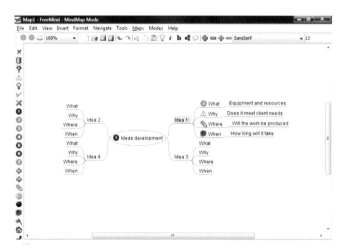

Figure 1.16 Mind map created using Freemind

Creating a visualisation diagram

Key points

● For the purpose of this unit, visualisation diagrams are for static (i.e. still image) media products such as print adverts, DVD covers, CD covers, posters, magazine covers.

● The visualisation diagram should illustrate what the intended final product will look like.

● A visualisation diagram could be used to show to a client or by a graphic designer to create the actual graphics.

● The layout should show where different assets and elements will be positioned and identify what colours could be used.

Physical visualisation diagram

You will most likely include a range of images, graphics and text. Annotations can clearly show your understanding of what content is needed and why.

Figure 1.17 Hand drawn visualisation diagram annotated with comments

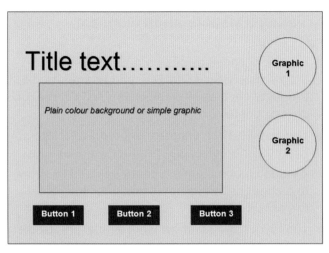

Figure 1.18 Digitally created visualisation diagram

Digital visualisation diagram

These can be produced in different types of software application such as Word, Publisher and graphics editing packages.

Figure 1.19 Hand drawn storyboard

Creating a storyboard

Key points

- The storyboard needs to show the flow of the story or sequence so that the viewer can get a good 'feel' or impression of what the final product will look like.
- Scenes should show the visual content and be supported by information such as camera shots, action and expected duration.

Physical storyboard

The content for each panel or scene will need visual images and annotations for duration, shot types, camera movement, dialogue and any action.

Digital storyboard

These can be produced in different types of software application such as Word, Publisher and graphics editing packages. You could start with a blank template that has panels for the sequence of scenes. Images can then be inserted into each panel.

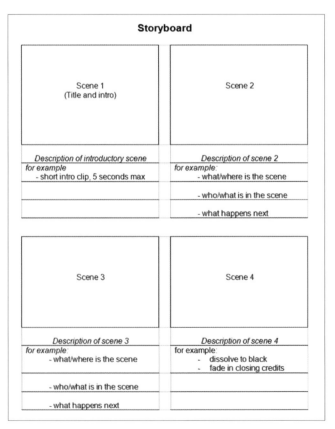

Figure 1.20 Digitally created storyboard

Analysing a script

In the exam you will only be asked to analyse a section of a script and not create one.

Key points

- The structure, layout and format of a script follow some conventions. This makes it easier to identify the different types of information.
- Analysing a script is called 'script breakdown'. From this you should be able to identify where the action takes place, what happens in the scene, the camera shot and movement, who features in the scene and what they say.

Typical script layout conventions

Font: Courier or other fixed width

Line spacing: Double

Scene: Left hand margin

Camera shot: Left hand margin

Action: Left hand margin

Character name: Indent 2", capital letters

Dialogue: Left indent 1", right indent 2"

```
                    SCRIPT - THE GAMING OFFICE

EXT. GAME DEVELOPER CAR PARK - DAY

Its early morning. Peter and Mary are walking into the
office.


                    PETER
          Hi Mary! Busy day today?


                    MARY
          Oh hi Peter! Yes - I need to fully
          test Level 6 of the new game by the
          end of the day.

                    PETER
          I take it that's a lot to do then? Do
          you need any help with it?

                    MARY
          Well if you want to volunteer that
          would be great but I know you have a
          lot to do as well. Paul will be
          working with me so I am hoping it
          will be fine.
```

Figure 1.21 An extract of a script

Know it!

Learn to recognise the layout of a script using the typical script conventions.

File formats and their properties

Pre-production document file formats

If pre-production documents are created by hand, they will need to be digitised (by scanning, for example) and then stored as an image file such as jpg, tiff or pdf.

If pre-production documents are created digitally, the file format will be influenced by the software that was used to create them. Examples are shown in this table:

Software application	Original file format	Alternative file format
MS Word	.doc, .docx	.pdf
MS Publisher	.pub	.pdf
Apple Pages	.pages	.doc, .pdf
MS PowerPoint	.ppt, .pptx	.pdf
Adobe Photoshop	.psd	.jpg, .tif, .pdf
Freemind	.mm	.pdf

The general rule is to save the pre-production files in the standard format for the software used so that it can be edited later. The file can then be exported in a format that can be viewed on a different computer system that may not have any specialised software.

Final media product file formats

Pre-production documents are used in the next stage of the creative process: production. This is where the media product is created, using the pre-production documents as a guide. The file formats for the final media products will be determined by the type of media product, intended platform and client requirements.

Here we will review file formats for these categories: images and graphics, audio and sound, moving images and video, animation.

Images and graphics

These are for still or static images i.e. images that do not have any movement.

File format	Properties and use	Limitations
.jpg	lossy compression to reduce the file size at the expense of image quality; used with digital cameras and websites	image quality with higher compression settings
.png	lossy compression and supports transparency. Intended for web use as an alternative to .gif files	not as widely supported (or popular) as jpg
.tiff	high quality lossless image files; used in high quality printing but losing popularity	large file sizes, which restricts transfer and distribution
.pdf	export format from image editing software which cannot be edited further; used with documents and print products with image content	cannot be edited directly – must use the original file format before being exported
.gif	small file sizes and supports transparency and animation; used in website pages for web buttons, logos and other basic graphics	limited range of colours and has licensing restrictions since the format is protected by copyright

Audio and sound

These are for sound files that can be heard through speakers or headphones.

File format	Properties	Limitations
.mp3	compressed file format that can be compressed using different bit rates, providing a range of options for the sound quality and file size; good for portable devices and widely supported	audio quality can be a limitation when using high compression in order to obtain small file sizes
.wav	uncompressed high quality audio files intended for Windows computers	file sizes can be large
.aiff	uncompressed high quality audio files and the default for Apple Mac computers	cross platform restrictions, not always widely supported
ogg vorbis	similar to mp3 but less widely used	not widely supported

Note: Newer formats that can be used for audio include .mp4 (a multimedia format for audio and video) and .m4a, which is for audio only. These are relevant but not currently listed in the specification.

Moving images and video

File format	Properties	Limitations
.mpg	video file format with lossy compression provides smaller file sizes for faster loading	compression can lower the video quality
.mp4	multimedia/video compression standard that enables high-quality video over low-bandwidth connections	
.mov	widely used for video files from digital cameras, providing good quality; originally developed for use with Apple QuickTime	
.avi	uncompressed video file format for high quality; often used when editing video before exporting in other formats	file sizes can be very large
.flv	flash video file, providing smaller file sizes; may be used with both video and animation products	not as widely supported and will be phased out

Animation

File format	Properties
.swf	compressed file formats provide small file sizes for fast loading speed online but not well supported by Apple platforms.
.gif	limited colour support but useful for short animations that are supported by web browsers
.flv	flash video file, providing smaller file sizes; may be used with both video and animation products
.mov	widely used for video files from digital cameras, providing good quality; originally developed for use with Apple QuickTime

Compression

The term compression has different meanings. For the purposes of pre-production skills and file formats of the final products, compression is the process of using compressed file types to reduce the file size. There are two types: lossless and lossy.

Lossless: no information is discarded or thrown away when saving the file. It retains all of the original information and quality but file sizes are higher.

Lossy: discards some of the original information in order to reduce the size of the file. This is useful for web use or to minimise the required storage capacity, at the expense of quality. A smaller file is faster to upload, download and share online. The amount of information discarded varies depending on what algorithm or settings are used (for example, jpg files typically have quality settings from 1–12, where 12 has the highest quality).

File naming conventions

Naming conventions apply to any documents and files that you create. The use of practical and descriptive names makes it easier to identify the content of the file. In addition to using a descriptive name, version control can also be included in the file naming.

Version control

Whenever documents are created, a version number or reference can be included as part of the file name, such as 'Ver_1'. Whenever changes are made, a new file name should be created that includes an updated version reference, such as 'Ver_2'. An alternative to a version numbering system is to use a date code for when it was created.

Version numbering examples

- Graphics_mindmap_Ver1
- Graphics_mindmap_Ver2

Date code examples

- Advertisement_script_26.10.2018.docx
- Advertisement_script_15.11.2018.docx

Know it!

Describe what pre-production documents would be suitable for:
1 a digital graphic
2 a website
3 an animation
4 a new computer game.

LO4 Be able to review pre-production documents

Getting started

It is important that you can look at your own work and identify its strengths and weaknesses. You can then think about ways to improve it. This learning outcome aims to develop that skill. To start, have a look at the work of other people. You can include some professional examples but locate some weaker pre-production documents as well so that you can find parts that clearly do not work.

How to review pre-production documents and identify areas for improvement

In the exam, you will most likely be asked to critically review one type of pre-production document. This means commenting on the

strengths and **weaknesses** in addition to how well it meets the client requirements. Keep in mind that the user for a pre-production document is not usually the final target audience. Pre-production documents are used by your client and a media developer, so your comments should be aimed at those people or whoever is identified in the exam paper question.

 Key terms

Strengths: the best parts about something; what works really well.

Weaknesses: the worst parts or those that need to be better.

Improvements: a description of what is needed to make the product better.

Key areas to cover in a review

- Do you understand what it is supposed to be showing? If not – why not?
- Could you make the media product based on the content shown in the pre-production document? If not, what else is needed?
- Check the original brief and client's requirements – does it do what was asked for?
- Document format: is it suitable for what media product is to be developed?
- Content: is it suitable for the intended purpose of the final media product?
- Identify and comment on the strengths, positives, advantages and benefits
- Identify and comment on the weaknesses, negatives, disadvantages and drawbacks
- Use technical language and terminology where possible and relevant

Areas for improvement

Once you have completed your review, the next stage should follow on naturally. Here you should think about and comment on further areas for **improvement**.

Areas to consider (depending on what type of product it will be) include:

- the user of the pre-production document; what extra information would they need?
- the use of colour; could these be more appropriate or complement each other in a better way?
- the range of content; could some of this be a better match for the brief?
- the layout; for example, use of white space, positioning of different elements
- the story flow; for example, for a comic, animation or video; what additional information is needed before you could record the entire range of video?

To complete your review, write a conclusion that summarises what you have written.

Know it!

In your review, you will be assessed on your use of written English; some marks will be for your use of spelling, punctuation and grammar. Keep this in mind and write your answer clearly, keeping your sentences well structured.

Assessment preparation

As part of this unit you will have learned about the importance of planning and pre-production when being involved with creative media projects. The three main areas covered by the exam are:

1. Knowledge of pre-production concepts, techniques, research, legislation and planning considerations.
2. Skills in creating and reviewing the different types of pre-production documents, whether mood boards, mind maps, visualisation diagrams or storyboards. You might also have to find and summarise information from a script that is supplied.
3. Understanding of pre-production concepts. You will be able to evidence your understanding by applying your knowledge to a specific scenario that is found in the exam paper.

Think about the individual performance you will need to undertake. Make sure you:

- know about the use and purpose of the different pre-production documents, suitability of different file formats, how to create work plans, legislation, health and safety
- understand how to apply planning techniques to creative media projects
- are able to create a mood board, mind map, visualisation diagram and storyboard, each with a good level of detail if aiming for the higher marks
- know how to review a pre-production document and its suitability for use by a target audience, which may be another creative team member and not necessarily the end user or viewer.

Read about it

My Revision Notes: OCR Cambridge Nationals in Creative iMedia L1/2: Pre-production skills and creating digital graphics, by Kevin Wells (Hodder Education, 2017).

Past papers from the OCR website.

R082 Creating digital graphics

About this unit

This is a mandatory unit for the Award or Certificate in Creative iMedia. In this unit, you will learn about the purposes, properties and planning of digital graphics, together with the tools and techniques needed to create them.

Resources for this unit

You need image editing software, such as Adobe Photoshop, Illustrator, Fireworks, Affinity Photo, Designer, Serif PhotoPlus, Corel® Paint Shop Pro®, Pixelmator or GIMP. Note that desktop publishing software is not generally considered to be a suitable alternative to image editing software.

Learning outcomes

LO1 Understand the purpose and properties of digital graphics
LO2 Be able to plan the creation of a digital graphic
LO3 Be able to create a digital graphic
LO4 Be able to review a digital graphic

How will I be assessed?

You will be assessed through an OCR model assignment, marked by your tutor and externally moderated by OCR. It is worth 25% of the overall mark when working towards a Certificate in Creative iMedia.

For LO1
Learners need to:
- understand how and why digital graphics are used
- know about different file types and file formats
- understand the properties of digital graphics and the suitability for different uses
- understand how different purposes and audiences influence the design and layout.

For LO2
Learners need to:
- be able to interpret the client requirements for digital graphics
- understand the target audience for a digital graphic
- produce a work plan for creating a digital graphic

- create a visualisation diagram for a digital graphic
- identify the assets and resources needed to create a digital graphic
- understand how legislation applies to creation of digital graphics.

For LO3
Learners need to:
- source assets for use in a digital graphic
- create assets for use in a digital graphic
- ensure the technical compatibility of assets
- create a digital graphic using a range of tools and techniques
- be able to create a digital graphic
- save and export a digital graphic in suitable formats
- know how to use version control when creating digital graphics.

For LO4
Learners need to:
- review a digital graphic
- identify areas for improvement and further development.

LO1 Understand the purpose and properties of digital graphics

Getting started

Have a look around the school and classrooms. Make a list of where images and graphics are used. You can include posters, leaflets, books and electronic platforms (such as television screens), displays and your school network.

Why digital graphics are used

Digital graphics can entertain, advertise, promote, inform or educate.

Entertain: examples include magazine features, graphic novels, comics and any still graphics used in games.

Advertise: there is a huge demand for creative graphics in advertisements. These are found in magazines, newspapers, billboards, posters, vehicle signage and digital advertisements on websites and social media.

Promote: similar to advertisements, but can be broader in scope (for example, to promote NHS campaigns).

Inform: examples include posters, leaflets and instructions, such as those created for events, new products or how to use something.

Educate: similar to inform, but with a clear and measurable objective (for example, to learn about different video camera shots or composition in photography).

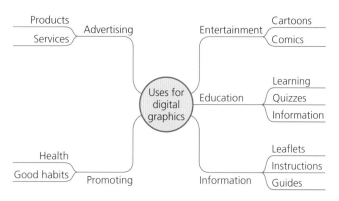

Figure 2.1 Possible uses for digital graphics

 Classroom discussion

Identify at least three graphic products for each category listed on the previous page. Discuss the differences in layout, size and style.

How digital graphics are used

Here are some of the areas where digital graphics are used.

- Print publishing (such as magazines, leaflets, newspapers, books, posters).
- Labelling and branding of products.
- Advertising (in print and digital graphic file formats).
- Websites (banners, navigation buttons and image-based content).
- Presentations (using eye catching graphics to encourage audience interest).
- Games (such as game box covers, still graphics used within the game and any advertising or promotion of it).

Graphics are often used in more than one format. If, for example, a film is distributed on DVD and Blu-ray, a front cover will be needed in two different sizes. The film would also require advertising posters to attract the target audience, and smaller versions of the graphics for retail websites and streaming services, such as iTunes and Netflix; these need fewer pixels to ensure the webpage or display loads quickly.

Types of digital graphics

There are two main types of digital graphic which have very different characteristics: bitmap and vector graphics.

Bitmap/raster graphics

Bitmap or raster graphics use pixels. They are produced by digital cameras or scanners. They are the most common type of file for any graphic that includes pictures. The pixels contain colour information as a mixture of red, green and blue. There is a limit to how far they can be enlarged or viewed at high magnification, because the image will become 'pixelated', that is, the eye can begin to see the individual pixel shape, colour and position.

Vector graphics

Vector graphics are independent of resolution and do not use pixels; they maintain crisp edges when resized, without any loss of quality. This is because they are based on mathematical formulae that represent curves and lines. Vector graphics are typically shapes and text that are drawn using the shape, pen or text tools. Vector graphics can be converted to raster images for further editing or use within a digital graphic.

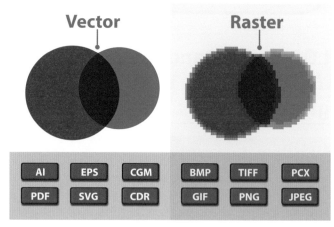

Figure 2.2 Comparison of bitmap and vector graphics at high resolution and associated file formats

File formats

The most important image file formats are shown in this table.

File format	Properties
.jpg	The most common image file format, used in digital cameras and supported by web browsers; gives a range of options for the amount of compression to reduce file size, at the expense of image quality.
.png	Portable Network Graphics; an alternative to .jpg with the benefit of supporting transparency; intended as a replacement for .gif images without any licensing restrictions for web use.
.gif	Graphic Interchange Format; has a limited range of 256 colours, so is more suitable for graphics and logos than photographs, but it does support animation and transparency.
.tiff	Tagged Image File Format is now less popular, partly due to its large file size; still used occasionally in print and desktop publishing applications because of its high quality with no loss of detail.
.eps	Encapsulated PostScript is used within high-quality desktop publishing applications.
.psd	Adobe Photoshop Document is the generic format used by Adobe in its graphics software; constructed of layers for complex editing.
.spp	Proprietary file format that is used by Serif PhotoPlus; supports image information such as layers in a similar way to Adobe .psd.
.dpp	Proprietary file format; used by Serif DrawPlus.
.svg	Scalable vector graphics file format; can be used across different vector graphic editing software applications.
.psp	Paint Shop Pro document; generic file format used by Corel in PaintShop® software applications.
pdf	Portable Document Format; widely used format for images, manuals, desktop publishing and other documents combining text and images. Not an image file format that can be edited, only exported for proofing and/or print use.
.bmp	Bitmap file format developed by Microsoft; usually uncompressed and supporting a range of different colour depths.
.wdp or .hdp	A file format used by Windows Media for high quality photo images with good tonal range; expected to be replaced with the .hdp file format.
.jxr	A newer jpeg XR format for professional high quality image editing using 48 bit colour depth.

Compression settings

Compression settings relate to file format – for example, jpg or tiff – and, potentially, what quality settings have been chosen. The purpose of compression is to reduce the file size. This can be either lossy or lossless compression. Jpg files are a good example of **lossy compression** and offers different quality settings affecting the final file size.

Properties of digital graphics and their suitability for creating images

Digital graphics *must* be fit for purpose; you need to choose the correct image properties – the **pixel dimensions** and **DPI resolution**. You will learn about these properties in LO1 and then apply them in LO3 when creating your graphics.

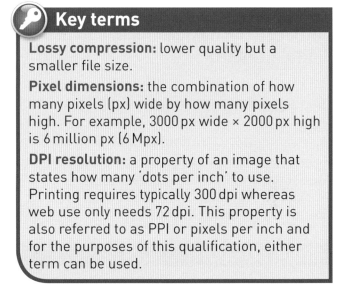

Key terms

Lossy compression: lower quality but a smaller file size.

Pixel dimensions: the combination of how many pixels (px) wide by how many pixels high. For example, 3000 px wide × 2000 px high is 6 million px (6 Mpx).

DPI resolution: a property of an image that states how many 'dots per inch' to use. Printing requires typically 300 dpi whereas web use only needs 72 dpi. This property is also referred to as PPI or pixels per inch and for the purposes of this qualification, either term can be used.

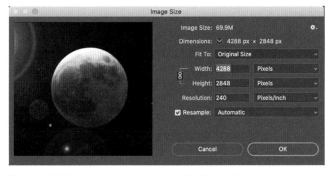

Figure 2.3 Properties of an image in Photoshop

How different purposes and audiences influence the design and layout of digital graphics

Design and layout considerations

Use of colour

Colours can stimulate different moods in the viewer. Red, orange and yellow are generally considered bright, energetic and warming, for example. But blue, green and purple are considered settled and cooling.

Neutrals can be used for large area, with highlight colours to attract the viewer's attention. The genre or theme of the product will also affect the choice of colours. A poster for a young children's film, for example, might use bright primary colours – but they wouldn't be suitable for a darker crime theme.

Composition

Composition refers to the layout of the different elements in the graphic, and includes:

- positioning of the main object or subject so that there is a focus point for the viewer
- use of lines and perspective to draw the viewer's attention to the main focus point
- use of balance (for example, are all the elements symmetrical or does one element stand out?)
- use of suitable typeface or font (for example, a science fiction theme probably wouldn't work with an antique style font)
- use of white space to separate the different elements; this is any area within the final graphic that is blank – it doesn't necessarily mean that it is 'white' as a colour, but could be any solid block of colour.

Content and style

This is related to the genre of the final work. It means that the overall style should be consistent with what would be expected, so antique fonts and sepia toned images would work for historical pieces, whereas digital style fonts and images of alien worlds could be used with science fiction.

Assessment preparation

Think about the individual performance you need to undertake. Make sure you:

- know a wide range of areas where graphics are used
- understand why print and web graphics need different image properties
- understand why the purpose and audience influence new projects.

LO1: Understand the purposes and properties of digital graphics		
Mark band 1	Mark band 2	Mark band 3
Produces a summary of how and why digital graphics are used, demonstrating a limited understanding of the purpose of digital graphics.	Produces a summary of how and why digital graphics are used, demonstrating a sound understanding of the purpose of digital graphics.	Produces a summary of how and why digital graphics are used, demonstrating a thorough understanding of the purpose of digital graphics.
Identifies a limited range of file types and formats, only some of which are appropriate to digital graphics.	Identifies a range of file types and formats, most of which are appropriate to digital graphics.	Identifies a wide range of file types and formats, which are consistently appropriate to digital graphics.
Mark band 1	Mark band 2	Mark band 3
Demonstrates a limited understanding of the connection between the properties of digital graphics and their suitability for use.	Demonstrates a sound understanding of the connection between the properties of digital graphics and their suitability for use.	Demonstrates a thorough understanding of the connection between the properties of digital graphics and their suitability for use.
Demonstrates a limited understanding of how different purposes and audiences influence the design and layout of digital graphics.	Demonstrates a sound understanding of how different purposes and audiences influence the design and layout of digital graphics.	Demonstrates a thorough understanding of how different purposes and audiences influence the design and layout of digital graphics.

Assessment guidance

The OCR set assignment

When completing your work for the OCR set assignment, you will need to:

- summarise your investigations into the use of digital graphics in a range of different areas. These should not be limited to the assignment scenario and your work for LO1 should be broad in scope
- describe a range of file types and formats, with typical characteristics
- show your understanding of image properties, i.e. pixel dimensions and dpi resolution, so that the graphics will be suitable for different uses, i.e. print and web/display
- describe how the purpose and audience influence the design and layout of some new graphics projects.

What do the command words mean?

Thorough understanding [of purpose]: can be demonstrated through depth, breadth or a combination. Breadth is the number of different areas, depth is the level of detail.

Wide range [file types]: generally means five or more.

Thorough understanding [connection between]: relates to the different image properties and how they relate to print and web use, which should cover the pixel dimensions and dpi resolution for both.

Thorough understanding [purpose and audience]: should be a forward-looking consideration of what might work in different types of new graphics projects.

LO2 Be able to plan the creation of a digital graphic

Getting started

Find a DVD or Blu-ray case for a film you like. Look at the content on the front and back covers. Make a list of the information that is useful to you. You are the target audience for the film so somebody will have thought about what you wanted to see when they were planning the layout.

Interpreting client requirements

Before starting work on creating a digital graphic, you must check what the client wants.

Read the client brief or specification carefully. Think about what the purpose is (you can refer back to your investigation in LO1 here). Then think about how to satisfy the brief using your creative talents and ideas. Jot down ideas on content, layout, composition, house style and specification of the graphics (image properties).

You could discuss your ideas with the client before starting work, which is a typical approach within the graphics industry. Make sure you know when the client wants to see your ideas so you can put timescales on a work plan.

You could record your interpretation of the client brief with a mind map or spider diagram, or a mood board with images, text and captions from similar products; this uses knowledge and skills from unit R081.

Key term

Interpretation of the brief: a key element of your planning as an aspiring graphic designer. It must be individual, fit-for-purpose, and express your creative ideas and understanding of digital graphics.

Understanding the target audience

The expectations, needs and requirements of the target audience must be considered if your digital graphic is to be successful. This is helped by categorising the target audience before thinking about their needs.

Links to other units

You can find further information on how to categorise a target audience in **unit R081**.

Once you have a clear idea about who the target audience is, you can consider what they want or need from the digital graphic. For example, do they want information or to be entertained?

Producing a work plan for graphics creation

Work (project) plans are structured lists of all the tasks and associated activities needed to create the digital graphic, with a timescale for each activity and estimated completion date for the overall project.

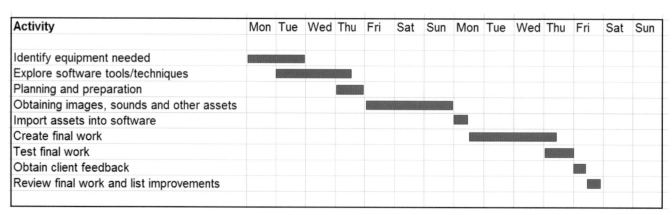

Activity	Mon	Tue	Wed	Thu	Fri	Sat	Sun	Mon	Tue	Wed	Thu	Fri	Sat	Sun
Identify equipment needed	█													
Explore software tools/techniques		█	█											
Planning and preparation				█										
Obtaining images, sounds and other assets					█	█	█							
Import assets into software								█						
Create final work									█	█	█			
Test final work												█		
Obtain client feedback												█		
Review final work and list improvements												█		

Figure 2.4 Work plan for a new film poster

A work plan does not have to be in any set format, but should include a range of activities that must be completed to create the digital graphic (and not the tasks in the assignment). When thinking about the effectiveness of the work plan, consider: 'could somebody else follow it?'

Links to other units

You can find further information on how to create a work plan or project plan in **unit R081**.

Producing a visualisation diagram

A **visualisation diagram** is a drawing or sketch to illustrate your ideas of what the final graphic could look like. The visualisation diagram can be produced in one of two ways.

1 **Hand drawn/sketched:** using paper and pencils or coloured markers. Sketch out what you want the graphic to look like. Annotate this with comments on colours, fonts and layout.

2 **Digitally produced:** using a software application. This does not have to be image editing software; you could use desktop publishing applications such as Microsoft Publisher, Microsoft Word and Apple Pages.

Think: 'Is the visualisation effective?' 'Could somebody else, such as a graphic designer, follow it?' Your visualisation diagram should have enough detail to be created by somebody else as well as giving your client a good idea of what you are intending to create. That might need some detailed annotations to illustrate your ideas.

Identifying assets needed to produce a digital graphic

In LO2, this is a planning activity completed before obtaining the assets in the first part of LO3. You need ideas about what could potentially be used, but you will also need to comment on their suitability. Assets could be from:

- **photographs**, whether taken by yourself or by others
- **scanned images**, from any printed material (but think about copyright restrictions)
- **image libraries**, from web-based picture libraries (conditions and costs of use to be identified)
- **graphics and logos**, these might be supplied by the client in a vocational or commercial context.

Links to other units

You can find information on taking photographs to use as assets in **unit R090**.

Figure 2.5 Visualisation diagrams (hand drawn and digital)

Using the internet to find images

Internet images can be found using an image search, but the results do not always show images that would be a suitable resolution for print. It is the pixel dimensions of the image that determine its suitability. Always check the pixel dimensions and divide these by 300 to determine how large they could be (in inches) as part of a print-based product. The second restriction is copyright – most internet images will be protected, even if it isn't clearly stated. Always check and record your findings.

Group activity

Make a list of the assets you might like to use in a practice graphics project. This could be produced as a table of potential assets.

Assets that could be used			
Image	Source	Legal issues	Potential use

Image: descriptive name or thumbnail picture.

Source: where the asset is from (state the URL, not 'Google images').

Legal issues: is it copyrighted, trademarked or royalty free, and how would you obtain permission for its use?

Potential use: this should be your own thoughts on how and where you could use the image in the digital graphic.

Figure 2.6 Resources are the equipment, hardware and software

Identifying resources needed to create a digital graphic

 Key term

Resources: defined as the computer hardware, equipment, peripherals and software application(s) needed to create the digital graphic. Note that you do not need to include software for the write up of the unit.

Peripherals for use in creating digital graphics

Scanner: Typically used when creating digital graphics to scan logos or images for one of the layers in a graphic montage.

Graphics tablet: An alternative to the standard computer mouse. Using a stylus pen on the tablet is similar to using a brush on paper, so it is popular with creative artists and designers. The thickness of a line can be changed by increasing or decreasing the pressure of the stylus on the tablet.

Digital camera: Refer to unit R090.

Choosing image-editing software

The following is a list of software applications that can be used to create and edit your digital graphics.

- **Adobe Photoshop:** A widely used industry standard application used with photographs and graphic design.
- **Adobe Illustrator:** Also an industry standard for professional use, but more popular for graphics design and the use of art based vector graphics.
- **Adobe Fireworks:** Popular with those using graphics within web development and animation work. It was taken over by Adobe and is being discontinued.
- **Affinity Photo and Designer:** Professional level image editing applications. Comparable with Adobe Photoshop and Illustrator.
- **Serif PhotoPlus:** (Discontinued) User friendly image editing software with wide range of tools available.

Figure 2.7 Affinity Photo

- **Serif DrawPlus:** (Discontinued) More suited to desktop publishing than image editing. Serif PhotoPlus would be a better choice for this unit.
- **Corel Paint Shop Pro:** Supports both bitmap and vector graphics.
- **Pixelmator:** Powerful image editing software application for the Apple Mac with some advanced features and capabilities.
- **GIMP:** A freely distributed open source program for photo retouching and graphical image creation.

Other applications can be used to edit graphics, such as Microsoft Publisher, Word, PowerPoint, iPhoto and Paint, but they are not considered good choices. Some are MS Office-based applications more suitable for desktop publishing.

Keep in mind what will be needed and why when planning your digital graphics projects so that you can make informed choices.

Legislation in digital graphics production

You need to document use of copyrighted, trademarked or intellectual property when creating digital graphics. This should include records of all sources and permissions obtained for material that is not your own.

Since this qualification is set in a commercial context, you will need to consider the use of all the image assets as if they are to be published in

the media industry. There are some allowances to use copyrighted material for educational use, but it is the commercial context that needs to be covered.

To use published resources, you must check the licensing restrictions. Even if there are none shown, you should:

1 contact the owner
2 ask for permission to use it
3 be prepared to pay a fee
4 obtain written permission to use the image.

For the purposes of digital graphics, you may need to include the use of certification and classification symbols, such as those from the BBFC and PEGI.

Links to other units

You can find more information on the legal issues of copyright, trademarks and intellectual property in **unit R081**.

You can find further information on model and property releases in **unit R090**. These are a way of obtaining permission to use photographs that include people or are taken on private property.

Group activity

Use a large sheet of paper to sketch a visualisation diagram for the following scenario.

A client wants some ideas for the front cover layout of a new magazine about social media. The content will be aimed at 15–16-year-olds and the forms of social media they use, together with the benefits and risks. The cover can have some text but the client also wants you to consider what image assets would be suitable to attract the audience. Annotations should be added to explain your reasoning. Make sure you all contribute some ideas to the visualisation diagram.

Know it!

1 Know what activities you must complete as part of creating a graphic and not just the tasks in the assignment.

2 Make a list of what sort of comments would be added to a visualisation diagram as annotations.

Assessment preparation

Think about the individual performance you will need to undertake. Make sure you:

- know what is expected from your own interpretation of a client brief and target audience
- are able to use additional knowledge and skills learned in other units
- are able to create work plans and visualisation diagrams
- know about the potential use of assets and purpose of resources
- understand legislation in the context of what you are going to create.

LO2: Be able to plan the creation of a digital graphic		
Mark band 1	Mark band 2	Mark band 3
Produces an interpretation from the client brief which meets few of the client requirements.	Produces an interpretation from the client brief which meets most of the client requirements.	Produces an interpretation from the client brief which fully meets the client requirements.
Produces a limited identification of target audience requirements.	Produces a clear identification of target audience requirements.	Produces a clear and detailed identification of target audience requirements.
Draws upon limited skills/knowledge/ understanding from other units in the specification.	Draws upon some relevant skills/ knowledge/understanding from other units in the specification.	Clearly draws upon relevant skills/ knowledge/understanding from other units in the specification.
Mark band 1	Mark band 2	Mark band 3
Produces a work plan for the creation of the digital graphic, which has some capability in producing the intended final product.	Produces a work plan for the creation of the digital graphic, which is mostly capable of producing the intended final product.	Produces a clear and detailed work plan for the creation of the digital graphic, which is fully capable of producing the intended final product.
Produces a simple visualisation diagram for the intended final product.	Produces a sound visualisation diagram for the intended final product.	Produces a clear and detailed visualisation diagram for the intended final product.
Identifies a few assets needed to create a digital graphic, demonstrating a limited understanding of their potential use.	Identifies many assets needed to create a digital graphic, demonstrating a sound understanding of their potential use.	Identifies most assets needed to create a digital graphic, demonstrating a thorough understanding of their potential use.
Identifies a few of the resources needed to create a digital graphic, demonstrating a limited understanding of their purpose.	Identifies many of the resources needed to create a digital graphic, demonstrating a sound understanding of their purpose.	Identifies most of the resources needed to create a digital graphic, demonstrating a thorough understanding of their purpose.
Demonstrates a limited understanding of legislation in relation to the use of images in digital graphics.	Demonstrates a sound understanding of legislation in relation to the use of images in digital graphics.	Demonstrates a thorough understanding of legislation in relation to the use of images in digital graphics.

When completing your work for the OCR set assignment, you will need to:

- produce your own interpretation of the client brief
- identify the target audience and what they will want from the graphic
- use knowledge and skills from other units such as R081
- produce a work plan to create the digital graphic
- produce a visualisation diagram of what you intend to create
- identify the assets and their potential use
- identify the resources and their purpose
- describe the legal issues of using assets in your graphic.

What do the command words mean?

Fully [interpretation of the brief]: needs to be your own individual ideas and thoughts on what is required that expands on what is given in the scenario and brief.

Clear and detailed [target audience]: should be a clear definition of who the target audience is and what they will want to gain from the digital graphics.

Draws on [knowledge, skills and understanding]: must be from other units and not something that is already in R082, such as a work plan or visualisation diagram.

Clear and detailed [work plan]: should break down the tasks and activities into small steps that must be completed in order to create the digital graphic. It is not for the completion of the unit or assignment, which also covers LO1.

Clear and detailed [visualisation diagram]: should be clear for somebody else so that they have a good idea of what you intend to create. Annotations may be added for clarification.

Thorough [understanding of potential use of assets]: should identify where you could use the assets, what makes them suitable. It can include assets that you decide not to use later on.

Thorough [understanding of purpose of resources]: should identify why you need to use the resources for creating the digital graphic.

Thorough [understanding of legislation]: should be applied to the actual image assets that you intend to use. Their use should also be in a commercial context and not just education.

LO3 Be able to create a digital graphic

This is where you create what you have planned in LO2. There is a sequence of activities to complete for this learning outcome.

1 Obtain the **assets** needed, by sourcing and creating them.
2 Prepare the assets for use in the final **graphic** and store them in a suitable location.
3 Create the graphic using a range of tools and techniques.
4 Save and export all the required versions for different uses.

Sourcing assets for use in digital graphics

Sources for images and graphics could be:

- the internet: a web can locate a wide range of images subject to restrictions
- stock libraries (most of these have a website to browse and purchase images)
- client: for their own logos
- photographers: commission-based work
- printed materials: these will need to be scanned.

When using the internet, an image search is likely to display many pages of results. A common limitation is image size (pixel dimensions and dpi resolution). If an image is used on a web page, it only needs to be 72 dpi and no larger than the display monitor. Unfortunately, that is not much use for a print product since resolution needs to be 300 dpi. An advanced search can be selected so that only images larger than a specified size are shown in the results. This ensures the image assets are technically compatible with what you want to do.

Another restriction is permission for use. Most content on the internet is protected by copyright and you may need permission from the owner to use it. If working in the media industry, you need to know how to obtain copyright clearance and permissions, so you should demonstrate this in your work.

Creating assets for use in digital graphics

When planning the final graphic you may identify the need for specific assets that you need to create. An example would be a logo, symbol or other graphic that would be part of the finished design. This may have to be drawn digitally in the image editing software application, or created from other assets that were a starting point.

Whether the image assets were sourced or you intend to create them, you need to start using image editing software. Collect all the assets into one folder – including logos, copy text and a range of images for the background and foreground.

Using image editing software with assets

Your digital workflow and processing of image assets

The basic editing techniques in most software applications are similar, so skills learned in one application can often be transferred into a different application.

If you learn a basic workflow – a standard sequence of editing techniques for every image and graphic – you can use it in whatever software application you choose.

Here is an example of a basic workflow.

1 Check the image quality.
2 Adjust levels, or brightness/contrast, if necessary.
3 Check the colour and adjust if necessary.
4 Crop to the required size, shape and resolution (this depends on the intended use).
5 Save the image in a suitable format and filename.

Let's look at the techniques and processes for each of these five basic steps, and apply them to a range of assets that we have sourced.

1 Check the image quality
If the image quality is not good enough, you want to know straight away before wasting any time. Use the zoom control to view the image at 100% magnification. Look closely to see whether it is blurred or out of focus on the important subject areas. If the image quality is poor, close the file and find something else.

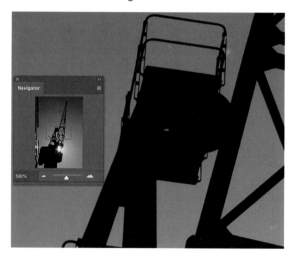

Figure 2.8 Checking the image quality at 100%

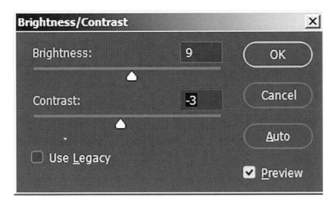

Figure 2.9 Using the brightness/contrast sliders

2 Adjust levels, or brightness/contrast

Adjusting this will make sure that the full tonal range is used in the image, which means the darkest (shadow) areas are a true black and the brightest (highlight) areas are true white. Without this optimisation, an image can look either 'washed out' or very dark.

You can use either the brightness/contrast adjustment sliders, which is accepted as a standard tool, or levels adjustment histogram in Adobe Photoshop, which is a more advanced way to achieve the same thing.

The brightness/contrast sliders are a basic tool that allow you to make manual changes visually on the screen. Move the sliders to the left or right until the best-looking result is achieved.

An alternative standard tool is to use the 'Auto Levels' function in Adobe Photoshop, which attempts to automatically decide the optimum settings. This doesn't always work well, so you might have to adjust the levels manually.

The benefit of making adjustments using the levels is that it displays a histogram of how the image is made up in terms of the brightest and darkest points together with everything in between. The darker levels are shown at the left-hand side and brighter levels at the right-hand side. To make adjustments for the levels, do the following.

- Move the black point slider inwards from the left until it is at a point where the black shading on the histogram just begins.
- Move the white point slider from the right-hand side to where the histogram just ends.
- Move the mid-point (gamma slider) to a position that makes the image look the best in terms of the overall brightness and contrast on the screen.

When using the levels adjustment, note the optimum positions for the black and white point sliders in the image as shown in Figure 2.10.

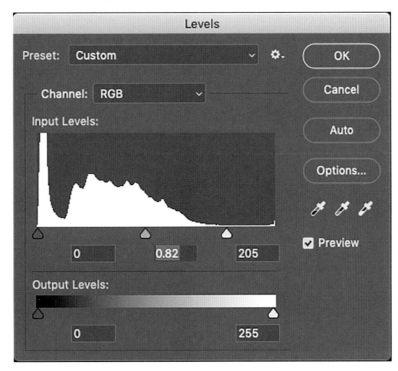

Figure 2.10 Levels adjustment

Figure 2.11 Colour adjustment

3 *Check and adjust the colour*
In Adobe Photoshop there are a number of options for adjusting the colour. Some of these are:

- Image menu → auto colour
- Image menu → adjustments → hue/saturation
- Image menu → adjustments → colour balance

The auto colour option may not work well with every type of image, depending on what range of colours is included. The hue and saturation are a set of sliders similar to brightness/contrast. They enable you to change overall colour tone and colour saturation. You can also reduce the colour saturation to zero, which removes all the colour to leave a black and white image.

4 *Cropping the image*
You may need to crop an image if it is not straight – for example, a scanned image that was not square on the scanner, or a photo from a digital camera where the horizon is not straight across the frame.

Or you may want to only use part of an image as an asset in a graphic, which you crop from the full picture.

Another reason for cropping is to obtain the size and shape that you need.

To crop and straighten an image in the same process:

1 select the 'Crop' tool from the Toolbox; if you want a specific size, enter it in the option bar fields found below the menu bar

2 draw a box around the area that is approximately how you want your composition to look

3 adjust the position of the corners and edges as needed; everything that is outside this crop window will be removed when you complete the crop command

4 rotate the crop window by positioning the mouse cursor just outside a corner of the box so that a 'rotate' icon is displayed for the mouse cursor; you can then freely rotate the box left or right as needed

5 press 'Enter' to perform the final crop, or click on the tick mark in the Options bar.

5 *Saving images and graphics*
Save your edited image and graphical assets onto your computer hard disk in an appropriate folder. It is a good idea to save a full size, high resolution

Figure 2.12 Cropping an image

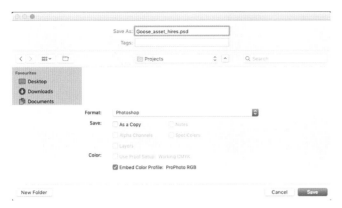

Figure 2.13 Saving an asset for use

image as your master file since it is easy to make this smaller later on (but not so easy to make something larger that is a high enough quality). Look back at the file formats from LO1 before deciding what format to use. Check that the pixel dimensions and dpi resolution are suitable for your intended purpose – once pixels or image quality are discarded, they cannot be recovered.

To save the image asset, from the 'File' menu, click on 'Save As'.

Ensuring the technical compatibility of assets

The technical properties of an image asset include the pixel dimensions and dpi resolution. Since you will be creating a print product to begin with, you will need to use assets that can be printed with 300 dpi at the intended size. Therefore, if you sourced an image from the web at 300 pixels wide, it could only be printed at 1 inch (25 mm) width. However, it is possible to edit image assets and crop or resize them to make sure they are technically compatible.

Using tools and techniques to create assets and graphics

The first step in creating an asset or graphic is to set up a new image file. The important part here is to make sure the image properties meet what is needed by the client brief (or your own criteria if creating an asset). So, if you are creating an A4 poster for print purposes, you need:

- print dimensions of 297 mm × 210 mm or approximately 11.69" × 8.27"
- resolution for print, 300 dpi.

Stretch activity

Find some low-resolution images from the internet (less than 300 pixels in width or height and only 72 dpi).

1 Open the image asset in your image editing software.
2 Check the image properties to view the pixel dimensions and resolution.
3 Check the box for resample image. Change the resolution to 300 dpi so that it will be suitable for print use. Enter 600 pixels in the pixel dimensions field so that it will be 2 inches.
4 Click OK – when the box closes you may notice the display changes with the new resolution.
5 Work through several different images, resizing to larger sizes so that they are technically compatible for use in a print product.
6 Make notes of the 'before' and 'after' pixel dimensions and resolutions.

Therefore, the pixel dimensions for A4 need to be 3508 × 2480 based on 25.4 mm per inch. You might need to check what units your image editing software is using to confirm this. It will be either imperial (inches) or metric (millimetres and centimetres). A quick conversion of 300 dpi is 118 pixels per cm. If you are creating an asset at this stage, you will need to think about what print size the asset will be and this will inform your choice of pixel dimensions.

Look at the following table with examples of products that need specific image properties.

Product	Print dimensions (size)	Pixel dimensions
Magazine advert (approx. ¼ page)	4" wide × 5.25" high (varies by magazine)	1200 × 1575
Magazine front cover	8 3/8" wide × 10 7/8" high (varies by magazine)	2512 × 3262
Blu-ray (front cover only)	126 mm wide × 148 mm high	1488 × 1748

Figure 2.14 Using a gradient

Drawing and painting tools

Shapes: These are created as vector-based graphics and are scalable for any size or resolution. There is also a library of shapes built in.

Pencil: The pencil tool allows you to draw thin lines or change the colour of individual pixels, which is similar to a very narrow brush.

Brush: The brush can be used with quick masks and for freehand painting or filling in shapes. There are different sizes but always larger than the pencil.

Eraser: This is used to permanently erase parts of an image. The eraser is considered a standard (basic) tool so you might want to consider using selection tools instead of just erasing a background.

Gradient: A gradient consists of two defined colours, foreground and background. Changing the foreground colour to transparent creates a natural blending effect. Gradients are best created on a new layer to allow editing and further modification.

Using and applying filters

There is a range of filters and effects available in Adobe Photoshop, some of the more popular examples are distort, liquefy, artistic (watercolour, paint daubs), and blur.

Filter effects can be applied to individual assets, such as background images or smaller image assets that have been placed on top of the background image. Try not to rely too much on filters, since it is easy to ruin a graphic that is basically sound.

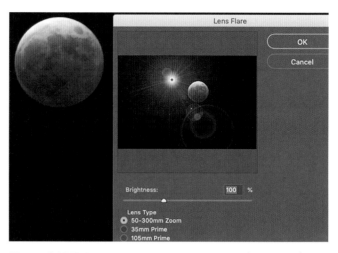

Figure 2.15 Using filters in Adobe Photoshop (lens flare)

Adding text

Most digital graphics will include some sort of text in the form of a title or information.

Select the type or text tool from the toolbar. Click on the graphic where you want to start and enter the text using the keyboard. The text can be formatted afterwards with font, size and colour.

Placing the assets and creating the digital graphic

The techniques and processes involved in creating the digital graphic are best learned by applying them to practice projects.

1 Create the new image file at suitable dimensions.
2 Import the assets to be used. These can be opened and then copied (or dragged) onto a new layer.

Figure 2.16 Adding text to a graphic

3   Use the move tool to position and scale the assets as needed. Try not to change the aspect ratio of the image.

4   Edit and enhance the visual effects on assets. This could include layer styles, gradients, blending and filters.

5   Add titles and any other text required.

Using advanced tools and techniques

As a starting point, we need to know the difference between standard tools and advanced tools. Some of these could be used when creating the individual assets and not just the final graphic.

Standard tools	Advanced tools
Brightness/contrast	Levels
Auto levels	Curves
Auto colour	Manipulating layers (with names)
Eraser	Using adjustment layers
Basic painting with a brush	Layer styles (on text, for example)
Adding text	Using selection tools
Adding basic shapes	Using feathering on edges
Applying filters	Cloning and healing tools
Move tool (to position assets)	Gradient effects
	Stroke and fill
	Text special effects
	Modifying shapes with effects
	Burn and dodge
	Using masks

Note that in the following sections, the use of advanced tools is identified using the {Advanced} tag.

Using the curves adjustments {Advanced}
This is a versatile tool that means you can brighten and darken an image together with adding contrast and adjusting the colours. It offers a wider range of adjustments compared to levels.Using the curves graph displays input and output levels, initially as a straight line. You can modify the image by changing the shape of the line. As an example, you can increase the contrast by changing the

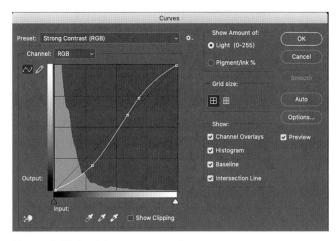

Figure 2.17 Applying a curves adjustment

shape of the curve to look like an S, or decrease the contrast with an inverted S shape.

Working with layers {Advanced}
The layers palette shows how an image is constructed. A new digital graphic has a single background layer. Each additional layer is transparent in the parts shown as a checkerboard pattern. Imagine that you are looking down on these layers from above – the top layer is seen first and you can see through all the transparent areas to anything that is underneath.

Individual layers can be added, turned off for editing, renamed or moved. Contents can also be changed and skilful use of layers is a great way to create complex digital graphics.

Using layer styles {Advanced}
These are typically used on text, shapes and sometimes objects that have been cut-out and placed on a new layer.

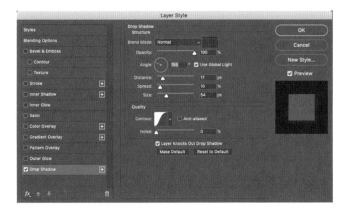

Figure 2.18 Adding a layer style to text

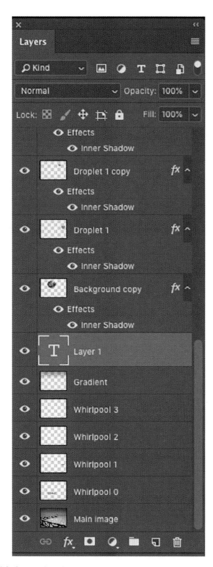

Figure 2.19 Complex layer stack

Figure 2.20 Using selection tools

The most common styles are drop shadow and bevel and emboss. You can experiment with the settings, such as light direction and depth.

Using selection tools {Advanced}
Selection tools allow you to define parts of the image so that you can make changes to those parts without affecting the remainder of the image. Another way to use selections is to copy and paste selected parts of an image onto other layers or different image files so that you can assemble a complex digital graphic. When using selections, an active selection area appears with a flashing dotted line around it, sometimes referred to as 'marching ants'.

Selection tools include marquee, lasso, magic wand and intersect.

Marquee: These use either rectangular or elliptical shapes for regular-shaped outlines in the image. If you hold down the keyboard 'Shift' key at the same time, this will enable you to draw a perfect square or circle.

Lasso: There are three types of lasso tool.

- The freehand lasso tool works like a pencil on the screen.
- The polygonal tool draws straight lines between mouse click points.
- The magnetic lasso tool attempts to trace the outline of an object by automatically recognising the edges.

Magic wand: This selection tool uses colour to recognise which pixels are to be selected. The options bar has a checkbox to control whether these are either contiguous (all joined together) or non-contiguous (anywhere within a colour tolerance).

New/add/subtract/intersect (Found on the options toolbar): Having created an initial selection, you can add extra areas or remove them using one of these modes. They are available with all selection tools.

Using the cloning tool {Advanced}

The purpose of the clone stamp is to duplicate parts of the image from one section into a different section. This is a very useful tool that can be used to remove unwanted details from an image, although practice is needed to build up your skill level.

How to use the clone tool:

- Click on the icon in the tool box once to select it.
- If needed, select the brush style from the 'options' bar although the soft-edged default brush works well on most images.
- Set the required brush size (use the left and right square brackets [ ] to decrease and increase size).
- Move the mouse onto the image and position it close to the feature that you want to remove, then press and hold down the 'Alt' key so that the mouse cursor changes to a 'target' icon.
- Single click with the left mouse button, then release the 'Alt' key.
- Carefully move the mouse across the image onto the part to be removed, remembering where you have just clicked for the clone source point.
- Click and hold down the left mouse button so that a cross hair and a circle are shown as mouse cursors. The tool works by copying the colour information from the cross hair (source) and pasting it into the circle (destination).
- Repeat as necessary.

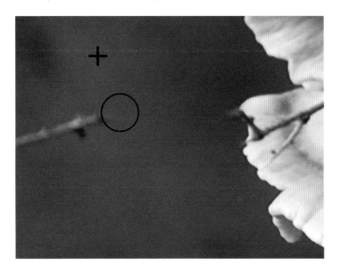

Figure 2.21 Using the cloning tool

Using healing tools {Advanced}

Adobe Photoshop has both healing and patch tools. You can use the healing brushes to remove small blemishes and spots by blending the colours and textures. Having selected a suitable tool size that is typically slightly larger than the blemish, you then click on it with the mouse. The patch tool is a large area healing brush and is used by first drawing a shape with the mouse. This area can be used as the 'source' or 'destination' for the blending.

Transformation techniques {Advanced}

This advanced technique allows you to modify the shape or perspective of an image. One example of a use for this technique is to straighten the vertical angles that are seen when photographing tall buildings from low down.

- Select the entire image from 'Select' > 'Select all'.
- From the 'Edit' menu, click on 'Transform' using one of the options provided.

In addition to using the 'Transform' menu, you can use 'Ctrl' click on any of the corners to adjust the individual transformation points.

Additional tools {Advanced}

Stroke tool: This can be used to create a solid line around the edge of a selection. The thickness of the edge can be set in the tool options.

Fill tool: This can be used to fill a defined area with a specific colour. Typically used with selection tools to create coloured shapes.

Smudge tool: This is a good way to 'push' colours around using the mouse. Think of an oil painting when the oils are still wet – you could push the colours around with a finger.

Blur tool: The blur tool is the opposite of sharpening and effectively blurs the area under the cursor. Used for softening edges.

Sharpen tool: This does the opposite of blurring, but is a fairly subtle effect.

Dodge tool: The name of this tool comes from a darkroom technique whereby the light is restricted from reaching the photographic paper. This makes the image lighter.

Burn tool: The name of this tool also comes from the darkroom and is the opposite to the dodge tool, so makes it darker.

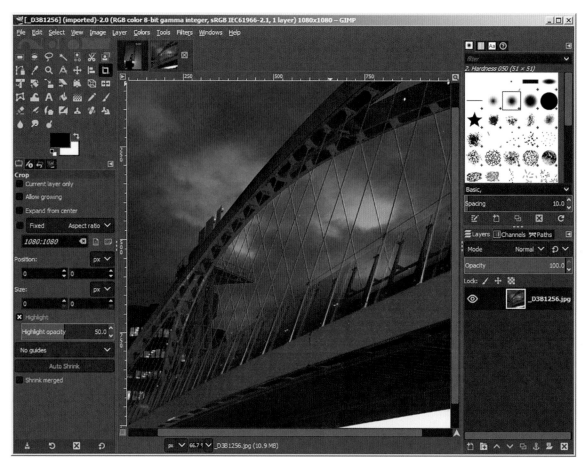

Figure 2.22 The basic sections in GIMP

Sponge tool: This is used to change the colour saturation of selected parts of the image. You can change the mode between saturate and desaturate to increase or decrease the colour intensity.

Saving and exporting a digital graphic in different formats

This is where you apply your knowledge from LO1 on file formats and image properties depending on where the graphic is to be used. Keep in mind that software specific file formats include .psd, .spp, .dpp, .svg, .psp, .wdp, .hdp. These are all working file formats, but final graphics should be exported in a standard image file format.

The second consideration is what the optimum image properties should be for the intended use. The image properties include both the overall pixel dimensions and the dpi resolution. This is a fundamentally important aspect of the unit.

Print use: Pixel dimensions to be based on print size using 300 dpi. To calculate the pixel dimensions, multiply the print size (in inches) by 300. If you need to convert mm to inches, use 25.4 mm = 1 inch.

Web or multimedia use: Pixel dimensions to be based on a conventional resolution of 72 dpi but the total pixel dimensions are also important to make sure the graphic fits the page and can be downloaded quickly. Unlike print products, there are no calculations as such for this – the pixel dimensions and dpi should be specified in the client requirements but double check the height and width are the right way around.

Links to other units

For more information on using version control in the filenames, refer to **unit R081**.

Using other image editing software

The screen layout varies, but the four basic sections are:

1 workspace/editing window
2 menus
3 toolbars with shortcut icons
4 tools panel.

The basic processes and concepts of creating digital graphics are the same whichever software is being used.

1 Obtain and store the image assets in a working folder.
2 Open the image assets and check the image quality.
3 Adjust brightness/contrast or levels.
4 Adjust/correct colours.
5 Complete any additional editing that is needed.
6 Save the assets with a descriptive filename in a high-quality format.

7 Create the final digital graphic to the required print dimensions by combining the image assets and editing as needed.
8 Save the final graphics with the high-resolution pixel dimensions and resolution required.
9 Resize the digital graphic for web or multimedia use as required by the brief. Save this version as a separate file – do not overwrite your high-resolution master file.

Know it!

1 Look at a list of assets. Decide what size they will be when finally printed. From this, calculate how many pixels they will need to be.
2 Make a list of 3–5 advanced tools that you are comfortable and confident with.

Assessment preparation

Think about the individual performance you need to undertake. Make sure you:

- understand asset properties to ensure they are technically compatible for print use
- are able to use a wide range of image editing tools and techniques
- understand graphics file formats and resolutions for print and web use.

LO3: Be able to create a digital graphic		
Mark band 1	**Mark band 2**	**Mark band 3**
Sources or creates a limited range of assets for use in the digital graphic.	Sources and creates a range of assets for use in the digital graphic.	Sources and creates a wide range of assets for use in the digital graphic.
Prepares the assets for use in the digital graphic, some of which are technically appropriate or compatible.	Prepares the assets for use in the digital graphic, most of which are technically appropriate and compatible.	Prepares the assets for use in the digital graphic, all of which are technically appropriate and compatible.
Mark band 1	**Mark band 2**	**Mark band 3**
Use of standard tools and techniques to create the digital graphic is limited and therefore creates a simple digital graphic which is appropriate to some aspects of the client brief.	Use of standard tools and techniques to create the digital graphic is effective and therefore creates a digital graphic which shows some detail which is appropriate to most aspects of the client brief.	Use of a range of advanced tools and techniques to create the digital graphic is effective and therefore creates a complex digital graphic which is appropriate for the client brief.
Occasionally saves and exports the digital graphic in formats which are appropriate.	Mostly saves and exports the digital graphic in formats and properties which are appropriate.	Consistently saves and exports the digital graphic in formats and properties which are appropriate.
Occasionally saves electronic files using appropriate file and folder names and structures.	Mostly saves electronic files using file and folder names and structures which are consistent and appropriate.	Consistently saves electronic files using file and folder names and structures which are consistent and appropriate.

LO4 Be able to review a digital graphic

Getting started

In a group, choose a number of finished graphic items to review. Make notes of what you like and dislike about them. From this, summarise how they could be made better. Share these decisions with the rest of the class.

How to review a digital graphic

All units of this qualification require you to independently review your own work; you must learn how to critically look at your work. This is important as a freelance designer in the media industry.

In this unit, you should look at the digital graphics created and comment on their strengths, weaknesses and how well they meet client requirements.

Key areas to cover in a review

- Does it meet the brief and client requirements?
- Is the format suitable? For example, a graphic for a web page is not suitable as a .tiff file.

- Is the content of the digital graphic suitable for what the client needs? For example, if promoting a film, are the images consistent with the film, its genre and storyline?
- Is the image content quality suitable in terms of brightness, contrast, sharpness, colour and composition?
- Is the editing of the graphics effective and pleasing to look at?
- Think about and describe the strengths, positives, advantages and benefits.
- Think about and describe the weaknesses, negatives, disadvantages and drawbacks.
- Use technical language and terminology where possible.

How to identify areas for improvement and further development

Having looked at what you have produced, you should be able to identify areas for improvement. Here are some common examples.

Size: Does the size or shape of the graphic need changing? Consider both versions (print and web use).

Resolution: Are changes needed to the pixel dimensions and resolution in any of the graphics?

Blurred: Do you need to use higher resolution images or change them for something else? If any of the image assets are pixelated this will be needed.

Text not readable: What could improve the readability? Are the font size and colour appropriate?

Poor layout: Could the different assets and elements be repositioned? Are things too close to an edge or out of balance, for example?

Colour (and contrast): Could you choose different colours, or make them brighter or more muted?

You may also need to think about how a graphic could be used in additional ways. For example:

Different formats: Where else might the graphic be used to promote the product? For example, you may have produced a magazine cover and a web version, and now need to think about an advertisement for inside the magazine to encourage people to buy it?

Enhanced versions: Perhaps the target audience reaction to the graphic was disappointing, so it may be necessary to create a new version that has more impact.

Know it!

1 Explain why it is important that your product meets the client brief.
2 Keep in mind the saying 'Excellence will be tolerated; perfection is our goal'. Nothing is ever perfect, so ask yourself where and how the graphics can be improved.

Assessment preparation

Think about the individual performance you need to undertake. Make sure you:

- know how to review your own work
- are able to justify further improvements and why they would make it better.

LO4: Be able to review a digital graphic		
Mark band 1	Mark band 2	Mark band 3
Produces a review of the finished graphic which demonstrates a limited understanding of what worked and what did not, making few references back to the brief.	Produces a review of the finished graphic which demonstrates a reasonable understanding of what worked and what did not, mostly referencing back to the brief.	Produces a review of the finished graphic which demonstrates a thorough understanding of what worked and what did not, fully referencing back to the brief.
Review identifies areas for improvement and further development of the final digital graphic, some of which are appropriate and sometimes explained.	Review identifies areas for improvement and further development of the final digital graphic, which are mostly appropriate and explained well.	Review identifies areas for improvement and further development of the final digital graphic, which are wholly appropriate and justified.

Assessment guidance

The OCR set assignment

When completing your work for the OCR set assignment, you will need to:

- produce your own review of the digital graphics that you have created
- comment on the final product and how this relates to the brief
- following on from the review, identify what could be improved further.

What do the command words mean?

Thorough [review]: means commenting on all the aspects and elements of the digital graphic (not the process through the unit).

Appropriate and justified [areas for improvement]: areas for improvement should be relevant and supported by your reasons why.

R083 Creating 2D and 3D digital characters

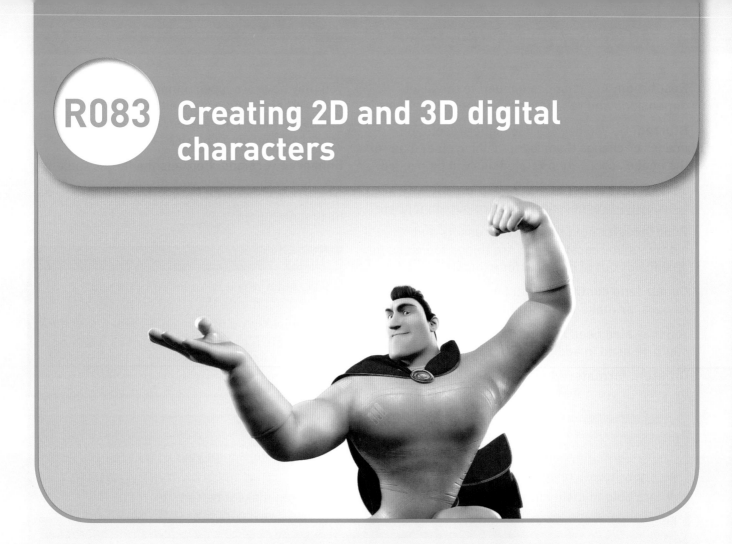

About this unit

R083 is about 2D and 3D digital characters. You will investigate where and why they are used before planning, creating and reviewing an original character of your own to meet a client brief.

Resources for this unit

2D image editing software: for example, Photoshop, Fireworks, DrawPlus, PhotoPlus, Affinity, Pixelmator or GIMP.

3D modelling software: for example, Google Sketchup, Blender and Autodesk® 3ds Max®.

Learning outcomes

LO1 Understand the properties and uses of 2D and 3D digital characters

LO2 Be able to plan original 2D and 3D digital characters

LO3 Be able to create 2D and 3D digital characters

LO4 Be able to review 2D and 3D digital characters

LO1 Understand the properties and uses of 2D and 3D digital characters

Getting started

Try creating a mood board of 2D and 3D characters. Find images of the characters; print them out for the mood board. See how many you can fit on a large sheet of paper – you can keep adding to it as you work through LO1.

Where they are used

Key areas

- Advertising (to include branding and promotion).
- Entertainment (in films, animations, games, and so on).
- Education (as a virtual teaching assistant to explain concepts, for example).

Target audiences

Considerations

- Age range.
- Why a character would appeal.
- How the audience relate to the character (cute, strong, lovable, powerful, for example).

Software for creation

2D characters

- Microsoft Paint
- Adobe Photoshop, Illustrator or Fireworks

- GIMP
- Serif PhotoPlus or DrawPlus
- Affinity Designer
- Krita

3D characters

- Google Sketchup
- Blender
- Autodesk 3ds Max
- Pixologic ZBrush

Physical and facial characteristics

This relates to the target audience and what makes them appealing. For example, many superhero characters are strong and muscular. Other characters used in computer games are fun and friendly, such as Mario and Luigi.

Classroom discussion

Make a list of as many 2D and 3D characters you can think of, from films, games and advertisements. Discuss what physical characteristics they have and why these characteristics are suitable for the character.

Group activity

Think about facial characteristics and what this means. In particular, comment on the eyes, ears, nose, mouth and facial expressions.

Assessment preparation

LO1: Understand the properties and uses of 2D and 3D digital characters		
Mark band 1	**Mark band 2**	**Mark band 3**
Demonstrates a basic understanding of when and where 2D and 3D digital characters are used.	Demonstrates a sound understanding of when and where 2D and 3D digital characters are used.	Demonstrates a thorough understanding of when and where 2D and 3D digital characters are used.
Lists a few 2D and 3D digital characters and a limited range of basic software that can be used to create them.	Describes a range of 2D and 3D digital characters and details a range of software that can be used to create them.	Describes a range of 2D and 3D digital characters and details a range of software, including some complex types, that can be used to create them.

Mark band 1	Mark band 2	Mark band 3
Demonstrates a basic understanding of physical and facial characteristics of a limited range of 2D and 3D digital characters.	Demonstrates a sound understanding of physical and facial characteristics of a range of 2D and 3D digital characters.	Demonstrates a thorough understanding of physical and facial characteristics of a wide range of 2D and 3D digital characters.

Assessment guidance

The OCR set assignment

When completing your work for the OCR set assignment, you will need to:

- describe a range of 2D and 3D digital characters together with when and where they are used
- describe a range of software applications used to create 2D and 3D digital characters
- discuss the physical appearance and facial features of a range of 2D and 3D digital characters.

What do the command words mean?

Thorough understanding [when and where used]: This can be demonstrated through depth, breadth or a combination. Breadth is the number of different areas/products in which 2D/3D characters are used whereas depth would be the detail in how, why and in what formats.

Complex types [software]: This relates to the complexity and level of skill needed to use different types of software, whether basic 2D image editing, complex 2D image editing and/or any 3D modelling software.

Thorough understanding [physical and facial characteristics]: This also can be demonstrated through depth, breadth or a combination. It can include the visual style, what is suggested by their appearance and how those physical and facial features give 'meaning' to the character.

LO2 Be able to plan original 2D and 3D digital characters

The content of this planning section applies techniques learned in the mandatory units R081 and R082.

Activity	Link to
Interpreting the client requirements for 2D and 3D digital characters (for a specific target audience, age group, print use, online use, and so on)	R081; R082
Understanding the target audience requirements for 2D and 3D digital characters	R081; R082
Identifying the assets needed to create 2D and 3D digital characters	R082
Identifying the resources needed to create 2D and 3D digital characters	R081; R082
Producing a work plan to create the digital character	R081; R082
Creating a visualisation diagram	R081; R082
Creating and maintaining a test plan	
Legislation (copyright, trademarks, logos, intellectual property use, permissions and implications of use)	R081

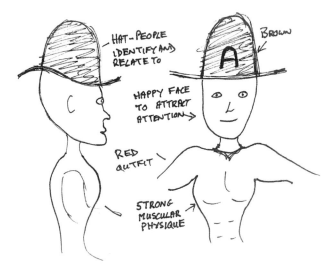

Figure 3.1 Visualisation diagram for a 2D character

Creating a test plan

The only element not covered by R081 and R082 is the test plan. For this, the concept of testing should be based around technical checks that the character will be fit for purpose and suitable for the client.

Technical checks for tests include:

File format: Bitmap or vector; how much can this be enlarged?

Image properties: Does it meet the minimum requirements for print and web use?

Resolution: Are the important features, such as words and logo, readable?

Colours: Does the brief need any specific colour schemes, and have they been used?

Assessment preparation

LO2: Be able to plan original 2D and 3D digital characters		
Mark band 1	**Mark band 2**	**Mark band 3**
Produces an interpretation from the client brief for a 2D or 3D digital character which meets few of the client requirements.	Produces an interpretation from the client brief for a 2D or 3D digital character which meets most of the client requirements.	Produces an interpretation from the client brief for a 2D or 3D digital character which fully meets the client requirements.
Produces a limited identification of target audience requirements.	Produces a clear identification of target audience requirements	Produces a clear and detailed identification of target audience requirements.
Identifies a few assets needed to create a 2D or 3D digital character, demonstrating a limited understanding of their potential use.	Identifies some assets needed to create a 2D or 3D digital character, demonstrating a sound understanding of their potential use.	Identifies many assets needed to create a 2D or 3D digital character, demonstrating a thorough understanding of their potential use.
Identifies a few of the resources needed to create a 2D or 3D digital character, demonstrating a limited understanding of their purpose.	Identifies some of the resources needed to create a 2D or 3D digital character, demonstrating a sound understanding of their purpose.	Identifies many of the resources needed to create a 2D or 3D digital character, demonstrating a thorough understanding of their purpose.
Produces a work plan for the 2D or 3D digital character, which has some capability in producing the intended final character.	Produces a work plan for the 2D or 3D digital character, which is mostly capable of producing the intended final character.	Produces a clear and detailed work plan for the 2D or 3D digital character, which is fully capable of producing the intended final character.
Draws upon limited skills/knowledge/understanding from other units in the specification.	Draws upon some relevant skills/knowledge/understanding from other units in the specification.	Clearly draws upon relevant skills/knowledge/understanding from other units in the specification.
Mark band 1	**Mark band 2**	**Mark band 3**
Produces a simple visualisation diagram for the 2D or 3D digital character.	Produces a sound visualisation diagram for the 2D or 3D digital character.	Produces a clear and detailed visualisation diagram for the 2D or 3D digital character.
Creates a test plan for the character which tests some of the functionality.	Creates a test plan for the character which tests most of the functionality, identifying expected outcomes.	Creates a clear and detailed test plan for the character which fully tests the functionality, listing tests, expected and actual outcomes and identifying re-tests.
Demonstrates a limited understanding of legislation in relation to the use of assets in 2D and 3D digital characters.	Demonstrates a sound understanding of legislation in relation to the use of assets in 2D and 3D digital characters.	Demonstrates a thorough understanding of legislation in relation to the use of assets in 2D and 3D digital characters.

Assessment guidance

The OCR set assignment

When completing your work for the OCR set assignment, you will need to:
- produce your own interpretation of the client brief
- identify the target audience and what they will want from the character

- identify the assets and resources needed to create the character
- produce a work plan to create the photoshoot
- use knowledge and skills from other units such as R081 or R082
- produce a visualisation diagram for the intended character
- create a test plan that checks the technical aspects of the digital character
- describe the legal restrictions regarding the re-use of any assets.

What do the command words mean?

Fully [interpretation of the brief]: This needs to be your own individual ideas and thoughts on what is required that expands on what is given in the scenario and brief.

Clear and detailed [target audience]: This should be a clear definition of who the target audience is and what they will want from the 2D/3D character.

Many [assets and understanding potential use]: This should identify how and where you could use the assets together with what makes them suitable. It can include assets that you decide not to use later on. Many can be accepted as a wide range, which is generally five or more.

Thorough [understanding of purpose of resources]: This should identify why you need to use the resources for creating the 2D/3D character.

Draws on [knowledge, skills and understanding]: This must be from other units and not something that is already in R083 e.g. a work plan or visualisation diagram.

Clear and detailed [work plan]: This should break down the main tasks into a sequence of relevant activities in order to create the 2D/3D character.

Clear and detailed [visualisation diagram]: This should be clear for somebody else so that they have a good idea of what you intend to create. Annotations may be added for clarification.

Clear and detailed [test plan – functionality]: The tests should be for the functionality and not the visual appeal or 'look' of the character. Functionality is more about whether the character will actually work, with consideration for the technical properties and formats.

Thorough [understanding of legislation]: This should be applied to the actual assets that you intend to use. Their use should also be in a commercial context and not just education.

LO3 Be able to create 2D and 3D digital characters

In this section, you will create a 2D or 3D digital character. If choosing a 2D character then the process is similar to creating digital graphics in R082.

The basic steps are:

1 Source and store assets.
2 Create the digital character using a range of tools and techniques.
3 Enhance the digital character to emphasise features and visual appeal (you can also create multiple views and/or close ups of facial features).
4 Save and export the character in suitable formats.
5 Organise files and folders.
6 Use version control during the character development.

Links to other units

You can find further information on sourcing and storing assets in **unit R082**.

Creating 2D digital characters

Many tools and techniques learned in R082 will enable you to create your 2D digital character. However, you are more likely to use shape and drawing tools.

Shapes and boxes can be filled with a colour using the paint bucket tool. You can add texture and shadow effects using layer styles. A drop shadow, together with bevel and emboss, can give a 3D effect to the character.

The finished character and development versions can be saved in the Photoshop .psd format to preserve the layers. Only when

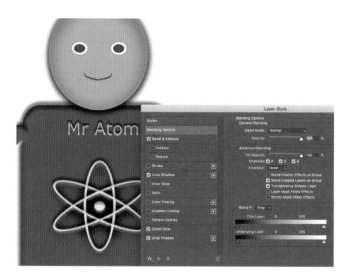

Figure 3.2 Enhancing the digital character

Links to other units

You can find further information on version control and file naming conventions in **unit R081**.

exporting for the client would the character be saved as a tiff or jpg file. If transparency is needed for the background, png file format would be a good choice.

Creating 3D digital characters

If creating a 3D character, software options would include Blender or Sketchup. The process is similar, but the choice of tools and techniques is different.

Having created a wireframe outline of the character, fill each element with colours and textures.

The 3D character is saved in the native format for the 3D software application so that further edits and work can be completed. The options for export will depend on the software chosen.

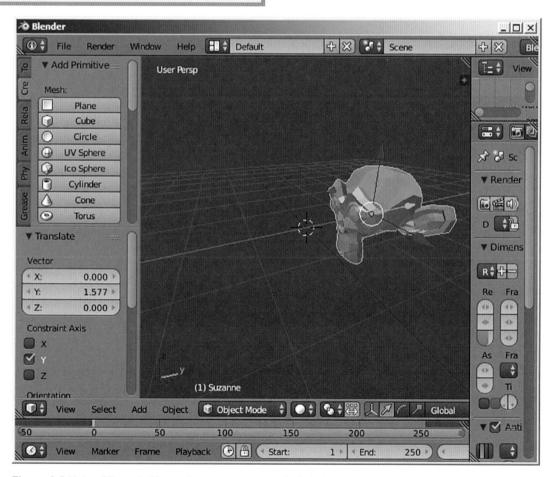

Figure 3.3 Using 3D modelling software to create a digital character

Assessment preparation

LO3: Be able to create 2D and 3D digital characters		
Mark band 1	Mark band 2	Mark band 3
Sources and stores a limited range of assets for use, occasionally uses appropriate methods. Creates a character using shapes or freehand drawing tools.	Sources and stores a range of assets for use, mostly uses appropriate methods. Uses a range of software tools and techniques to create the visualised character. Adds and applies a range of effects to enhance the character.	Sources and stores a wide range of assets for use, consistently uses appropriate methods. Uses a wide range of software tools and techniques to create the visualised character. Adds and applies a wide range of effects to enhance the character.
Mark band 1	Mark band 2	Mark band 3
Occasionally saves and exports the 2D or 3D digital character in appropriate formats. Occasionally saves electronic files using appropriate file and folder names and structures.	Mostly saves and exports the 2D or 3D digital character in appropriate formats. Mostly saves electronic files using file and folder names and structures which are consistent and appropriate.	Consistently saves and exports the 2D or 3D digital character in appropriate formats. Consistently saves electronic files using file and folder names and structures which are consistent and appropriate.

Assessment guidance

The OCR set assignment

When completing your work for the OCR set assignment, you will need to:

- source and store a range of assets to be used when creating the digital character
- use a range of tools and techniques when creating the character
- enhance the character e.g. through colour, texture and features
- save and export the character in suitable formats to meet the client requirements
- use appropriate file and folder naming conventions to organise your work.

What do the command words mean?

Wide range [of assets]: This is accepted as five or more. Consistently using appropriate methods means saving in a suitable format and location.

Wide range [software tools and techniques – creation]: This is accepted as five or more.

Wide range [effects to enhance]: This is accepted as five or more. To enhance the character means making it look more effective than a basic character.

Consistently [saves and exports]: This means the exported formats for the character must be suitable for use by the client and that they would meet the requirements of the brief.

Consistently appropriate [files and folders]: This means that the development of the character should be documented using different version numbers and with descriptive file names, with assets stored in suitable folders.

LO4 Be able to review 2D and 3D digital characters

Reviewing your character

Key areas to cover in a review:

Size/resolution: Are the size, pixel dimensions and resolution suitable?

Quality: Is the digital character clear and well defined at the intended size?

Features (such as text and logos): Can these be seen and read easily by a viewer?

Colour (and contrast): Do the colours work, or do they need to be brighter and bolder?

Areas for improvement

Using this information, you can think about how to improve the digital character.

Links to other units

You can find further information on this topic in **unit R082**.

Read about it

Disney Pixar Character Encyclopedia (DK Children, 2011).

The Art of Pixar: the Complete Color Scripts and Select Art from 25 Years of Animation, by Amid Amidi (Chronicle Books, 2011).

The Art of DreamWorks Animation, by Ramin Zahed (Abrams, 2014).

YouTube – character design video tutorials.

Assessment preparation

LO4: Be able to review 2D and 3D digital characters		
Mark band 1	Mark band 2	Mark band 3
Produces a review of the finished character which demonstrates a limited understanding of what worked and what did not, making few references back to the brief.	Produces a review of the finished character which demonstrates a reasonable understanding of what worked and what did not, mostly referencing back to the brief.	Produces a review of the finished character which demonstrates a thorough understanding of what worked and what did not, fully referencing back to the brief.
Review identifies areas for improvement and further development of the final character, some of which are appropriate and sometimes explained.	Review identifies areas for improvement and further development of the final character, which are mostly appropriate and explained well.	Review identifies areas for improvement and further development of the final character, which are wholly appropriate and justified.

Assessment guidance

The OCR set assignment

When completing your work for the OCR set assignment, you will need to:

- produce your own review of the digital character that you have created
- comment on the final character and how this relates to the brief
- identify what could be improved further.

What do the command words mean?

Thorough [review]: This means commenting on all the aspects and elements of the 2D/3D digital character (not the process through the unit).

Appropriate and justified [areas for improvement]: The areas for improvement should be relevant and supported by your reasons why.

R084 Storytelling with a comic strip

About this unit

This unit allows you to explore the history of comic strips and their characters. You will learn to use this knowledge to plan, develop and create your own multipage comic strip to fit a client brief. You will build on your reflective skills to review your work.

Resources for this unit

There are a range of different software options that could be used to create a comic strip; some are specific comic creation software and some are more general software. Examples include Microsoft Publisher, Comic Life, Pixton Comic, iStudio Publisher and Adobe Illustrator/Fireworks/Photoshop.

Learning outcomes

LO1 Understand comic strips and their creation
LO2 Be able to plan a multipage comic strip
LO3 Be able to produce a multipage comic strip
LO4 Be able to review a multipage comic strip

How will I be assessed?

You will be assessed through an OCR model assignment, which is marked by your tutor and externally moderated by OCR. It is worth 25% of the overall mark when working towards a Certificate in Creative iMedia.

For LO1

Learners need to:

- investigate the origins and history of multipage comic strips and their target audiences
- demonstrate understanding of comic strip characters and their physical and non-physical characteristics
- describe software that can be used to create comic strips and tools that can be used
- demonstrate understanding of panel placement and story flow.

For LO2

Learners need to:

- plan an original script and storyline for the comic strip, meeting the client brief and the requirements of the target audience
- create an accurate storyboard to plan the key aspects of the comic strip

- identify assets and resources needed to create the multipage comic strip
- demonstrate understanding of legislation in relation to the use of assets in multipage comic strips.

For LO3

Learners need to:

- appropriately source and store assets for use
- prepare comic strip layout and place assets to produce a multipage comic strip
- create a comic strip with a coherent storyline in line with the plan
- save and export the comic strip in suitable formats using appropriate file and folder names.

For LO4

Learners need to:

- review their finished comic strip, referencing back to the brief
- identify areas for improvement and further development of the comic strip.

LO1 Understand comic strips and their creation

Getting started

Search for and look at a range of comics and comic strips. Make notes on the storyline, characters and panel layout. In a group, discuss why these are different to other ways of telling a story.

The first objective focuses on the core features of comic strips and their creation. To understand comic strips it is important to consider their history, **origins**, and potential purpose and audience.

Key term

Origin: where something came from or began (the *origins* of a story or concept).

Multipage comic strips

Genres

The genre and topic of a comic strip influences its style and design; this is closely linked to its target audience. Comic strips can be created in black and white or colour. Some of the more popular genres of comic include:

Key terms

Panel: a container used to contain one scene in a comic strip.

Story flow: the path of the story from beginning, to middle, to end.

- **Science fiction:** Often set in the future; can use blue, grey and silver colour schemes and bold metallic appearance and futuristic fonts.
- **Superhero:** Usually have a main character that represents good or evil; characters often have distinctive, identifying costumes.
- **Manga:** Distinctive bold character design and specific **panel** placement and **story flow**.
- **Horror:** Often characterised by predominant use of black, red and green, and stereotypical horror style fonts (such as those replicating dripping blood from the letters).

Target audience

Comic strips can appeal to all age ranges; the image-based method of storytelling makes them particularly suitable for children and young adults.

Target audience influences a number of design features, such as the amount of text on each page depending on the audience age and reading ability. For a young target audience, you would aim to convey the main storyline using mostly images. For an adult target audience, you can include more text, and more complex vocabulary and storylines.

Content and number of pages should also reflect the target audience; you need to consider how many pages are suitable to tell a story to different age groups. Young children, for example, would require a shorter comic than teenagers and adults.

Origins and history

The idea of telling stories using a series of images goes back to Egyptian hieroglyphics. And in Europe, in the seventeenth century, series

of images were used for propaganda and to convey religious and moral messages. So it is challenging to pin point *exactly* when and where the first comics were created.

The first comic strip as we recognise them, however, was published in the Hearst New York American in 1896. It was called 'The Yellow Kid' and was created by Richard Felton Outcault.

For the purposes of this unit, we will look at the development of popular comics since the 1930s.

Rodolphe Töpffer

Rodolphe Töpffer, a Swiss teacher, was one of the first European comic strip creators. And his book, *Histoire de M. Vieux Bois*, is one of the first European comic books. It was based on comic style black and white sketches with caption boxes below to outline the story, which were usually humorous fictional tales.

Manga

Manga refers to Japanese comic books. It is thought to be centuries old, but came to prominence in the 1940s and 1950s when America occupied Japan. The Americans brought their style of comic to Japan which had a lasting influence on Manga comics. The Manga artist Osamu Tezuka created one of the first modern style Manga comics featuring the character Astro Boy, which demonstrates the style of graphics we associate with Manga today.

Figure 4.1 Example Manga character

Morning Journal

The first weekly newspaper comic supplement was released in the Morning Journal in the US in 1896. Comic strips became increasingly popular and were present in many newspapers in the 1900s. They were so popular that collections of comic strips began to be collected and made into comic books. The comic strips published in the newspapers were in black and white, but with the advances in printing comics could eventually also be printed in colour.

Superheroes

From the 1930s to the 1950s, the range of genres expanded significantly, including action genres and superheroes. Some of the earliest comic strips of this genre were Tarzan (1929) and Flash Gordon (1934). The English comic Dandy began in 1937, and Beano shortly after in 1938. There were some British comics in this time, but American comics were more popular.

DC and Marvel

DC and Marvel Comics are two of the most prominent names in 20th century comics. Their influence is immense. Both were launched in the 1930s – which later became known as the **Golden age** of comics.

In recent years, both ranges have been successful and have divided the loyalties of their audiences.

They share similarities, but there are core differences in terms of characters and storylines. DC base its characters and storylines on super human heroes, such as Superman and Wonder Woman, often portrayed as the hero coming to save the human race from disaster. In contrast, Marvel creates characters based on humans who gain their powers or abilities to become superheroes. An example would be Peter Parker and his alter ego Spiderman, or the Hulk and his alter ego Bruce Banner. These characters are often more flawed, the storyline tends to depict their weaknesses as well as their strengths, and they are often overcoming issues within their own life as well as defeating the villain of the story.

Key terms

The last 80 years have been characterised into different 'ages'. Your research should include these.

Golden age: 1938–1954
Silver age: 1956–1969
Bronze age: 1970–1980
Late Bronze age: 1980–1984
Modern age: 1985–present day

Marvel and DC are still very successful; they have introduced many characters over the last eight decades and they still attract large numbers of readers.

They have, however, started to move away from the idealistic themes of the hero saving the day to darker storylines which are a little more realistic and appeal to the modern reader.

Comic strips characters

Physical characteristics

Physical characteristics include body size and shape, facial features, hair styles and outfits.

A character's appearance is used consistently throughout the comic and other strips within the series; this allows the reader to easily identify the core characters throughout the storylines.

Many comic book characters are represented by a signature look or outfit, from Superman's blue suit and red cape, to Tintin's quiff.

Physical characteristics are often exaggerated – Manga characters, for example, have very large eyes and small mouths. The eyes are often used to show the character's feelings. They also have distinctive hairstyles in a range of colours.

Non-physical characteristics

Non-physical characteristics often link to the genre of the comic strip. For example, in a horror comic strip, characters may have characteristics such as dishonesty and deviousness. Children's comic books characters will have more simplistic characteristics, such as happiness, sadness or humour.

Superheroes' non-physical characteristics are, typically, exaggerated strengths and weaknesses. These often link the hero and the villain, and go back to the origins of how they became adversaries.

Other non-physical characteristics often relate to the superhero or villain's powers, such as mind reading, telepathy, X-ray vision. Some are more conventional characteristics, such as high intellect and technical ability (for example, Tony Stark as Iron Man).

Characters in comic strips often have characteristics that the reader can relate to, such as a personality trait, skill, fear or insecurity.

Group activity

In a small group, select a comic strip character and complete this fact file.

Comic character fact file	
Name	
Comic genre	
Physical characteristics	
Non-physical characteristics	
Other characters in series	

Software and tools for creation

Software

There are a range of applications to create a comic strip. There are comic specific software and more generic software.

Some software you could consider:

- Comic Life
- Microsoft Publisher
- Pixton Comic
- iStudio Publisher
- Adobe Illustrator/Fireworks/Photoshop

Tools

You need to be able to link the tools to the creation of a comic strip – not simply state all the tools available in the software. Consider what elements you need to create to construct your comic strip, and then think about which tools you may use to complete that task.

You might consider creating:

- panels and page layout
- backgrounds for each panel
- characters
- speech and thought bubbles
- caption/narration boxes
- text to use for speech, thought, captions and narration.

Panel placement and story flow

Comic strips have clear layout and story flow, unlike many other **illustrated** story telling methods. Comic strips conventionally display their artwork in a sequence of boxes, which are read left to right across the page. These typically have six to nine panels on a page. Panel shape can indicate different action in the comic strip; for example, a long panel can indicate an extended length of time or distance. Figure 4.2(left) shows a typical example of story flow in a comic strip.

Key term

Illustrate: to add images to support the story or information provided in the product.

Western comic flow

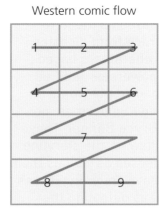

Manga comic flow

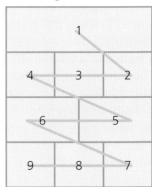

Figure 4.2 Examples of typical story flow in Western style and Manga comics

In Manga comic strips, the story flow is different – it reads from right to left. This also applies to the speech and thought bubbles. Figure 4.2(right) demonstrates the story flow in a Manga comic strip.

When creating a story flow, it is important to let your audience know where the story is set. This is called an *establishing shot* and precedes the panels that focus on the action.

There should be a good variety of images to keep the audience's attention. If the same image is used in a range of scenes, consider how you might make the storyline more concise to allow the imagery to move with good pace. This applies to panel layout too – try to create variety in the layout of the panels and match this to the story flow. Larger panels tend to slow down the pace of the story, while a series of smaller panels will speed it up.

Text-based conventions are also used to explain a story, such as **narrative** and caption boxes that are usually around the edges of the panels. These boxes can narrate a scene, or clarify a change in the location or situation.

Speech and thought bubbles

Speech or thought bubbles show character's speech or thought. Their shape and style indicate the type of communication they contain.

Speech bubbles are usually square or circular, with a pointed 'tail' in the direction of the character who is speaking. The style can also indicate the tone of the speech. For example, a spiky outlined bubble might suggest shouting or anger, whereas a bubble with a dotted outline might represent whispering. A bubble representing speech from a radio, television or phone is usually shaped like a lightning bolt, or has a lightning bolt 'tail'.

Thought bubbles tend to be a cartoon cloud shape; there are usually two or three smaller circles leading towards the character who is thinking.

It is good practice to avoid crowding your panels with speech and thought bubbles; up to two or three per panel is a good guide. Think carefully about where to place them – they should read left to right across the panel in the order you want the reader to read them.

Figure 4.3 Examples of speech and thought bubbles

Key terms

Narrative: explaining events by speaking or writing them down.
Onomatopoeia: a word that sounds like the thing it is describing, such as *slurp*.

Stretch activity

Onomatopoeia – such as CRASH! or ZOOOOM! – can be used for emphasis. When spoken, they sound like, or suggest, the sound that they describe. In comics, they are usually in a large, bright font, with an exclamation mark, and occupy a lot of space over the action displayed in the panel. Find examples of onomatopoeia in the comics you have available.

Figure 4.4 Examples of onomatopoeia

Group activity

In small groups create a three-sentence story using as many onomatopoeias as you can.

For example, it was lunchtime on a murky January day, in the school dinner hall, the dinner ladies' wet shoes squeaking and squelching as they moved across the tacky lino floor. Stephen slurped slimy cabbage soup, which squelched as he squashed in his crumbly bread. Tommy sat next to him, glugged his fizzy pop, then belched loudly.

Stretch activity

List comic book genres. For each genre, identify some physical and non-physical characteristics you might expect of the characters.

Know it!

Explain the difference between a physical and non-physical characteristic.

Assessment preparation

Think about the individual performance you will need to undertake. Make sure you:

- know the different software that can be used to create a comic and tools within the software that could be used
- understand comic strips and their creation and the characteristics of the characters found in comic strips.

LO1: Understand comic strips and their creation		
Mark band 1	Mark band 2	Mark band 3
Demonstrates a limited understanding of the origins and history of multipage comic strips, which shows limited awareness of their target audiences. Demonstrates a basic understanding of comic strip characters and limited knowledge of their respective physical and non-physical characteristics.	Demonstrates a sound understanding of the origins and history of multipage comic strips, and shows some awareness of their target audiences. Demonstrates a sound understanding of comic strip characters and some knowledge of their respective physical and non-physical characteristics.	Demonstrates a thorough understanding of the origins and history of multipage comic strips, and shows a clear awareness of their target audiences. Demonstrates a thorough understanding of comic strip characters and detailed knowledge of their respective physical and non-physical characteristics.
Mark band 1	Mark band 2	Mark band 3
Identifies software that can be used to create a comic strip and some of the tools that can be used in its creation. Demonstrates a basic understanding of panel placement and story flow.	Identifies software that can be used to create a comic strip and a range of tools that can be used in its creation. Demonstrates a sound understanding of panel placement and story flow.	Describes software that can be used to create a comic strip, accurately describing a range of tools that can be used in its creation and explains how these relate to the layout and features of the pages. Demonstrates a thorough understanding of panel placement and story flow.

Assessment guidance

The OCR set assignment

When completing your work for the OCR set assignment, you will need to:

- produce a report or presentation summarising the origins and history of multipage comic strips and their target audiences
- produce a report or presentation on the physical and non-physical characteristics of a range of comic strip characters
- describe a range of software that can be used to create multipage comics and what tools are used for this purpose
- describe the options for panel placement and story flow for different approaches to multipage comics.

What do the command words mean?

Thorough [understanding comics]: can be demonstrated through depth, breadth or a combination. Breadth would be the number of different origins and comics whereas depth is the level of detail.

Thorough [understanding characters]: can be demonstrated through depth, breadth or a combination. Breadth would be the number of different characters with their physical and non-physical characteristics whereas depth is the level of detail.

Accurately [describing tools]: can be demonstrated through knowledge of relevant tools within software applications that are used to create the key elements of a comic, such as the panels, scenes, characters and dialogue.

Thorough [understanding panel placement]: can be demonstrated by describing the options for panel layout on different pages and how the story should flow between them so that it is logical for the reader.

LO2 Be able to plan a multipage comic strip

Getting started

Read through the brief below. Make a list of the key elements you need to think about when planning this comic.

Brief

You are working for a zoo; they are running a campaign to raise awareness of endangered species. You have been asked to create a comic strip to give out with the children's lunch boxes in the restaurant. It should explain the problems faced by endangered species, particularly the Giant Panda. Your comic needs to be in a format that can be printed for the lunch boxes and displayed on the zoo's website.

Key term

Interpretation: reviewing the information provided and taking the relevant information from the text.

Links to other units

You can find further information on this topic in LO2 of **unit R081**.

The client brief

The client brief is vital to creating an effective comic script. If you do not pay attention to the brief, you could make an excellent comic product that doesn't satisfy the client's needs and is, therefore, unsuccessful.

Key questions to think about when analysing and **interpreting** the brief:

- Who is the client?
- What is the product?
- Who is the audience?
- What are the main features of the product? For example, how many pages are needed? What is the main message? What content must be included?

Target audience requirements

First, think about the characteristics of the target audience, such as:

- age
- gender
- income
- location.

From this core information you can develop a picture of the target audience and their requirements. For example, let's consider the brief in the 'Getting started' box.

We can summarise the following details from the brief.

- The audience are children.
- Children eating the children's lunches are probably younger than teenagers.

- The aim is to help them understand about endangered species, so we can assume they are older than toddlers.
- So, we can put the age range at approximately 4 to 10 years old.
- Now we need to consider the literacy levels of the audience. With this age range the text will need to be simple and short to allow the younger readers to access the information.
- The content should not include imagery that is too adult or graphic for young people.
- Since the audience are at the zoo, we can assume that have some interest in animals.
- The requirement is to raise awareness of endangered species, so the comic should provide information and entertain, not promote or sell a product.
- So, the focus of the story will be on factual information displayed in an entertaining way to engage the audience.

Script, storyline and storyboards

The script and the storyboard go hand in hand when planning your comic strip. You will know the basics of planning techniques from unit R081, LO2. However, there are additional guidelines for creating a script and storyboard for a comic strip. The story flow through the comic is important as this is what will take your reader through the story. If the plot is confusing or difficult to follow, the reader will not have a good experience of reading the comic and is unlikely to fully understand the purpose or meaning of the story.

There are three core stages to planning out the comic:

1 Draft out an outline for the story. This could be a simple series of bullet points which outline the key points and create a clear beginning, middle and end for the story. Or it could be a short paragraph of text.

2 Create a script. This is for recording the characters' speech and information on captions, narrative and the staging of each panel and page. When the script is complete, it can be used to look at the flow of the story to decide where the page divides will fall and what

> *Storyline (part 1): Ryszard is talking to Sarah about going to the cinema using a smartphone messaging app on social media*
>
> **SCRIPT**
>
> AT HOME IN LOUNGE, MESSAGING VIA SOCIAL MEDIA on SMARTPHONE
>
>   **Ryszard**
>
>   How about going to see the new film that opens today?
>
>   **Sarah**
>
>   Yeah great, let me know what time?
>
>   **Ryszard**
>
>   Starts at 6.30 – meet outside at 6.00|
>
>   **Sarah**
>
> STANDING OUTSIDE THE CINEMA
>
>   **Ryszard**
>
>   Hi Sarah – over here!
>
> RYSZARD AND SARAH GO INSIDE

Figure 4.5 Example script for a comic

the individual panels will contain. Refer to unit R081, LO3 for the content and layout of a script.

3 Create the storyboard. This is an important planning document as it allows the other elements of the plans to come together – the creator can visually plan how the comic will look, and consider any changes that are needed to allow the reader to have the best experience when reading the comic. First, plan the panels on the pages and sketch out the graphics for each scene, being sure to label the **focal points** of each panel. Add the speech, thought and narrative, taking care to follow the left to right reading convention.

Creating the storyboard allows the creator to review the story flow to make sure it is clear and coherent, and reflect and make any changes to ensure that the brief and target audience requirements are met.

Key term

Focal points: the place in a panel where the creator wants the reader's eye to be focused.

Assets

Assets are the different elements you need to create the panels on the comic strip; they include:

- background images
- characters
- communication assets, such as speech and thought bubbles
- font styles.

You need to be able to explain *why* you need each asset and what the purpose of it will be in your comic strip.

Consider the audience and purpose of the product to make sure you plan the best assets to meet the brief. Also consider the source of the assets. For example, which assets do you plan to create yourself, how will you create them, and which assets will you source elsewhere?

Resources

Resources refers to the equipment you need to make your comic strip. Make sure you have everything you need to allow you to complete the project on time. It is likely that you will need computer hardware, such as computer, keyboard, mouse and screen, as well as peripheral devices, as:

- digital camera
- graphics tablet
- scanner.

You also need think about what software you require for the construction of the comic strip, and to prepare and locate the assets you plan to use in the comic.

You need to be able to explain the reasons for your choice of resources, and how they will enable you to create the comic strip.

Legislation

You will have seen information on **legislation** in the chapter on R081 LO2. So, how does this information link to the comic?

You need to be able to explain copyright issues and comply with relevant legislation when creating your comic, particularly the assets.

Intellectual property is also relevant when deciding on themes and ideas; you must make sure they are original.

There's a chance that defamation may also be a consideration, especially if you base a character on a real person. Think about the steps you need to take to make sure you don't create anything considered defamatory.

Key terms

Assets: the content collected or created for the final product, such as images, sound and video.

Resources: software or hardware that is used to create part or all of the product or planning.

Legislation: a collection of laws.

Group activity

Use your three-sentence story with onomatopoeias (from a previous group activity) to create a three panel sketch storyboard. Label the

- focal points
- speech and thought bubbles
- narration.

Know it!

Explain which elements of legislation might need to be considered when creating a comic strip.

Read about it

www.britannica.com/art/comic-strip

www.freecomicbookday.com/Article/116248-Genres--Categories

www.cartoonmuseum.org/explore/history-of-cartoons-comics

https://comicsforbeginners.com/

Assessment preparation

Think about the individual performance you will need to undertake. Make sure you are able to:

- assess the client brief, the requirements of the target audience and plan
- create a comic strip that follows the plans and meets the requirements of the brief.

LO2: Be able to plan a multipage comic strip		
Mark band 1	**Mark band 2**	**Mark band 3**
Produces an interpretation from the client brief for a multipage comic strip which meets few of the client requirements.	Produces an interpretation from the client brief for a multipage comic strip which meets some of the client requirements.	Produces an interpretation from the client brief for a multipage comic strip which fully meets the client requirements.
Produces a limited identification of target audience requirements.	Produces a clear identification of target audience requirements.	Produces a clear and detailed identification of target audience requirements.
Creates a script and storyline with some elements of originality.	Creates a script and storyline which is mostly original.	Creates a script and storyline which is fully original and appropriate for use in a multipage comic strip.
Draws upon limited skills/knowledge/ understanding from other units in the specification.	Draws upon some relevant skills/ knowledge/understanding from other units in the specification.	Clearly draws upon relevant skills/ knowledge/understanding from other units in the specification.
Mark band 1	**Mark band 2**	**Mark band 3**
Creates rough sketches to plan the comic strip, including a panel layout which has limited accuracy.	Creates a storyboard of rough sketches and a script with reasonable accuracy that includes panel layout, characters, storyline, communication, and focal points.	Accurately creates a storyboard of sketches and a script that includes characters, storyline, panel layout, communication, focal points and locations.
Identifies a few assets needed to create a multipage comic strip, demonstrating a limited understanding of their potential use.	Identifies some assets needed to create a multipage comic strip, demonstrating a sound understanding of their potential use.	Identifies many assets needed to create a multipage comic strip, demonstrating a thorough understanding of their potential use.
Identifies a few of the resources needed to create a multipage comic strip, demonstrating a limited understanding of their purpose.	Identifies some of the resources needed to create a multipage comic strip, demonstrating a sound understanding of their purpose.	Identifies many of the resources needed to create a multipage comic strip, demonstrating a thorough understanding of their purpose.
Demonstrates a limited understanding of legislation in relation to the use of assets in multipage comic strips, which is occasionally accurate.	Demonstrates a sound understanding of legislation in relation to the use of assets in multipage comic strips, which is mostly accurate.	Demonstrates a thorough understanding of legislation in relation to the use of assets in multipage comic strips, which is accurate.

Assessment guidance

The OCR set assignment

When completing your work for the OCR set assignment, you will need to:

- produce your own interpretation of the client brief
- identify the target audience and what they will want from the comic
- produce an outline script for the intended comic
- use knowledge and skills from other units such as R081 and R082
- produce a storyboard based on the storyline and script
- identify the assets needed to create the comic and why
- identify the resources needed to create the comic and their purpose
- describe the legal restrictions on any planned assets.

LO3 Be able to produce a multipage comic strip

Getting started

Comics are all about storytelling. Think about your favourite comic. What is the storyline about? In a small group, write down some ideas for a new storyline that features your favourite characters.

Sourcing and storing assets

You now need to source the assets you identified in LO2, then organise and store them to create the comic strip. When identifying assets, consider whether you will create them yourself, or source them. When sourcing assets, make sure you comply with relevant legislation, such as copyright law. Search engine settings allow you to search for assets which are not subject to copyright. Or, if you choose to use assets which are subject to copyright, follow the copyright legislation (as discussed in R081 LO3) and use a source table to record the relevant information.

You also need to think about how you store your assets so they are easy to locate when you need to use or edit them. Remember to use version control to store the assets in a logical way, especially when editing, so you can chart changes and make sure you use the correct version.

Panel layout and inserting assets

The layout of the panels is key to conveying the storyline. Think about the size and shape of each panel, and the number of panels on each page. Each one needs enough space to ensure assets and communication can clearly be seen. The number of panels per page will impact on the story flow. For example, if you are planning a cliff hanger scene you need to make sure this panel is the final panel on the page. The shape of the panels can impact the reader. Lay out assets in each panel so the key parts of the story are clear to the reader.

A typical process:

1 Create the panel layout for the page.
2 Import the image assets and place in the panels.
3 Crop/adjust/scale the panel content as required.
4 Add speech bubbles and dialogue (use the script for reference).
5 Add any special effects.
6 Proofread the comic page.
7 Save the comic page.

Focal points

Focal points allow the reader to follow the story from one panel to the next. The focal point is the main element in each panel where you want to the reader to look – this will depict the key point of that panel and that part of the storyline.

Figure 4.6 Example of focal point

Integrating the script

Integrating the script creates and maintains the story flow throughout the comic. When placing the communication items in the panels, ensure they do not obstruct the focal points. It is also good practice to consider the styling – text size and font style, for example – of the communications; they have an impact on the overall look and feel of the comic strip. The font styles are often informal, imitating a hand drawn style, rather than formal styles that you might find in a book or a letter.

Figure 4.7 Example of comic style font

Figure 4.8 Adding speech bubbles to the comic

Saving and exporting your comic strip

The brief requirements are key to saving and **exporting** the comic strip, so it's important to have the brief to hand. This will allow you to ensure that the comic strip is suitable for the client needs. As you will have seen from your work in R081, the file type selected for the product has significant influence on the properties of the comic. Some of the things you need to consider when choosing the file format are:

- **File size:** does the comic strip need to be emailed or shared on the internet?
- **Image quality:** does the comic strip need to be high quality or low quality?
- **Product format:** does the comic strip need to be in print or electronic format?

You also need to remember the work on version control and file names from R081 to ensure that the final document is easily identifiable to the client, in terms of both the file name and an indication that the version they are looking at is the finished product.

> 🔑 **Key term**
>
> **Export:** to change the format of a product that is published for use by the client.

For example, if we return to our earlier brief we can consider how we might export this comic strip:

You are working for a zoo; they are running a campaign to raise awareness of endangered species. You have been asked to create a comic strip to give out with the children's lunch boxes in the restaurant. It should explain the problems faced by endangered species, particularly the Giant Panda. Your comic needs to be in a format that can be printed for the lunch boxes and displayed on the zoo's website.

We can see that there are two core requirements: it needs to be printed for the lunch boxes, and used in an electronic format on the website.

There are a number of ways to approach this. You could create a PDF version of the comic strip; this would protect the formatting for print and electronic formats, while keeping the file small enough to be uploaded and downloaded quickly. An alternative would be to create two versions – a high-quality image file with high resolution for printing (a .tiff file would be suitable) and a second version using compression (a .jpg or .png would be suitable).

Links to other units

You can find further information on this topic in LO3 of **unit R082**.

Stretch activity

You are required to create a comic that can be emailed to readers and printed in large scale A3 for a sample poster. What file types would you use for each requirement and why?

Know it!

What resolution would the images need to be, to be suitable for a printed comic strip?

Assessment preparation

Think about the individual performance you will need to undertake. Make sure you are able to:

- source assets appropriately
- create a comic strip that follows your plans and meets the requirements of the brief.

LO3: Be able to produce a multipage comic strip		
Mark band 1	**Mark band 2**	**Mark band 3**
Sources and stores a limited range of assets for use, occasionally using methods which are appropriate.	Sources and stores a range of assets for use, mostly using methods which are appropriate.	Sources and stores a wide range of assets for use, consistently using methods which are appropriate.
Prepares the page layout for the comic strip with panels, not all of which are complete.	Prepares the page layout for the comic strip with panels which are mostly complete.	Prepares the page layout for the comic strip with complete and detailed panels.
Mark band 1	**Mark band 2**	**Mark band 3**
Inserts some basic assets into the comic strip panels, sometimes establishing appropriate focal points.	Places assets into the prepared panels to produce an illustrated story over several pages, establishing some key focal points.	Places assets into the prepared panels to produce an illustrated story over several pages, consistently establishing key focal points for the story.
Creates a story and narrative within the strip of limited coherence, which is occasionally in line with the plan.	Integrates the script with the visual storyline to produce a mostly coherent comic strip storyline, which mostly follows the plan.	Integrates the script with the visual storyline to produce a fully coherent comic strip storyline, which closely follows the plan.
Saves and exports the comic strip occasionally using appropriate formats.	Saves and exports the comic strip mostly using appropriate formats.	Saves and exports the comic strip consistently using appropriate formats.
Occasionally saves electronic files using appropriate file and folder names and structures.	Mostly saves electronic files using file and folder names and structures which are consistent and appropriate.	Consistently saves electronic files using file and folder names and structures which are consistent and appropriate.

Assessment guidance

The OCR set assignment

When completing your work for the OCR set assignment, you will need to:

- source and store a wide range of assets
- prepare the page layout and provide evidence of this
- place your assets into the panels, ensuring the focal point for the viewer is clear
- combine the storyline with the script, ensuring that the finished comic has a clear story flow for the reader
- save and export the comic in suitable formats and with appropriate names.

What do the command words mean?

Wide range [of assets]: means five or more.

Consistently [using storage methods]: assets should be stored in a separate folder with clear naming conventions.

Complete and detailed [panels]: comic should be multipage and complex in its layout.

Consistently establishing key [focal points]: should be relevant elements of the story that the reader is attracted to when looking at the comic.

Fully [coherent comic]: means that all elements work effectively as intended.

Consistently appropriate [formats]: comic should be exported in electronic file format for use and distribution by the client.

LO4 Be able to review a multipage comic strip

Getting started

In a small group, choose one story from a comic. Look at the panel layout and flow of the story. Write down a list of five things that work well.

This objective links to R081. You have learnt that the main aim of the review is to reflect on the product you have created and how well it fits the brief, and to think about developments and improvements that you could make. The key to writing a good review is to link this to the client brief (the success criteria for the product). Remember this is not a diary of the project; you have demonstrated the other areas of the skills in the other objectives, so focus on discussing the final completed product.

Links to other units

You can find further information on this topic in LO4 of **units R081** and **R082**.

Know it!

Make a list of five things that should be considered when reviewing a comic.

Assessment preparation

Think about the individual performance you will need to undertake.

Make sure you are able to reflect on what did and did not work in relation to the comic strip and its suitability for the brief and suggest further developments and improvements to the comic to help it better suit the brief and audience.

LO4: Be able to review a multipage comic strip		
Mark band 1	Mark band 2	Mark band 3
Produces a review of the finished comic strip which demonstrates a limited understanding of what worked and what did not, making few references back to the brief.	Produces a review of the finished comic strip which demonstrates a reasonable understanding of what worked and what did not, mostly referencing back to the brief.	Produces a review of the finished comic strip which demonstrates a thorough understanding of what worked and what did not, fully referencing back to the brief.
Review identifies areas for improvement and further development of the finished comic strip, some of which are appropriate and sometimes explained.	Review identifies areas for improvement and further development of the finished comic strip, which are mostly appropriate and explained well.	Review identifies areas for improvement and further development of the finished comic strip, which are wholly appropriate and justified.

Assessment guidance

The OCR set assignment

When completing your work for the OCR set assignment, you will need to:

- produce your own review of the multipage comic that you have created
- comment on the final comic and how this relates to the brief
- identify what could be improved further.

What do the command words mean?

Thorough [review]: means commenting on all the aspects and elements of the multipage comic (not the process through the unit).

Appropriate and justified [areas for improvement]: areas for improvement should be relevant and supported by your reasons why.

R085 Creating a multipage website

About this unit

In this unit you will be introduced to the basics of website design and creation. You will need to use the client brief to guide the creation of your website. You will also need to use your skills from R081 to help you plan your project. You will need to consider the function as well as the design and visual appearance of your product.

Resources for this unit

Hardware: Computer system.

Software: for example, Adobe Dreamweaver®, Serif WebPlus, Microsoft Expression.

Learning outcomes

LO1 Understand the properties and features of multipage websites

LO2 Be able to plan a multipage website

LO3 Be able to create multipage websites using multimedia components

LO4 Be able to review a multipage website

How will I be assessed?

You will be assessed through an OCR model assignment, marked by your tutor and externally moderated by OCR. It is worth 25% of the overall mark when working towards a Certificate in Creative iMedia.

For LO1

Learners need to:

- investigate the purpose and component features of multipage websites
- investigate devices to access webpages
- investigate methods of internet connection.

For LO2

Learners need to:

- interpret the client brief and target audience requirements for the project
- create a work plan for the website creation
- plan using a site map and visualisation diagram for your website
- plan and prepare the assets you will need for your project
- plan the resources you will need to use for the project
- make a test plan for use as you create your website

- understand the legislation implications of creating your website.

For LO3

Learners need to:

- create folder structures to allow effective organisation of webpage and assets
- find and import assets that are needed to create your website
- make a master page for your website
- use tools and techniques within the web authoring software to create your website
- insert a range of assets into the website layouts
- create a functional navigation system for your website
- save and publish the website in an appropriate location and format, using effective version control.

For LO4

Learners need to:

- review your website and consider areas of further improvements and developments to the website project.

LO1 Understand the properties and features of multipage websites

Websites and the internet are part of everyday life; they are used for any number of purposes and are often the first port of call for access to information and services because most websites are **public domain**.

Getting started

How many different types of website can you think of; for example, retail or education?

 Key term

Public domain: for the purposes of the research in LO1, this means available to the public on the internet; this is different to a 'Public Domain' status that applies to a piece of creative work where the copyright has expired (see R081).

Multipage websites

Multipage websites have several pages that are linked in one or more ways. Websites can have different purposes and features.

Purposes of websites

Websites serve many purposes, from paying bills to applying for a passport, shopping to reading the news ... and much more.

Education

These could be school websites, revision websites, or educational websites for the general public, such as One You, the NHS healthy lifestyle website.

Online retail

Retailers often expand their customer base by offering an online presence as well as their high street shops. Some retailers are solely online, such as Amazon. There are also auction and private selling websites, such as eBay and Gumtree.

Information and services

Examples include travel information, such as Transport for London, weather information, such as the Met Office, or services such as passport applications or local authority permits.

Promotion

Examples include websites to promote music events, musicians and bands.

Entertainment

These could be websites for television and radio stations, games or social media websites.

Features of websites

There are a huge range of features that can be built in to websites, but there are a number which are frequently used in most websites.

Most websites have an evident house style, or prominent identity. This can include colours which are characteristic with the company, their brand, font styles and logos that the user can instantly identify as belonging to the company. Many websites indicate the brand identity with a large banner which spans the top section of each page of the site.

Functioning multipage websites need to incorporate navigation features such as a navigation bar or hyperlinks to other pages. Convention states that the navigation bar is found horizontally across the top of a web page or vertically down the left-hand side. On more complex websites there may be a main

Key term

Graphical User Interface (GUI): a term used for the layout and display of the display screen, which forms the basis of the way that the user interacts with the product. An effective GUI will be intuitive and easy to use.

website navigation bar and some sub navigation for more specific needs. The navigation bar is consistently positioned on each page of the website so that the user always knows where to find it and how to get from page to page. This is an important design feature of the **Graphical User Interface (GUI)**.

In order to allow users to locate the information they need, many websites have a search facility that allows users to type in key criteria for the information they want and to locate the relevant page. The placement of the search bar varies, but it is often found in the top right-hand corner of each page.

At the bottom of most websites is a footer, which is usually less prominent than the rest of the content of the website. It often contains text-based links and information. This area of the page is usually used for information such as the website terms and conditions, privacy policies

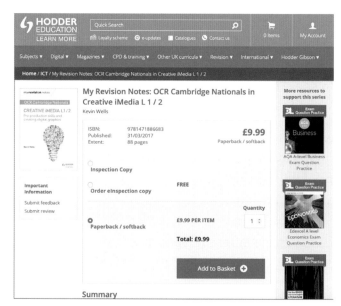

Figure 5.1 Web page with content and features

and contact details. While these details are not the main focus of the site, they contain important information that the user needs to be able to access should they need to.

Images are a key feature of most websites. These can be in the form of thumbnail images, scrolling banners or large-scale images which are the core focus of the page. Images increase the interest and draw of a page. They also make pages easier to access; images can often provide information much quicker than text alone.

Keep in mind that you should be investigating the features of *websites*, not just the *homepage*. Each page may have additional features, such as video, forms, tables, lists, maps, ordering forms and downloadable content, to name a few. This list of features is extensive.

Classroom discussion

Think of your favourite website. What features make it your favourite? What makes you like it?

The devices used to access webpages

There are an ever-increasing range of devices that can be used to access webpages. They fall into a number of categories.

Laptops and personal computers

Desktop personal computers (PCs) are made up of component parts with a monitor, keyboard and mouse. Webpages viewed on a desktop PC are viewed in a large scale, so content is easy to see. There are a range of settings that can be changed, such as screen resolution, text size and colour contrast; these allow people to view the website in the format most accessible to them.

Laptop PCs have similar features to desktop PCs, but the components are combined into a single package. The screen is usually fairly large, sometimes detachable, and the settings are adjustable to allow for optimum viewing. The main difference is that laptops are designed to be portable; they are smaller, can be folded away, and have a battery so they can work without mains power.

Tablets

Tablets provide all their functions and tools in one hand-held device. Unlike a laptop, they are made of one piece that is a fixed shape and size. In order to make the device more robust and compact the tablet does not have a separate screen and keyboard but uses a touch screen to access the functions on the device. While tablets are made to view webpages, they tend to behave and be viewed in a different way to a laptop or desktop PC. This is known as the 'mobile' site version instead of the full sized 'desktop' site. The size of the screen and the touch screen functionality is usually considered when creating professional webpages for tablets and mobile devices but outside the scope of this unit.

Mobile devices and smartphones

Mobile devices and smart phones are similar in make up to a tablet, though they tend to have a smaller screen on which to view the website. One consideration is that the orientation of the page when being viewed on a mobile device is the opposite of a desktop PC or laptop screen (portrait rather than landscape). This is something to consider when creating the settings for your webpage design.

Game consoles and digital television

Some game consoles and digital televisions can be used to access web pages. Since they are viewed on a large screen, the functionality of the website is the same as the desktop. Browsing may be different, though. A television browser, for example, is often controlled by your television remote control, which is harder to use than a mouse or trackpad when navigating a website.

Methods of internet connection
Wired broadband

Wired broadband requires a router and, possibly, micro filters for the phone sockets (modern routers have micro filters built in). The router connects the computer(s) and the phone socket, so you can connect the wired local area network in the building to the wide area network (the world wide web). An internet service provider manages access. Wired broadband is typically used to access the internet on static devices such as PCs and smart televisions rather than mobile devices, which have a wireless connection to the router.

Wi-Fi

Wi-Fi provides broadband internet access and typically connects via a wired router. Wi-Fi is often used to connect laptops, tablets and mobile devices to the internet. It is frequently used in homes, and public places – such as cafes – often provide customers with Wi-Fi. A broadband router connects to a wireless transmitter, which connects to the computer or mobile device via radio waves. This type of network is known as a wireless local area network or WLAN. Devices can join this network by connecting to the router, often known as a wireless hotspot in public locations. Devices need a Wi-Fi adapter to connect; most have this built in as standard. The Wi-Fi signal has a limited range, and walls and other obstacles can reduce the strength of the signal. Depending on the location of the wireless network, it is possible to make a private local area network with encryption and passwords. This is something you should have in your home where it is possible to restrict devices' access to the network. In a public area you are likely to have a public hotspot which allows any device access, sometimes without any encryption or security.

3G, 4G and 5G wireless broadband

3G, 4G and 5G provide wireless broadband via the mobile network using radio wave transmission. This allows internet access to be provided using mobile phone signals for most smart phones and some tablets. The speed and availability of the internet using wireless broadband depends on the mobile network signal coverage in the location of the device. This affects the signal strength and the speed of the internet provided. All smart phones are now equipped with the ability to use wireless broadband. However, the amount you can use the internet on a mobile device is likely to be limited by your mobile phone provider and dependent on the amount of data available to you on the tariff you pay for on your device. The page load time for a website depends on the page content and this can be quite slow when only a poor mobile broadband signal is available. This is an important consideration when designing and building a website.

Know it!

1 Identify three purposes fulfilled by websites.

2 Investigate a mobile device that could be used to access web pages and what connection methods are available.

Assessment preparation

Think about the individual performance you will need to undertake. Make sure you:

- understand the range of purposes a website can fulfil
- can describe devices used to access websites
- understand methods used to connect to the internet.

LO1: Understand the properties and features of multipage websites		
Mark band 1	Mark band 2	Mark band 3
Produces a summary of the purpose and component features of websites in the public domain which demonstrates a limited understanding.	Produces a summary of the purpose and component features of websites in the public domain which demonstrates a sound understanding.	Produces a summary of the purpose and component features of websites in the public domain which demonstrates a thorough understanding.
Provides a limited description of the devices used to access web pages.	Provides a sound description of the devices used to access web pages.	Provides a detailed description of the devices used to access web pages.
Demonstrates a limited understanding of internet connection methods.	Demonstrates a sound understanding of internet connection methods.	Demonstrates a thorough understanding of internet connection methods.

Assessment guidance

The OCR set assignment

When completing your work for the OCR set assignment, you will need to:

● investigate the purpose and component features of websites in the public domain, summarising your findings; these should not be limited to the assignment scenario or just the homepage for it to be broad in scope

● describe a range of devices used to access web pages, identifying their typical characteristics to demonstrate your knowledge

● discuss a range of internet connection methods, identifying their characteristics in an applied context to demonstrate your understanding.

What do the command words mean?

Thorough understanding [of websites]: can be demonstrated through depth, breadth or a combination. Breadth is the number of different areas whereas depth is the level of detail.

Detailed [devices]: can be demonstrated by describing a range of devices, identifying their features and properties.

Thorough understanding [connection methods]: should be discussed by applying your knowledge of connection methods to scenarios in order to demonstrate your understanding.

LO2 Be able to plan a multipage website

When creating a multipage website, it is vital to plan the work you are going to carry out. There are many different elements to the planning process which we will cover in this section.

Getting started

In a small group, look at a website of your choice and list what pages are available from the home page. This will be the first level of a **site map**.

Key term

Site map: a visual method to show how a website is constructed and what pages are linked together in a hierarchy.

Links to other units

You can find further information on these topics in LO2 and LO3 of **unit R081**.

Interpreting the client requirements and target audience

Understanding client requirements is vital when creating a successful product. When reviewing the client brief you need to be able to interpret clearly what the client needs you to make and the elements the website needs to have.

You must understand the *purpose* of the website. For example, is it selling a product or providing entertainment or information? Understanding the purpose will help you craft the website.

As well as style and design, you need to think about the functional elements, such as:

● number of pages

● media content

● information on each page

● type of navigation

● additional requirements of your client.

You also need an understanding of the requirements of the target audience. The target audience will shape many of the features on the website. Some key elements are:

● categorisation of the target audience (see R081)

● literacy levels

● accessibility needs

● devices and the connection method they might use.

These elements, among others, will link to your design in numerous ways. For example, the age and literacy levels of your audience will influence how much text you include on each page and the vocabulary you will use. The devices used and connection method will also affect the page load time – audiences don't like to wait long for a page to display properly.

Producing a work plan

When creating a complex project, such as a multipage website, it is particularly important to plan your time. There are many different tasks and features that need to be incorporated into a plan to ensure you create a working website, which meets the client brief and is delivered on time.

There are a range of elements to consider when planning your project; you looked at these in detail in R081.

Make sure you know when your product deadline is. Then you can build all tasks into a plan that can be completed on time.

Tasks and activities

The tasks are the main sections of a plan. When creating your website these could be elements such as sourcing media assets for the website; creating a master page for the website; creating

written content for website pages. The activities are the smaller pieces of work which make up each task that you are completing. For example, if we were to break down the task of creating the written content for the pages, you might have an activity based around researching the content, then outlining the content for each page, then creating the full content for each individual page. With a website of multiple pages this can break down into a significant number of individual activities.

Workflow: the order that the tasks and activities are carried out in. For example, if you were planning to complete the master page for your website you would need to make sure that items such as your page banner were complete so that you were able to put it straight into your master page.

Resources: could be anything from pencil and paper to sketch out a site map and page designs or the software to create your website master page and associated site pages.

Milestones: key stages such as completing the master page or completing the page content.

Contingencies: the spare time slots which can be used to make up for any delays or unforeseen problems that may come up during the project. If you do not need to use the contingency you may finish ahead of time!

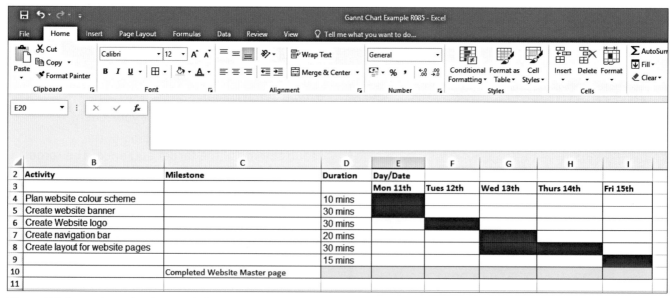

Figure 5.2 Gantt chart plan for a website

The following table shows an example of a basic table based work plan.

Task	Activities	Duration	Resources
Create website master page	Plan website colour scheme	10 mins	Computer with internet
	Create website banner	30 mins	Image creation software
	Create website logo	30 mins	Image creation software
	Create navigation bar	20 mins	Website creation software
	Create layout for website pages	30 mins	Website creation software
Contingency		15 mins	

Creating a site map

Site maps allow you to see clearly the pages of the website and how they link together with navigation features. You can also plan the user's route between the pages. They are also a good opportunity to see if the website structure is practical.

There are several ways to create a site map, by hand or the computer.

Visualisation diagram

The visualisation diagram allows you to plan out the content and layout of each individual web page. It is unlikely that you would include all the content for each page; rather, you plan where each item will be positioned on each page. You can use the visualisation diagram to identify fonts, colour schemes and house style items.

Assets

There are a number of pages, and the product is interactive, so there are likely to be a significant number and variety of assets needed. These may include backgrounds, banners, navigation buttons, shapes, text and fonts. You can include multimedia assets in your plan such as:

- images
- video
- sound.

Think about the quality of the assets and their suitability for the purpose of your website. You need to consider the resolution and size of your media assets to ensure they are a suitable resolution and file size for internet use.

For each asset you plan, you need to be able to demonstrate that you know *why* you need that asset for your project.

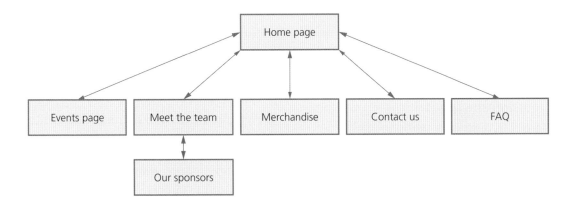

Figure 5.3 Example of a website page visualisation diagram.

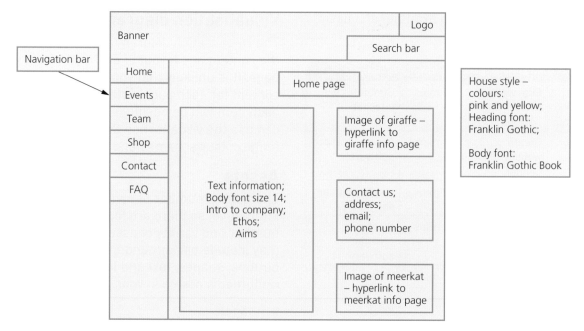

Figure 5.4 Example of a site map

Resources

Resources are everything you need to complete the project, from the most basic equipment, such as pencils and paper, to computer hardware and software. These items will vary based on the task and the facilities you have available.

Stretch activity

Identify and explain the additional resources you might need to get your finished website on the internet.

When planning the resources, you should consider the types of task that you will carry out throughout the creation process. You need to be able to explain the purpose of each resource. Consider the following tasks:

- Searching for and sourcing suitable assets.
- Editing assets.
- Creating your website pages.
- Saving and publishing your website.

Test plans

There is a range of elements that all need to work to produce a successful product. To ensure that the website functions effectively you need to be able to test your work. To do this thoroughly, you need to create a plan for the tests that you can use to structure your work. There are a number of functions of your website you need to test:

- Navigation to allow the user to access all the pages.
- Links to take the user to the correct page.
- Display of images and content.
- Playback of videos and audio.

Create a test table. This allows you to record the tests you plan and creates a space to record the results, any remedial action you might take, and the results of re-tests.

Legislation

You should be familiar with legislation covered in this course from your work on R081 LO2. For this unit, you need to think about the elements that apply to sourcing, creating and using assets on your website. You need to consider the source of the assets and identify how copyright law is complied with in a commercial context (not educational). You also need to think about the originality of your website – make sure your ideas and designs do not infringe on anyone's intellectual property. If you use links to external websites, you need to be sure that they are secure and suitable for your users.

Stretch activity

Imagine you are designing a website to be viewed on a range of different mobile devices. What design elements would you need to consider?

Know it!

- Identify three characteristics of the target audience you might need to consider.
- Describe four features you will need to test on your website.
- Explain the function of a milestone in a work plan.

Assessment preparation

Think about the individual performance you need to undertake. Make sure you:

- can identify the key elements of the brief and your target audience
- can plan assets and resources needed for the project
- understand the legislation that is relevant to this project
- can create a test plan to test the website.

LO2: Be able to plan a multipage website		
Mark band 1	**Mark band 2**	**Mark band 3**
Produces an interpretation from the client brief for a multipage website which meets few of the client requirements.	Produces an interpretation from the client brief for a multipage website which meets most of the client requirements.	Produces an interpretation from the client brief for a multipage website which fully meets the client requirements.
Produces a limited identification of target audience requirements.	Produces a clear identification of target audience requirements.	Produces a clear and detailed identification of target audience requirements.
Draws upon limited skills/knowledge/understanding from other units in the specification.	Draws upon some relevant skills/knowledge/understanding from other units in the specification.	Clearly draws upon relevant skills/knowledge/understanding from other units in the specification.
Produces a work plan for the creation of the multipage website which has some capability in producing the intended final website.	Produces a work plan for the creation of the multipage website, which is mostly capable of producing the intended final website.	Produces a clear and detailed work plan for the creation of the multipage website, which is fully capable of producing the intended final website.
Applies some basic planning techniques to show what the website will look like but with limited consideration to the client requirements.	Applies sound planning techniques, including some reference to a house style, that take into consideration some of the client requirements.	Applies complex planning techniques in a well-organised way, including detailed reference to a house style showing clear consideration of the client requirements.
Mark band 1	**Mark band 2**	**Mark band 3**
Identifies a few assets needed to create a multipage website, demonstrating a limited understanding of their potential use.	Identifies some assets needed to create a multipage website, demonstrating a sound understanding of their potential use.	Identifies many assets needed to create a multipage website, demonstrating a thorough understanding of their potential use.
Identifies a few of the resources needed to create a multipage website, demonstrating a limited understanding of their purpose.	Identifies some of the resources needed to create a multipage website, demonstrating a sound understanding of their purpose.	Identifies many of the resources needed to create a multipage website, demonstrating a thorough understanding of their purpose.
Creates a test plan for the website which tests some of the functionality.	Creates a test plan for the website, which tests most of the functionality, identifying expected outcomes.	Creates a clear and detailed test plan for the website, which fully tests the functionality, listing tests, expected and actual outcomes and identifying re-tests.
Demonstrates a limited understanding of legislation in relation to the use of assets in websites.	Demonstrates a sound understanding of legislation in relation to the use of assets in websites.	Demonstrates a thorough understanding of legislation in relation to the use of assets in websites.

When completing your work for the OCR set assignment, you will need to:

- produce your own interpretation of the client brief
- identify the target audience and what they will want from the website
- use knowledge and skills from other units such as R081
- produce a work plan to create the website
- produce a site map and visualisation diagrams for the website pages, clearly identifying the house style to be used
- identify the assets and their potential use
- identify the resources and their purpose
- develop a test plan for the website that you intend to create
- describe the legal issues of using assets in your website.

What do the command words mean?

Fully [interpretation of the brief]: needs to be your own individual ideas and thoughts on what is required that expands on what is given in the scenario and brief.

Clear and detailed [target audience]: should be a clear definition of who the target audience is and what they will want from the website.

Draws on [knowledge, skills and understanding]: must be from other units and not something that is already in R085.

Clear and detailed [work plan]: should cover all the tasks and activities for planning, creating, testing and reviewing the website.

Complex [planning techniques]: should include a site map in a standard format plus annotations to visualisation diagrams for the pages identifying the house style.

Thorough [understanding of potential use of assets]: should identify where you could use the assets and what makes them suitable. It can include assets that you decide not to use later on.

Thorough [understanding of purpose of resources]: should identify what equipment and software together with why needed for creating the website.

Thorough [understanding of legislation]: should be applied to the actual assets that you intend to use on the website. Their use should also be in a commercial context and not just education.

LO3 Be able to create a multipage website using multimedia components

Getting started

In a small group, list the types of media asset that you could include in your website to enhance the user experience.

Folder structure

Ensure that you create folders to store the assets you need to appear on your website *and* the website pages themselves. They must be stored in a clear and consistent location to enable you to link the documents together.

Your authoring files must also be separate from the published site files. Most of these should be managed through careful use of the web authoring software to make sure you do not end up with broken links to assets.

Save your files using suitable names that indicate *clearly* the content of each file (for example, the home page should be index.html).

Setting up your website

Spending a few minutes setting up your website correctly will save you a lot of work later on.

In both Serif WebPlus X8 and Adobe Dreamweaver you can set up a site and then add your pages to it, though the setup is a little different for each.

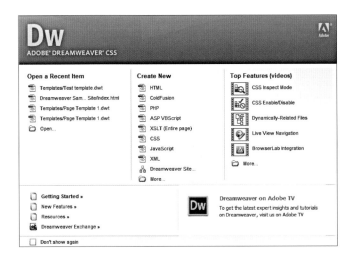

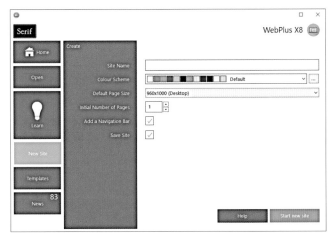

Figure 5.5 Website set up in Adobe Dreamweaver

Figure 5.6 Website set up in Serif WebPlus X8

In Adobe Dreamweaver you can select the new site option from the start menu and select where the site is going to be saved.

In Serif WebPlus X8 there is a pop up box which appears when opening the software which provides you with the option to create a new site, you will then see a menu which allows you to name your site, and select from a range of setup options for your pages.

Master pages

A master page is like a page template; it allows you to create a page design which can be applied to all the pages on the website. Using a master page allows you to create a consistent and professional design style for your website. The method for creating a master page will change depending on the software you choose to use. In Figure 5.7, you see an example of creating a Master page in Serif WebPlus X8 and Adobe Dreamweaver.

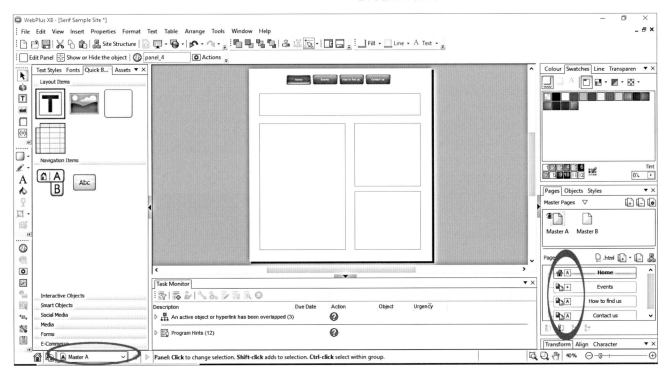

Figure 5.7 Using Serif WebPlus X8 you can switch to the master page in the bottom menu and in the right-hand menu you can see which master page each page is based on

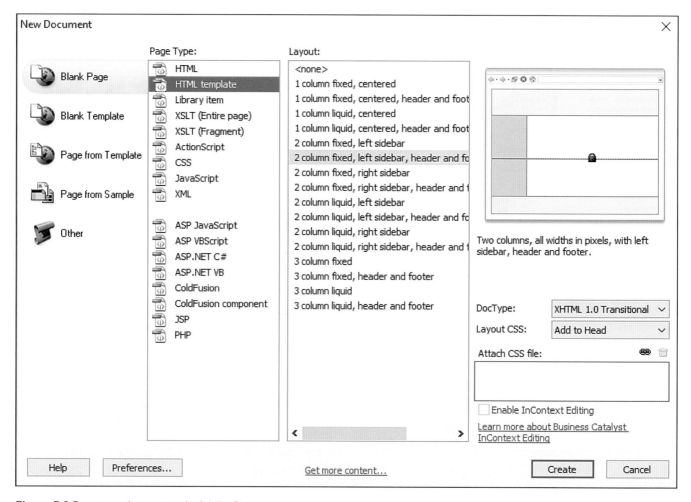

Figure 5.8 Page template set up in Adobe Dreamweaver

Serif WebPlus X8 allows you to create a master page using the same tools you would use to create a website page. However, if you create this using the master page you can then apply the master page to each page of your site to ensure a consistent design. You can also create more than one master page to allow you to keep a consistent style but build in some variation to your pages, by choosing to apply one of a few master pages to your page design.

In Adobe Dreamweaver, the setup of a master page is different; it is called making a page template. You can select this option by selecting File > New at the top of the page, this will create a menu; this allows you to set up a new page template. Once the template is created, you will need to create editable regions to allow you to edit the template.

Tools and techniques

The tools and techniques you will require to construct your website will vary based on the requirements of the brief. Here we will discuss some of the key tools and techniques you may need.

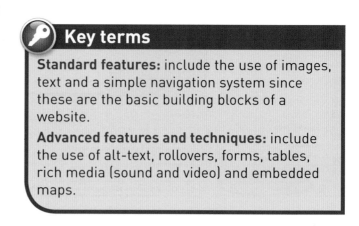

Key terms

Standard features: include the use of images, text and a simple navigation system since these are the basic building blocks of a website.

Advanced features and techniques: include the use of alt-text, rollovers, forms, tables, rich media (sound and video) and embedded maps.

Making a page from a master page

Once you have created a master page (or page template) you can use it to create the pages for your website. In Adobe Dreamweaver, select File > New; this will create a new pop up box from which you can select the option to create a page from template and choose the template you want to use.

To create a page from a master page in Serif WebPlus X8, you can add a page from the insert menu by selecting the blank page option, this will apply master page A by default. You can also do this from the page menu on the right tool bar, by clicking the plus page symbol.

External links

External links allow the user to navigate from your website to other websites. The link could be text, an image, a button or an element of a navigation bar. To create an external link in Adobe Dreamweaver, click the element you want to link, then add the full web address of the external website to the link box in the properties section at the bottom of the page. Make sure you include the http:// or https:// part.

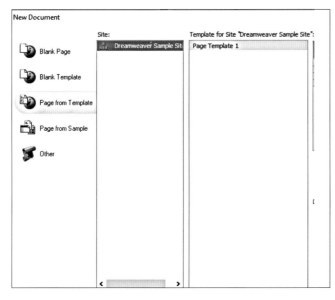

Figure 5.9 Creating a page from template in Adobe Dreamweaver

Adding an external link in Serif WebPlus X8 is a similar process. Right click on the element that you would like to link and select the hyperlink option. From the menu, select the internet page option and insert the address of the external website.

Email links

You can add a link to your website that, when clicked, can send an email to an address of your choosing (usually the contact details on the website). In Adobe Dreamweaver this is done from the insert tab: here you will find an email link option; this creates a pop-up box where you can insert the text that will appear on your page and the email address you want the text to link to. In Serif WebPlus X8 you need to create the text which you will use for the email link and select this text. Right click on the text and select the hyperlink option. In the menu box that appears select the Internet email option and insert the details of the email address you would like the user to contact.

Preview in browser

This is part of your testing during production. Before you complete your website, you will need to check how it will look when viewed in a browser. Use the 'preview in browser' tool. In Adobe Dreamweaver, from the file menu, select 'preview in browser' and click on the browser you would like to view your site in. Remember that not all browsers will display the page in the same way, so it is good practice to check your site on more than one browser. The process is similar in WebPlusX8; select the file menu, 'preview site', and click on the browser you would like to use.

Sourcing and importing assets

In LO2 you are required to plan the assets for your website pages. Here, you source and import what is needed. Sourcing an asset means either finding an asset which meets the needs of your plans, or creating the asset yourself.

When sourcing assets, ensure you comply with copyright. Record where the assets came from and any editing you did. You could create an assets source table which will store all the information about the assets you use. You will have come across assets source tables in R082 LO3.

Consider the properties of the assets, such as resolution and file size. For example, image files for internet use should have a resolution of 72 dpi. If the file size is too big, it won't be uploaded and downloaded quickly enough.

Inserting assets

Text

Adding text to a webpage is done slightly differently in Serif WebPlus X8 and Adobe Dreamweaver.

In Adobe Dreamweaver, once on the correct page, you can type directly onto the page.

In Serif WebPlus X8, you need to create a text frame, and then type within the frame.

Lists

Lists can help you organise text on your page. You can use bullet points or numbers to help display your list.

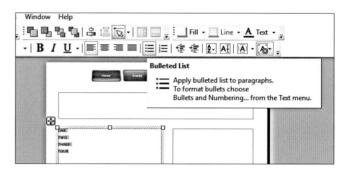

Figure 5.11 Adding lists in Serif WebPlus X8 and Adobe Dreamweaver

In Serif WebPlus X8 you can select text and then use the text properties menu to select the list format you need. In Adobe Dreamweaver, the list options are in the top menu bar under the format tab.

Images

Images are a core part of the construction of websites. Figures 5.12 and 5.13 are examples of how this could be carried out in Serif WebPlus X8 and Adobe Dreamweaver. It is important to include accessibility features to your image, such as alternate text.

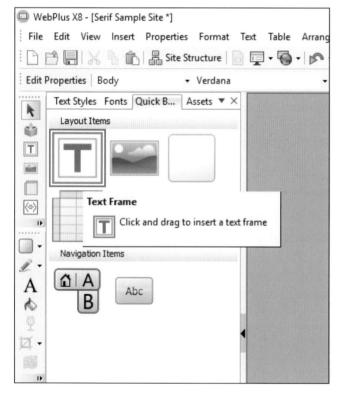

Figure 5.10 Creating a text frame

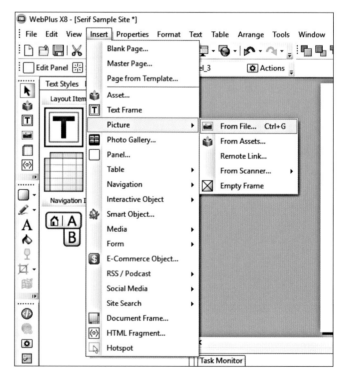

Figure 5.12 Inserting an image in Serif WebPlus X8

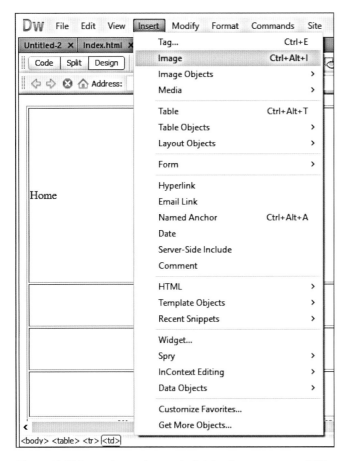

Figure 5.13 Inserting an image in Adobe Dreamweaver CS5

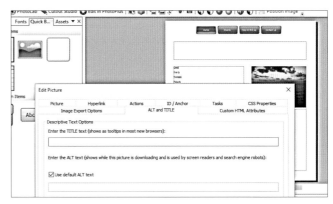

Figure 5.15 Adding alternate text in Serif WebPlus X8

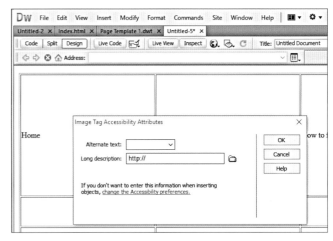

Figure 5.16 Adding alternate text in Adobe Dreamweaver CS5

Tables

To add structured information to a page, or to provide a structure to different elements of the page, you can add a table to your web pages.

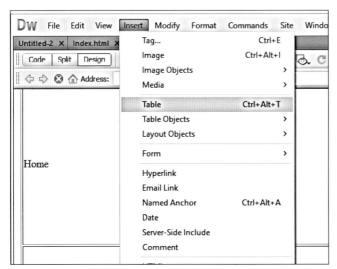

Figure 5.14 Inserting a table in Adobe Dreamweaver CS5

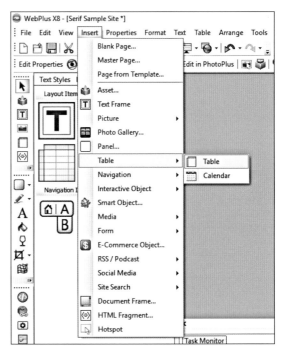

Figure 5.17 Inserting a table in Serif WebPlus X8

Rollover images

A rollover image changes to display a different image when the mouse is moved over it. Sometimes these images are used as a hyperlink. You can create a rollover image in Adobe Dreamweaver by selecting the insert menu, then image object and rollover image. In the menu box that appears you can name the image, and select the two images you want to be in the rollover. You can also create a hyperlink from here.

In Serif WebPlus X8, the rollover tool is in the insert section. Select interactive object, then rollover. A menu box allows you to add the details of your rollover image.

Media assets

There are a many media assets that you could add to your website, such as sound, video and animation. In both Serif WebPlus X8 and Adobe Dreamweaver, the tools to do this are in the insert menu under the media tab.

Forms

Forms are useful if you want to collect information from your users, such as comments, questions or bookings. Both Serif WebPlus X8 and Adobe Dreamweaver have tools to create

website forms. This is found in the insert menu in both softwares.

In Serif WebPlus X8, select the insert menu. The form option opens a menu with the option to select the form type, style, questions and options for data location.

In Adobe Dreamweaver, select insert, then form. This creates the online form area. You will then need to go back into the form menu to select the types of fields you would like in your form, such as text field, button or check box.

Maps

Maps allow users to see, for example, the location of a premises or event. This is classed as an interactive object.

In Serif WebPlus X8, use the insert, interactive object menu, and select the Google map option. This opens a menu which allows you to find the location you would like to link to and provides you with options to label the embedded map.

In Adobe Dreamweaver, you use Google maps to locate the section of map you would like to include *first*, then select the share and embed a map option to get the code for your map. Once you have copied this link, open your webpage in split view

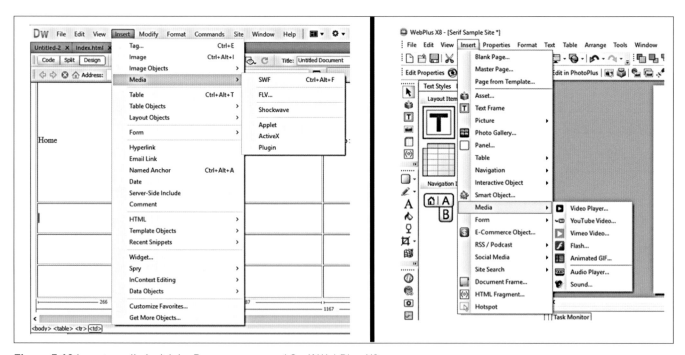

Figure 5.18 Insert media in Adobe Dreamweaver and Serif WebPlus X8

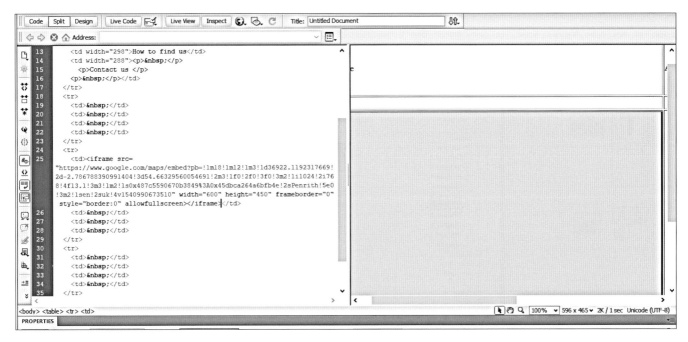

Figure 5.19 Adobe Dreamweaver in split view with code to embed map

so you can see the code and the design view. On the design view side, place your cursor where you would like the map to appear; this should put the cursor on the code side in the correct place. Paste the code into this space. You should see a grey box on the design view side where the map will appear. To check the map, take a look at your page using 'preview in browser'.

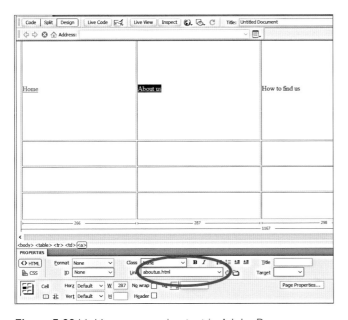

Figure 5.20 Linking pages using text in Adobe Dreamweaver CS5

Navigation system

The navigation of a website is vital. Without a functioning navigation system that allows the user to access all the pages, you will not achieve the requirements of the client brief. There are a range of ways to link pages together. Navigation bars are the most common way of navigating a website; users simply click on buttons to select the page they want to go to.

You can also link pages using text or image links. Figure 5.20 shows how to set this up in Adobe Dreamweaver. Select the text or image you want to link *from* and, using the link box properties bar on the bottom tool bar, add the file name of the page you would like to link *to*.

Saving and publishing websites

When working on your website it is important to save your work as you go. Using version control (see R081) allows you to create multiple chronological versions of your pages so that you can track back through the changes in your website or revert to an earlier version should you need to.

Convention states that you should name the home page of your website as **index**. This allows a browser to identify the correct page of a website

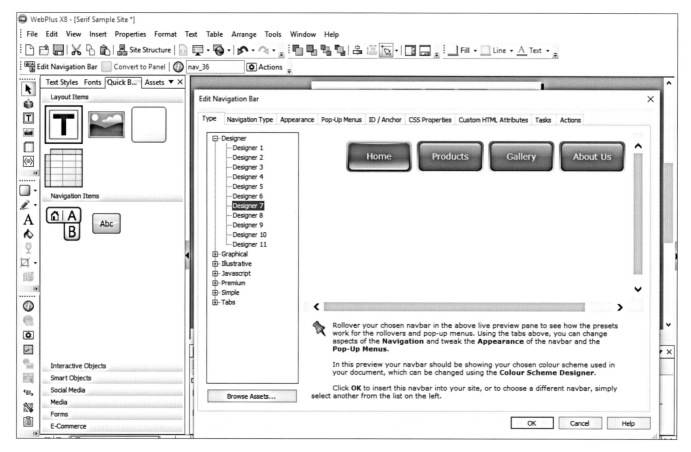

Figure 5.21 Set up for a navigation bar in Serif WebPlus X8

to display to the user when it searches for the website. Keeping your page names simple is good practice, as this reduces the number of potential errors with tasks such as linking pages.

Publishing to disk folder

When you have completed the pages for your website, you may wish to publish your website locally to a disk folder. This will allow you to view your website as a finished product using a browser on your computer. This does not make your website available online but allows you to see what it would look like and how it would function in an online environment. This is also how you will submit your assignment work.

This option is available in Serif WebPlus X8. To ensure you publish correctly you need to ensure that you select the correct folder location for your website and ensure that you select the option to publish all pages.

Figure 5.22 Publishing to disk folder in Serif WebPlus X8

Publishing to the web

You may also wish to publish your website on the internet. You will need to save your pages as HTML files and obtain space on a web server to host your files. You can then upload your files to the web server. To make your website accessible, register a domain name for your website (such as yourname.co.uk). Then link your domain name to your web server space; when you type your domain name into the browser, your website will load. Note that your assignment should *not* be published to the web, but you should *know* about the process.

Group activity

In pairs, decide who will be the creator and who will be the instructor. The instructor tells the creator what to do to create the elements of the website listed below. The creator can only do exactly what the instructor says. After each task, switch roles.

- Create a master page/page template.
- Insert an image.
- Add alt-text for the image.
- Embed a map.
- Add an email link to your page.

Assessment preparation

Think about the individual performance you will need to undertake. Make sure you:
- know how to source and prepare assets and store them in a suitable folder structure using appropriate names
- are able to create website pages using a master page/template and insert appropriate assets on the pages
- are able to save and publish a multipage website appropriately.

LO3: Be able to create multipage websites using multimedia components		
Mark band 1	**Mark band 2**	**Mark band 3**
Creates basic folder structures which are occasionally used appropriately.	Creates clear folder structures which are mostly used appropriately.	Creates logical and well-structured folder structures which are consistently used appropriately.
Sources and imports a limited range of assets for use, occasionally using appropriate methods.	Sources and imports a range of assets for use, mostly using appropriate methods.	Sources and imports a wide range of assets for use, consistently using appropriate methods.
Creates a basic master page as a template, in which the house style is only occasionally clear or consistent.	Creates a sound master page as a template which uses a clear house style.	Creates an effective and appropriate master page which uses a clear and appropriate house style.
Applies standard techniques with some effects created in the software to create the multipage website, using a limited range of assets.	Applies some advanced techniques and effects of the software to create the multipage website, using a range of assets.	Applies a range of advanced techniques and effects of the software, appropriately and effectively, to create the multipage website using a range of assets.
Combines components to produce a basic navigation system when creating the multipage website.	Combines components to produce a clear working navigation system when creating the multipage website.	Combines components effectively to produce a clear and coherent working navigation system when creating the multipage website.
Saves and publishes the website and related files occasionally using appropriate formats. The website will seldom load quickly and correctly.	Saves and publishes the website and related files mostly using appropriate formats. The website will frequently load quickly and correctly.	Saves and publishes the website and related files consistently using appropriate formats. The website will frequently load quickly and correctly.
Occasionally saves electronic files using appropriate file and folder names and structures.	Mostly saves electronic files using file and folder names and structures which are consistent and appropriate.	Consistently saves electronic files using file and folder names and structures which are consistent and appropriate.

Read about it

https://helpx.Adobe.com/uk/dreamweaver/user-guide.html

www.serif.com/media/community/pdfs/webplusx8-us.pdf

Know it!

1 Why is it good practice to use a master page or page template to create your website pages?

2 What is alt-text and what would you use it for in your website design?

LO4 Be able to review a multipage website

Getting started

In small groups, review your school website and make a list of what works and what could be improved.

Reviewing your website

You will be familiar with the requirements of LO4 from the previous units you have studied. There are two important parts to the review in this unit.

First, look critically at your finished website. Consider the visual appeal, layout of components, colour schemes, readability and ease of navigation.

Second, make sure you understand the client brief. Your brief will indicate the requirements that should have been met. So, your review looks at *what* you have done and *whether it meets the brief*. If you did not meet a requirement of the brief, you can reflect on why this happened and consider how you might change your approach in the future.

Think of the review in this unit as a larger task compared with some other units, since there are multiple pages and navigation to look at.

Links to other units

You can find further information on this topic in LO4 of **unit R082**.

Improvements and further developments

Build on your review comments and consider how you might develop and improve your website. Each point you make can be linked to the client brief and the audience. Remember you are not commenting on improving the process – only the finished website product.

Know it!

How can you use the results of testing to inform your review?

Assessment preparation

Think about the individual performance you will need to undertake. Make sure you:

- understand the client requirements and target audience and can use them to inform the reflection on your finished website
- are able to discuss further developments and improvements you could make to the website to enable it to more fully meet the requirements of the brief.

LO4: Be able to review a multipage website		
Mark band 1	Mark band 2	Mark band 3
Produces a review of the finished website which demonstrates a limited understanding of what worked and what did not, making few references back to the brief.	Produces a review of the finished website which demonstrates a reasonable understanding of what worked and what did not, mostly referencing back to the brief.	Produces a review of the finished website which demonstrates a thorough understanding of what worked and what did not, fully referencing back to the brief.
Review identifies areas for improvement and further development of the final website, some of which are appropriate and sometimes explained.	Review identifies areas for improvement and further development of the final website, which are mostly appropriate and explained well.	Review identifies areas for improvement and further development of the final website, which are wholly appropriate and justified.

Assessment guidance

The OCR set assignment

When completing your work for the OCR set assignment, you will need to:

- produce your own review of the website that you have created
- comment on the final website and how this relates to the brief
- identify what could be improved further.

What do the command words mean?

Thorough [review]: means commenting on all the features, content, pages and navigation of the website (not the process through the unit).

Appropriate and justified [areas for improvement]: areas for improvement should be relevant and supported by your reasons why.

R086 Creating digital animations

About this unit

Digital animation is used in a wide range of applications within the media industry. In this unit you will learn about the basics of animation. You will plan a digital animation, create a digital animation, store, export and review your final product. This unit builds on skills learnt in the mandatory units R081 and R082.

Resources for this unit

Hardware: Computer, display, mouse, graphics tablet.

Software: Adobe Flash®, Adobe Animate, Serif DrawPlus (for example).

Learning outcomes

LO1 Understand the purpose and features of animation

LO2 Be able to plan a digital animation

LO3 Be able to create a digital animation

LO4 Be able to review a digital animation

How will I be assessed?

You will be assessed through an OCR set assignment, marked by your tutor and externally moderated by OCR. It is worth 25% of the overall mark when working towards a Certificate in Creative iMedia.

For LO1

Learners need to investigate and understand:

- the purpose and uses of animation
- animation types
- the features of animation techniques.

For LO2

Learners need to:

- interpret client requirements for a digital animation to a given brief
- understand what the target audience requires for the digital animation
- be able to create a storyboard for a digital animation
- identify the resources and assets to be used in the digital animation
- identify different file formats that could be used for the digital animation
- understand how legislation applies to the assets, ideas and concepts that will be used in the digital animation whether sourced or created.

For LO3

Learners need to:

- source and store digital assets
- use animation software to create a digital animation using a range of tools and techniques (such as frame-by-frame, onion skinning, key frame, inbetweening, still motion, squash and stretch, layering, user-interaction)
- create and maintain a test plan to test the digital animation during production
- use a range of functions within software to enhance and animate movement
- save a digital animation in a format appropriate to the software being used
- export a digital animation in a format appropriate to client requirements
- use version control when creating your animation.

For LO4

Learners need to:

- review a digital animation against the brief
- identify areas for improvement and further developments for a digital animation.

LO1 Understand the purpose and features of animation

Getting started

Using a small pad of paper, draw out a simple stick person/animal and on each page move the position slightly to create a simple flip book animation. Aim for between 10 and 20 pages to get the impression of movement.

Animation has been used largely for entertainment in the form of flip books, cartoons and more recently feature-length films. Interest in animations really started with the works of Ray Harryhausen who in 1949 won an Oscar for his work on *Mighty Joe Young* using stop motion animation or as he called it 'dynamation'. His subsequent work was based very much on mythology and he influenced many of today's producers and directors, not least Nick Park. The work of Nick Park began with his creation of Morph, a plasticine character that appeared with Tony Hart in 1978 which started his interest in animation and short animated film. Nick Park later produced classic clay-modelling animation with the characters Wallace and Gromit.

Animation in many forms (including cel animation, made famous by Disney, and computer-generated animation) has found a large market at cinemas with the likes of Aardman, Pixar, Dreamworks and Disney all developing animated films such as *Toy Story*, *The Incredibles* and *Monsters Inc*. However, digital animation is also widely used on a smaller scale by way of moving logos and characters or objects on website pages. Adobe (previously Macromedia) Flash is widely used for creating digital animation in this field and can be used to produce short computer animation films as well.

Types of animation	File types for animation
Time-lapse, flipbook, cel animation, stop motion, cut out, digital	Gif, swf, mov, flv, html

Purpose and use of animation

Animations are used in a number of ways across multimedia products, such as websites, computer games and films.

Animations are used by businesses for marketing, promotion and information (often called dynamic promotions). They can be more effective than a static image as they attract the viewer's attention and communicate a message with moving text and images across multiple frames. More information can be displayed in a smaller space.

The entertainment industry uses animation in games and films. Huge international companies such as Aardman, Dreamworks and Pixar all use animation to make blockbuster movies.

Animation can be used to convey meaning or enhance narration. Animations are, therefore, used within education to explain concepts. They keep students motivated and engaged.

Types of animations

Flipbook

A flipbook is a series of sketches (or photographs) that change gradually from each page to the next. Images can be drawn on each page of a small book, starting at the back and working towards the front. The book is then 'flipped' through to show a rapidly changing picture that gives the impression of movement.

Cel animation

In cel animation, each frame is produced from a number of individual 'cels', which are either drawn or painted on. Each cel is produced on clear acetate film, so that only the parts of the frame that are moving need to be modified on the relevant cel. If the background is not moving, then the same background cel can be used for a number of frames, which reduces the amount of work for the animator. These cels are then photographed one-by-one using a camera that shoots frame by frame and then, similar to a flip book, they are put together to give the illusion of movement. The technique was used by the likes of Disney and Warner Bros Studios before computer animation.

Stop motion

This is a process of photographing physical objects that are moved very slightly between each frame. By keeping the changes small each time, the effect of movement is created when the frames are viewed in rapid succession. Any objects can be used, for example, moving a pen across a table, taking bites out of an apple or using Lego® characters to move across a surface.

Figure 6.1 Ray Harryhausen – *The 7th Voyage of Sinbad*, 1958

Modelling

Modelling animation uses clay, 'ColourClay' or other types of plasticine. Small models of characters and objects are created by hand and photographed using stop motion. Larger models may have a wire framework to support them; this also makes the adjustments easier and the model does not lose its shape or pose.

Cutout animation

This uses cloth, paper, card or any other form of flat material. Characters, backgrounds and props are created and then moved in small steps and photographed to create the illusion of movement.

Time lapse photography

Time lapse usually refers to objects that move naturally without being modelled by the animator. Examples would be a flower that opens up or stars moving in the night sky. Hundreds or thousands of photographs are taken, and then stitched together, like stop motion.

Digital

This is where the entire animation is created using software applications. An example would be Adobe Flash where objects are drawn and then animated using techniques such as keyframes and tweening (see next section for what this means). More advanced and complex digital animations are full length feature films using computer generated imagery (CGI).

Features of animation techniques

Frame by frame

The whole scene or stage is redrawn rather than a small part of it.

Onion skinning

The process of creating each new frame is made easier by using onion skinning or semi-transparent layers to see what is behind. This means you can redraw a minor change or movement for the next frame in the sequence. This technique is quite advanced for level 2, but you may still be able to experiment with the possibilities.

Key frame

This is the point in the timeline whereby the animation changes; for example, for a new sequence of movement. In general, it can be thought of as the starting point and/or ending point of the movement. Sometimes they are very close together as with stop motion but otherwise are used with tweening.

Inbetweening (or tweening)

A process whereby the frames in between the start and end keyframes are generated by the animation software. Incremental changes are made so that a smooth motion is created. In digital animation, such as using Adobe Flash, this can be a shape or motion tween.

Still motion (or stop motion)

Where objects are moved a small amount each time and a new frame (or photograph) taken. When the successive frames or photographs are viewed rapidly, it gives the effect of smooth motion. Each frame is effectively a key frame. This is how many animated movies are created, such as Wallace and Gromit. The intention of this unit, though, is to animate movement using software rather than stop motion.

Squash and stretch

A technique that makes animated objects look more real or lifelike. For example, when a bouncing ball hits the ground, it squashes, and then stretches again as it moves away. Without this, objects and movement can look very 'wooden' or unreal.

Layering

Used within the animation software. It is a way of reducing the work to create a scene. For example, a person walking along would have animated movement for each step (which can use onion skinning) but the background may be static. Therefore, the layers in the software would have just the person on one layer and the background image on a different layer, which is used for all the frames.

Group activity

1   In a group, divide tasks up as follows.
    - Look at a range of websites and identify the animations used and why they have been used.
    - Look on YouTube for animations and identify the type and use for the animation.
    - Research different animated films and look at the types of animations that were used.
2   Create a mind map (linking to unit R081) of the whole group's findings that can be shared with the rest of the class.

Know it!

Choose up to three animated films and write down the type of animation used and the techniques that were most likely used to create them.

Read about it

Animation: The Global History, by Maureen Furniss (Thames and Hudson, 2017).

Timing for Animation, by Harold Whitaker and John Halas (Routledge, 2009).

The Illusion of Life: Disney Animation, by Frank Thomas and Ollie Johnston (Hyperion, 1997).

Assessment preparation

Think about the individual performance you will need to undertake. Make sure you:
- know where and why animations are used.
- understand the different types and techniques of animations together with their advantages and disadvantages.

LO1: Understand the purposes and features of animation		
Mark band 1	Mark band 2	Mark band 3
Demonstrates a basic understanding of the purposes and uses of animations.	Demonstrates a sound understanding of the purposes and uses of animations.	Demonstrates a thorough understanding of the purposes and uses of animations.
Lists a limited range of animation techniques and types, demonstrating a basic understanding of the advantages and disadvantages of each.	Describes a range of animation techniques and types, demonstrating a sound understanding of the advantages and disadvantages of each.	Describes a wide range of animation techniques and types, demonstrating a thorough understanding of the advantages and disadvantages of each.

Assessment guidance

The OCR set assignment

When completing your work for the OCR set assignment, you will need to:
- demonstrate your knowledge of where and why animation is used to evidence your understanding of the purpose and uses
- describe the different types of animation and the techniques used
- demonstrate your understanding of animation types by describing the advantages and disadvantages.

What do the command words mean?

Thorough understanding [of purpose]: can be demonstrated through depth, breadth or a combination. Breadth is the number of different areas whereas depth is the level of detail.

Wide range [animation techniques]: generally means five or more.

Thorough understanding [advantages/disadvantages]: relates to the use of animation techniques and their advantages/disadvantages, which could relate to the resources needed, time available and cost to create.

LO2 Be able to plan a digital animation

Planning is an important part of any digital animation creation. You need to know what the clients wants, and then think about how to create this animation. Timescales need to be planned to meet the client's deadline.

Getting started

Think about your favourite animated films. In a small group, discuss what animation techniques would have been used to create them. Then make notes on what steps you think would be needed to create the films.

The client brief and target audience

Consider the requirements of the client brief, and how you are going to achieve this, with the software that you have available.

If the animation is aimed at children, for example, then you need to think about the different kind of text and images that might appeal to them compared to adults. If the animation is advertising a product, it must encourage the target audience to buy the product.

To understand the client's requirements you may need to:

- read a client brief
- discuss their requirements with them directly
- interpret a client's specification.

Clarify anything you do not understand and use your own creative ideas to meet the brief.

Links to other units

You can find further information on pre-production topics LO2 and LO3 in **unit R081**.

Storyboarding

Storyboarding is used to show the progression of movement with time. It is an important part of the planning and development process for any moving image project.

frame 1	frame 2	frame 3	frame 4	frame 5	frame 6
○					
	○			○	○
		○			
			○		

Figure 6.2 Frame sequence for a bouncing ball

This sequence of six **frames** in Figure 6.2 will produce a bouncing-ball effect when animated. If this was viewed at 12 frames per second (fps), the whole sequence would take 0.5 seconds. The **frame rate** is an important part of the animation – if it is too low, the movement will not be smooth or realistic. If it is too high, it will take a long time to produce because of the number of frames needed. The table below shows the total number of frames needed for an animation sequence at a range of frame rates.

When stop-motion techniques are used, it soon becomes clear how much work is involved in creating feature-length animation films.

Key terms

Frames: a single scene, drawing or image that forms an animation when multiple frames are viewed in rapid succession.

Frame rate: the number of frames per second (fps) that are used to create the effect of movement. Examples would be 6, 12 or 24 fps.

	10 seconds	20 seconds	30 seconds	60 seconds
	Number of frames needed			
3 fps	30	60	90	180
6 fps	60	120	180	360
12 fps	120	240	360	720
24 fps	240	480	720	1440

Assets and resources

Assets: can be images, sounds, graphics, text and shapes. These may be created by you or sourced from other places. A good approach is to log all of your assets in an asset table that identifies the sources and other key information. This would allow a client to agree or make suggestions to make sure they meet the brief provided.

Resources: include any hardware, software and other devices you may need.

File formats and players used

Animation files are commonly created as:

.gif: graphics interchange format, typically used for small animated objects on websites.

.swf: originally Shockwave Flash Format but now known as just .swf, it is commonly used for animated web graphics but requires the Flash Player plug-in to be installed (a free download from www.Adobe.com).

.html: Can be used to produce animated files when saved and published with supporting files from Flash.

.mov: Apple QuickTime movie format with players available for both PC and Apple Mac computers.

Legislation

You need to document any copyrighted, trademarked or intellectual property that you use. This is not restricted to images and can include the use of established characters and character names. Keep records of all sources and permissions obtained for any material that is not your own.

Links to other units

You can find further information on legislation in **unit R081**.

Group activity

In small groups research how copyright law affects the use of images and text as assets. Present your findings back to the rest of the class.

Know it!

You want to create an animation that forms an advert for use on a website. This should be viewable on any platform (PC, Mac or smartphone) and be a very small file size that does not affect the page load time significantly. What file format might you use and why?

Read about it

Storyboarding Essentials (SCAD Creative Essentials), by David Harland Rousseau and Benjamin Reid Phillips (Watson-Guptill, 2013).

Assessment preparation

Think about the individual performance you will need to undertake. Make sure you:

- know how to interpret a client brief and be able to explain how you would meet their brief
- understand suitable file formats to meet the brief
- are able create a storyboard
- understand the legal issues that surround any assets or information to be used in the animation.

LO2 – Be able to plan a digital animation		
Mark band 1	**Mark band 2**	**Mark band 3**
Produces an interpretation from the client brief for a digital animation which meets few of the client requirements.	Produces an interpretation from the client brief for a digital animation which meets most of the client requirements.	Produces an interpretation from the client brief for a digital animation which fully meets the client requirements.
Produces a limited identification of target audience requirements.	Produces a clear identification of target audience requirements.	Produces a clear and detailed identification of target audience requirements.
Draws upon limited skills/knowledge/understanding from other units in the specification.	Draws upon some relevant skills/knowledge/understanding from other units in the specification.	Clearly draws upon relevant skills/knowledge/understanding from other units in the specification.
Describes file formats and their properties with limited accuracy. Judgement of suitability for the digital animation is sometimes accurate.	Describes file formats and their properties with some accuracy. Judgement of suitability for the digital animation is mostly accurate.	Describes file formats and their properties with accuracy. Judgement of suitability for the digital animation is almost always accurate.
Mark band 1	**Mark band 2**	**Mark band 3**
Creates a basic storyboard which identifies a limited range of resources and assets to be used. These choices are occasionally appropriate to the client requirements.	Creates a sound storyboard which identifies a range of resources and assets to be used. These choices will mostly be appropriate to the client requirements.	Creates a detailed storyboard which identifies a wide range of resources and assets to be used. These choices will consistently be appropriate to the client requirements.
Demonstrates a limited understanding of legislation in relation to the use of assets, ideas and concepts in digital animations.	Demonstrates a sound understanding of legislation in relation to the use of assets, ideas and concepts in digital animations.	Demonstrates a thorough understanding of legislation in relation to the use of assets, ideas and concepts in digital animations.

Assessment guidance

The OCR set assignment

When completing your work for the OCR set assignment, you will need to:

- produce your own interpretation of the client brief
- identify the target audience and what they will want from the animation
- use knowledge and skills from other units such as R081
- discuss what file formats would be suitable
- produce a storyboard of what you intend to create
- identify the assets and resources needed
- describe the legal issues of using assets in your animation.

What do the command words mean?

Fully [interpretation of the brief]: needs to be your own individual ideas and thoughts on what is required that expands on what is given in the scenario and brief.

Clear and detailed [target audience]: should be a clear definition of who the target audience is and what they will want to gain from the animation.

Draws on [knowledge, skills and understanding]: must be from other units and not something that is already in R086.

Accuracy [file formats]: should identify the file formats that can be used for animation together with the properties that would make them suitable to meet the client brief.

Detailed [storyboard]: should be clear for somebody else so that they have a good idea of what you intend to create. Annotations may be added for clarification.

Wide range [assets and resources]: generally accepted as five or more.

Thorough [understanding of legislation]: should be applied to the actual assets that you intend to use. Their use should also be in a commercial context and not just education.

LO3 Be able to create a digital animation

It is possible to create a digital animation in software such as Adobe Flash, Adobe Animate and Serif DrawPlus using images that are created in the software itself or images that are imported into the library or directly onto the stage (or a combination of both). You can use the tools and techniques that were covered in LO1.

Getting started

Find out what resources you have available in your school. Write down what could be used to create a digital animation (not just a stop motion animation). In particular, look for software applications (more than one if possible).

Sourcing and storing assets

Think about the size of the animation stage and the properties of the image-based assets (such as pixel dimensions). One option is to create some assets using skills from R082 digital graphics. Make sure the image assets do not have high resolution or large file size, since this can introduce problems with creation and playback. The assets should be stored in suitable file locations, using good naming conventions, so they can easily be found to import into your chosen animation software. More information on naming conventions can be found in R081.

Creating and maintaining a test plan

The animation needs to be tested before it is presented to the client to ensure that it works as intended. Create a test plan for different aspects of the animation. This might include the following.

Frame size: is this correct for the viewing platform (phone screen, computer monitor or website banner, for example)?; the size might be specified in pixels.

Frame rate: is this correct to ensure the animation runs smoothly?

File size: does the animation need to be compressed depending on the delivery method, whether using 4G, wireless or wired connections?

Duration: does the length of the animation meet the client requirements (time from start to finish)?; is there enough time to read any text?

Movement: are the transitions smooth?

It may be that some of these parameters need to change because of what is found during the testing. So, the test plan should be kept up to date as necessary.

Version control when creating a digital animation

You need to remember the work on version control and file names from R081 to ensure that the final animation is easily identifiable to the client, in terms of both the file name and an indication that the version they are looking at is the finished product.

Using tools, techniques and functions in the animation software

Using Adobe Flash

Some of the main features of the Adobe Flash workspace are:

- **Toolbox:** a collection of tools for selection drawing, editing the assets imported to the stage.
- **Properties inspector:** used to define the properties of a selected object or asset.
- **Stage:** the central area where the graphical content of the animation is produced.
- **Timeline:** used to control how and when the objects or assets move during the animation sequence.
- **Panels:** for managing library assets, alignment, colours and other features.

Figure 6.3 Adobe Flash start-up screen

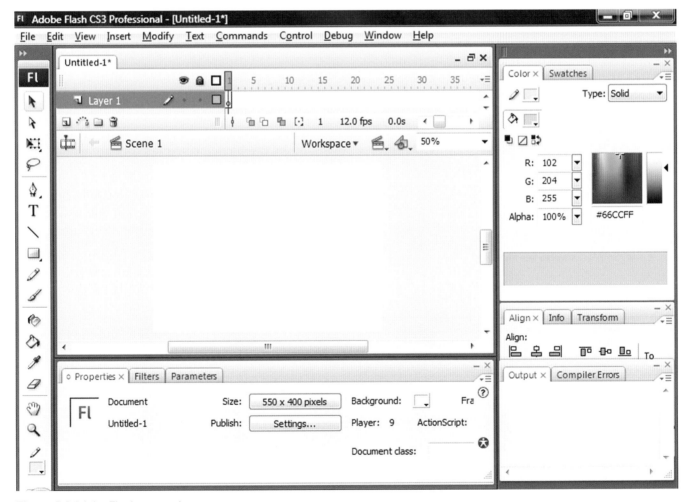

Figure 6.4 Adobe Flash screen layout

Figure 6.5 Adobe Flash Toolbox

Animation techniques using Adobe Flash

The process of producing an animation begins with creating or importing the assets. The movement is then animated over the timeline. The default frame rate in Adobe Flash is 12 fps. So, for a two-second animation, you need 24 frames. You do not have to create each frame, but you must define the content during playback.

Keyframes are those that signify a change to the animation and they are effectively the start and end point of a section. In between keyframes, tweening can be used to fill in the positions and shapes of objects. Using this method, Adobe Flash will work out what happens to the object in between the first and last keyframe, whether it needs to change the shape or move it to a different position, hence creating the content of the frame for you. If stop-motion images are to be used in a frame-by-frame animation, then every frame will be a keyframe.

Figure 6.6 Adobe Flash document properties

Working with symbols, instances and the library

In Adobe Flash, a symbol is defined from any single object or set of objects. These are stored in the library. Each time a symbol is used in the animation, this is called an instance. One benefit is that the overall size of the file is minimised because it only has to store the symbol once. Objects must be converted into symbols before they can be used on the stage in a motion or shape tween.

There are three types of symbols that can be created:

1 **Movie clip:** has its own timeline, which is different to the main timeline of the animation.
2 **Button:** used when adding user interactivity to animation (for example, click to start something or jump to a different page).
3 **Graphic:** used with graphics that will be part of a simple animation, such as one you may produce for Levels 1 and 2.

Creating a basic animated object

In this example, we will look at how to create a simple banner for use on a website. This is not a comprehensive guide to using Adobe Flash but will cover the basic principles that are essential to animating movement.

Find a suitable image that you can use to practice with. In this example, we are using one called raindrop. You could find something similar.

From the File menu, select New (this can also be done from the start-up screen). Choose ActionScript® 3.0 (or use the latest version available in your own software).

Set the size of the stage in pixels and the frame rate.

Import images/assets into the project

Select File > Import > Image to stage.

Position the image on the stage. If the image has been prepared to the correct size, check that the X, Y coordinates (top, left corner) are 0.0, 0.0 so that it fully covers the stage area. These coordinates can be found in the properties inspector.

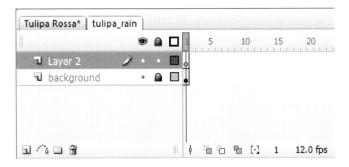

Figure 6.7 Layers/timeline panel

Double-click on the Layer 1 name to give it a suitable name, such as 'background'.

To make sure this background image is not moved when adding additional layers, lock it by clicking on the lock icon in the timeline alongside the layer name.

- Create a new layer and change the name to rain1.
- File > Import > Import to stage > raindrop image.
- Position the raindrop on the stage. From the Modify menu, select Convert to symbol (or press the F8 key). Choose a suitable name such as rain_symbol and type Movie clip. This conversion allows the image to be animated.
- Create a keyframe in frame 1 by pressing the F6 key. This function can also be found in the Insert or Modify > Timeline menu.
- Create a second keyframe at frame 15.
- Reposition the raindrop in frame 15 so that it is below the original frame 1 (as if it had fallen).
- In the properties inspector, click on the Tween option and select Motion.
- Drag the background frame out to align with the end of the rain frames on the timeline.
- Create additional rain layers with raindrops in different positions so that the rain effect is constant when the animation is looped (replayed continuously).
- At any time, you can play the animation by pressing the Enter key on the keyboard (or Control > Play).
- A preview of the final animation can be seen by pressing F12 or selecting the 'File' menu > 'Publish Preview'.

Adding text

Create a new layer and rename it 'text' (or something suitable if there will be more than one text layer). Select the Text tool in the toolbox and set the font/size/colour in the properties inspector. Click on the stage where you want to place the text and type the words using the keyboard. You can choose the Selection tool from the toolbox to move or modify the text. You can also align the text to any part of the stage using the Align panel. If this panel is not shown, select Window > Align. When complete, lock the text layer at the side of the timeline view.

Working with the library

Items that have been imported to the stage will be shown in the library panel. After converting to a symbol, they can be dragged and dropped onto the stage as needed.

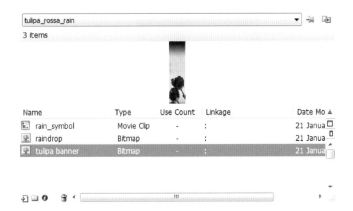

Figure 6.8 Adobe Flash library panel

Animate the sequence

Adobe Flash provides the facility to tween movement between keyframes. As the animator, you decide the position of an object at a start point and end point on the timeline. These points are defined as the keyframes. Adobe Flash will then calculate the content for each frame 'in between' the keyframes to give a smooth transition of shape and/or motion.

In this example, we will animate the text layer with a motion tween. To start with, add keyframes in frame 1 and frame 40 by pressing F6 or selecting Modify > Timeline > Convert to keyframes.

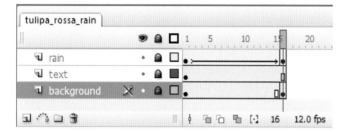

Figure 6.9 Adobe Flash timeline tween

In the properties inspector, select Tween > Motion between frame 1 and frame 40 to the text layer. At frame 1, the text is in the lower half of the stage. In frame 40, it has been positioned near the top of the stage. The motion tween calculates the position of the text for each frame in between. An alternative is a shape tween from the properties inspector, which modifies the overall shape of the object between the keyframes. After the tween has been applied, stretch the background layer out to frame 40 as well so it is always displayed during playback.

Figure 6.10 The final animated graphic

Tools and editing techniques

Adding timeline effects

These are built-in animation effects that provide an easy way to create styles of movement and motion. You can choose from copy, blur, expand, explode, spin and fade in or out. To use an effect, first select an object on the stage. Then Insert > Timeline Effects. The sub-menu options are Assistant, Effects, and Transform, with the following choices.

- **Assistant:** copy/duplicate.
- **Effects:** blur, drop shadow, expand and explode.
- **Transform:** transition (fade and wipe), transform (rotate, spin and change colour).

Note: To customise or remove the effect, select Modify > Timeline effects.

Selection tools

The main selection tool is found at the top of the toolbox. With this tool, click on any item or object in the stage and the properties will be shown in the properties inspector. In the banner, the text can be aligned to the centre of the banner from the Align panel (if it is not shown, select Window > Align). Make sure that To Stage is enabled and use the alignment buttons to position the selected object. By using the To Stage option, Adobe Flash will position the text with reference to the stage rather than other objects, for example, so that it is exactly in the middle of the stage (or banner in this example).

If you have several objects to be moved together, use the selection tool to click on each one while holding down the Shift key. This allows multiple objects to be selected, all of which can then be moved or aligned as before. If the objects are to be animated together, you can also group them first, Modify > Group.

Using drawing tools

In the banner animated object, we looked at how to import images and animate them. Another way to produce the rain drops would be to draw them within Adobe Flash, which is another option to consider. The toolbox includes tools to draw lines,

Figure 6.11 Adobe Flash drawing

shapes and use fill colours. You can refer to the diagram with the list of tools in the drawing section to identify these in your own version of software.

In Figure 6.11, the sun was created with the oval tool. The yellow fill can be set with the fill colour tool or changed in the properties inspector afterwards. Gradient fill effects can also be used for more realistic 3D objects. The stroke setting in the properties inspector is used to create an outline around the object drawn, with options for both the stroke width and colour. The eraser tool is used to remove unwanted parts of any objects drawn. It works on all layers that are not locked. Use the lock icon to protect them from the eraser if needed.

The background sky and grass are on separate layers. The layers for the stick person and the 'Media' text are above the background layers; otherwise they would not be seen.

Both the pencil and brush tool have automatic smoothing of the edges. Use the selection tool to move, straighten or bend the lines and shapes drawn. Click and drag on any segment of the shapes.

Using stop motion with Adobe Flash animation

Adobe Flash can be used to produce an animation from photographs, for example, using stop-motion modelling or time lapse photography. For the final work to be suitable for use on a website, the original photographs must first be processed in a digital graphics application. This is to resize them to a practical working size, such as 550 pixels wide × 400 pixels high, which is the default size of the stage. If each image is resized to 100 kB and there are 20 images in the animation, the file will be at least 2 MB (megabytes) in size unless further optimisation is done.

To produce the animation, place the resized images on successive frames in the timeline. Titles in the form of text boxes can be added for the opening and closing credits. By using different layers on the timeline, you can start the stop-motion animation after the introduction section has completed.

Saving and exporting animation files

Files saved from Adobe Flash have the file extension .fla, which keeps the structure of the layers and timeline intact. This format can only be viewed from within Adobe Flash so the file must be published for use on a web page or other computer. The recognised format for publishing is .swf. This is played using Adobe Flash Player, which is a free plug-in for a web browser. If your target computer does not have Adobe Flash Player, it can be freely downloaded

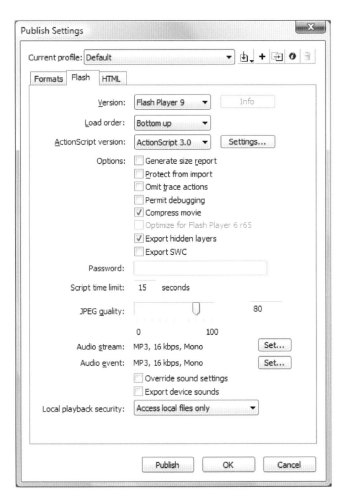

Figure 6.12 Adobe Flash tab of the settings dialogue box

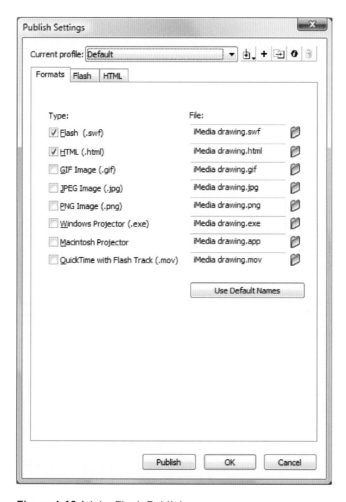

Figure 6.13 Adobe Flash Publish screen

from the Adobe website. Before publishing your work, check the publish settings from the File > Publish settings. The output formats that will be created are shown in a list, with detail tabs shown for each of the selected formats. If static (non-animated) images are required, choose the .jpg or .png options.

On the Adobe Flash tab of the settings dialogue box, you will see the file settings that will be used. The version of Adobe Flash Player and ActionScript needed to play the file can be chosen along with the JPEG quality and audio stream. In general, leave these at the most recent (highest) versions available unless you really need to make it compatible with older versions. Lower values for JPEG quality and audio stream will reduce the size of file that is produced, but quality may also be reduced.

Before publishing your animation, check that it works using Control > Test Movie. This will display your animation in a new window. If it does not display correctly, you will need to correct any problems found.

Once the settings have been configured, publish your animation, File > Publish.

Using Serif DrawPlus

This is not a comprehensive guide to using Serif DrawPlus but will cover the basic principles or creating an animation.

When you open DrawPlus you are given two options: stopframe and keyframe animation. In stop frame animation, objects are animated frame by frame (like page by page in a flip book). In keyframe animation, you set up the start and end frame and DrawPlus fills the steps in between automatically (rather like tweening in Flash).

Keyframe animation in Serif DrawPlus

Click on keyframe animation in the start-up wizard. You will be presented with a page setup window where you can pick your page size (think about your client's requirements and where the animation will be displayed).

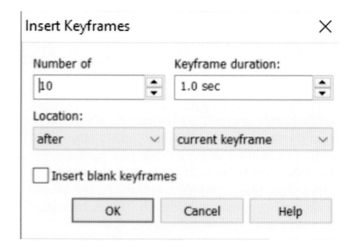

Figure 6.14 Image of dialogue window

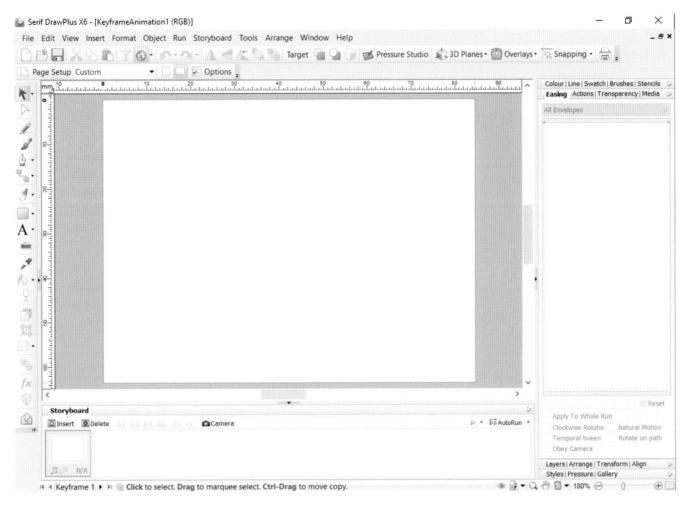

Figure 6.15 Serif DrawPlus Workspace

Importing assets

You will need to add any background you want to the animation and then import your asset that you want to animate or create them within the software.

Text can be created using the text tool, but an image or pre-created word could be imported into the software with Insert > Picture > From file. This can be resized using the resize handles as you would in most software.

Keyframe animation

Place the item where you want it to start animating. To make it move, add keyframes. In the storyboard tab (at the bottom of the screen) click Insert then, in the dialogue window, enter the number of keyframes you want, how long each keyframe is to last, and where you want the keyframe to be.

Once you click OK, the inserted keyframes appear on the bottom storyboard tab as exact copies of your first frame. To animate, select the last keyframe in the storyboard tab and drag your asset to where you want to animate it to. This creates a path across the stage that the animation will move across.

Changing movement

You may notice that, above each keyframe, the path has a node added to it. To change the path that the asset moves along you can move the node around to make the movement less linear. You can preview to test the movement using the play button at the top right of the storyboard tab.

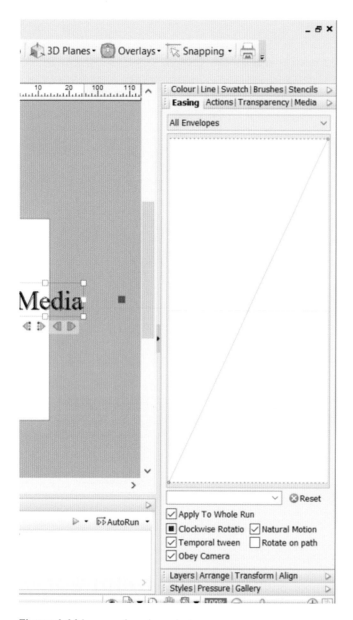

Figure 6.16 Image of easing window

Changing speed

You can change the speed of the animation, to make it more interesting. Use the easing window on the right-hand side of the screen. This allows a drop down into different envelopes (try these out and see what each one does). Choose the position envelope; once selected, a blue line appears under it. The line is straight – this is because, at the moment, the animation is moving at a constant rate. You can change the speed with one of the pre-set movements below the line (experiment until you are happy with the results).

Stop motion animation in DrawPlus

Click on stop frame animation in the start-up wizard. You will be presented with a page setup window. Pick your page size (think about your client's requirements and where the animation will be displayed).

Creating the animation

The asset that you have inserted appears in the first frame in the Frames tab. To animate it you need to clone the frame so that an exact replica appears next to it (click on clone frame in the frames tab). With the second frame selected, move your asset and then repeat this process (a bit like drawing a flip book animation).

If you click on the onion skin in the frame tab, you can see where the asset was in the previous frame. This will allow you to move the asset along in a more even motion.

As with a flipbook, continue to add frames (like extra pages) and keep moving the asset along the stage.

Exporting from DrawPlus

Stopframe can only be exported as an animated GIF or video, whereas Keyframe can be exported as an animated GIF, Video or SWF file. Take this into consideration when choosing which method you use, depending on the client brief.

To export a as a Flash file, choose File > Export > Export as Flash SWF. Choose a suitable file name

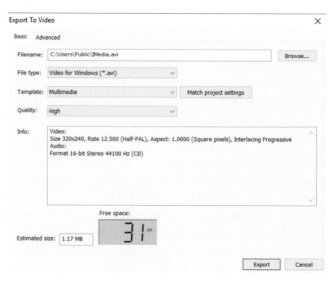

Figure 6.17 Video export window

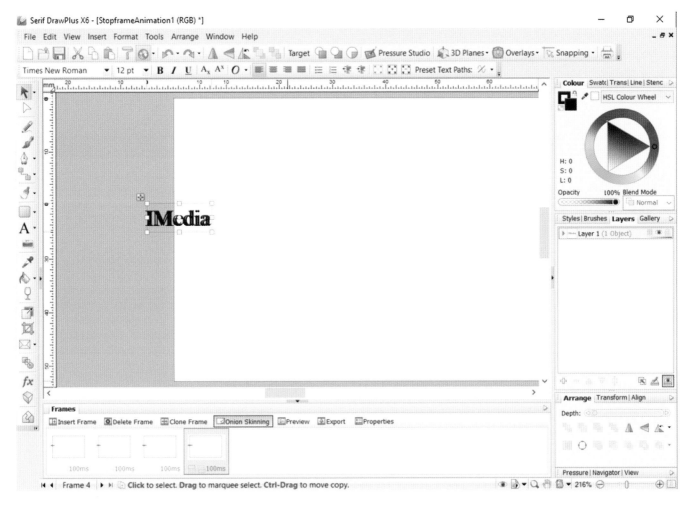

Figure 6.18 Onion skinning in Serif DrawPlus

and folder location. An export progress box will appear as the Flash file is created.

To export as a movie file, choose File > Export > Export as Video. Choose the export type (Quicktime, mov, Video for Windows .avi, or Windows Media audio and video .wmv). Select the export quality in the Quality drop down (from Draft to Very Best). Choose a suitable name and folder location.

Stretch activity

Explore the capabilities of the tools and techniques in the software you are using. For example, later additions of DrawPlus and Adobe Flash have a joint tool or a bone tool that allow the animator to create the look of natural movement by rotating two separate objects around a joint.

Know it!

Thinking about the software that you have available, what options would you have to animate the movement of a person walking across the stage or scene?

Read about it

DrawPlus User Guide:
dl.serif.com/pdfs/DrawPlusx8.pdf
Adobe Flash User Guide:
www.Adobe.com/support/documentation/archived_content/en/flash/cs3/flash_cs3_help.pdf

Assessment preparation

Think about the individual performance you will need to undertake. Make sure you:

- know how to source and store assets
- understand how to create and use a test plan
- are able to use tools and techniques within your software to produce an animation to the client's brief
- know what file formats are available for exporting.

LO3: Be able to create a digital animation		
Mark band 1	**Mark band 2**	**Mark band 3**
Sources and stores a limited range of assets for use, occasionally using methods which are appropriate.	Sources and stores a range of assets for use, mostly using methods which are appropriate.	Sources and stores a wide range of assets for use, consistently using methods which are appropriate.
Mark band 1	**Mark band 2**	**Mark band 3**
Produces a test plan for the animation which tests some of the functionality. Uses tools and techniques within the animation software some of which address the client brief, to create the digital animation. Uses a few functions within the animation software to enhance and animate movement. Carries out limited testing of the digital animation during production. Occasionally saves and exports the digital animation in an appropriate format. Occasionally saves electronic files using appropriate file and folder names and structures.	Creates a test plan for the animation which tests most of the functionality, identifying expected outcomes. Uses tools and techniques within the animation software most of which address the client brief, to create the digital animation. Uses some functions within the animation software to enhance and animate movement. Carries out sound testing of the digital animation intermittently during production. Mostly saves and exports the digital animation in an appropriate format. Mostly saves electronic files using file and folder names and structures which are consistent and appropriate.	Creates a clear and detailed test plan for the animation which fully tests the functionality, listing tests, expected and actual outcomes and identifying re-tests. Uses tools and techniques within the animation software to fully address the client brief, to create the digital animation. Uses many functions within the animation software to enhance and animate movement. Carries out thorough testing of the digital animation at regular intervals during production. Consistently saves and exports the digital animation in an appropriate format. Consistently saves electronic files using file and folder names and structures which are consistent and appropriate.

Assessment guidance

The OCR set assignment

When completing your work for the OCR set assignment, you will need to:

- source and create the assets that you need
- use a range of tools and techniques using software to create the animation and animate the movement
- create and use a test plan
- save and export the animation in suitable format and properties to meet the brief
- use appropriate file and folder naming conventions.

What do the command words mean?

Wide range [of assets]: generally accepted as five or more.

Fully [tests functionality]: means that the animation should be tested to ensure each section works correctly.

Fully [address client brief]: means that the type of animation and associated tools/techniques should meet the brief for a digitally created animation.

Many [functions to enhance and animate]: similar to a wide range, this is generally five or more.

Thorough [testing at regular intervals]: means that the test plan must be used during the production stages and records kept of the results.

Consistently [saves and export]: means that the animation should be exported in a suitable file format for the intended platform and also meet the brief.

Consistently [saves files]: means that the development of the animation should be documented using different version numbers and with descriptive file names, with assets stored in suitable folders.

LO4 Be able to review a digital animation

By the end of this learning outcome you will be able to review your digital animation and identify areas that could be improved. This is essential, because you need to ensure that the final version meets the client brief. Identifying ways it could be improved might be helpful for the client, and will help you when working on your next animation.

Getting started

Browse a number of websites to find three animated advertisements. Comment on each one in terms of what you like, what you don't like and what could be improved.

Digital animation review

Your review of your digital animation needs to cover both the content and file size/format of the final work. The functionality testing of the animation should make sure that all aspects of the motion and movement work as expected and planned on the storyboard.

Consider the following questions.

1 Does the content of the animation show what the client actually wanted?

2 Is the total duration correct as requested by the client?

3 What is the final size of the animation file and is it suitable for use on a website?

4 What is the file format of the animation and what will be needed to view the file (for example, Adobe Flash Player version 8/9/10)?

5 Will the download speed be suitable on the expected internet connection speeds?

6 Are the colour schemes suitable and any text easy to read?

7 Does the final work demonstrate a conventional or creative/innovative approach? There is no right or wrong here – just recognise what has been produced.

8 What improvements could be made (for example, frame rates, number of frames, animation techniques, colours, effects)?

Links to other units

You can find further information on how to review your work in LO4 from **units R081** and **R082**.

Know it!

What would be the impact of creating a web advert the wrong way round? Let's say the brief asked for a skyscraper advert, 160 pixels wide by 600 high, for use at the side of a web page. If the animated advert is created 600 pixels wide by 160 pixels high, what would the client think?

Assessment preparation

Think about the individual performance you will need to undertake. Make sure you:

- know what worked well and what did not in your animation with regards to the brief you have been given
- are able to identify areas for improvement and further development of your digital animation.

LO4 – Be able to review a digital animation		
Mark band 1	Mark band 2	Mark band 3
Produces a review of the digital animation which demonstrates a limited understanding of what worked and what did not, making few references back to the brief.	Produces a review of the digital animation which demonstrates a reasonable understanding of what worked and what did not, mostly referencing back to the brief.	Produces a review of the digital animation which demonstrates a thorough understanding of what worked and what did not, fully referencing back to the brief.
Review identifies areas for improvement and further development of the digital animation, some of which are appropriate and sometimes explained.	Review identifies areas for improvement and further development of the digital animation, which are mostly appropriate and explained well.	Review identifies areas for improvement and further development of the digital animation, which are wholly appropriate and justified.

Assessment guidance

The OCR set assignment

When completing your work for the OCR set assignment, you will need to:

- produce your own review of the digital animation that you have created
- comment on the final product and how this relates to the brief
- identify what could be improved further.

What do the command words mean?

Thorough [review]: means commenting on all the aspects and elements of the digital graphic (not the process through the unit).

Appropriate and justified [areas for improvement]: areas for improvement should be relevant and supported by your reasons why.

R087 Creating interactive multimedia products

About this unit

Interactive multimedia products are used in computer games, mobile phone applications, online advertising, e-publishing, streaming services and many other areas. This unit helps you to understand the basics of what interactive multimedia products are – including their purpose, features and properties – and how they are made. You will be able to plan and create an interactive multimedia product to a client's requirements. You will learn how to review the final product, evaluate how you met the client brief and decide how you could improve your work.

Resources for this unit

To produce an interactive multimedia product you may need access to, and be able to use, different types of software and hardware.

Examples of the software that you will require access to include:

- **Serif WebPlus X8**: This software can be purchased from various outlets on the internet. Whilst Serif have discontinued this officially, it is likely that many schools will have access to this package and it can be used for this unit.

- **Microsoft PowerPoint**: This software is part of the Microsoft Office suite and allows you to create interactive multimedia products that can be viewed on a variety of devices.

- **Google Web Designer**: This software can be downloaded free from Google. It allows you to make interactive web content without the need for coding skills but you can design all the interactive functions.

- Image editing software, such as **Adobe Photoshop**, **Fireworks** or **GIMP**: This is used to repurpose and change the format of graphics.

- Video editing software, such as **Windows Movie Maker**, **Apple iMovie**: This software can be used to repurpose and change the format of digital video.

Typical hardware devices include:

- Digital still cameras, digital video cameras to take photographs, record video and audio.
- A PC or laptop that is powerful enough to allow you to create and repurpose assets.

Learning outcomes

LO1 Understand the uses and properties of interactive multimedia products

LO2 Be able to plan an interactive multimedia product

LO3 Be able to create an interactive multimedia product

LO4 Be able to review an interactive multimedia product

How will I be assessed?

You will be assessed through an OCR model assignment, marked by your tutor and externally moderated by OCR. It is worth 25% of the overall mark when working towards a Certificate in Creative iMedia.

For LO1

Learners need to:

- investigate how and where different interactive multimedia products are used and their purposes across different industry sectors
- understand the elements you need to consider when designing an interactive multimedia product
- investigate the hardware, software and peripherals you will need to create an interactive multimedia product
- understand the limitations you may have when accessing and viewing interactive multimedia products caused by connections, broadband bandwidth and data transfer.

For LO2

Learners need to:

- plan an interactive multimedia product to meet a client brief
- produce an identification of the target audience for an interactive multimedia product
- produce a workplan for the production of an interactive multimedia product
- produce a series of visualisation diagrams for an interactive multimedia product
- identify the assets and resources needed to create an interactive multimedia product

- create and update a test plan to test an interactive multimedia product throughout production
- discuss the legislation in relation to the use of assets, such as video and sound content, when creating an interactive multimedia product.

For LO3

Learners need to:

- source assets to be used to create an interactive multimedia product
- create original and re-purpose assets to be used in an interactive multimedia product
- store assets to be used in an interactive multimedia product
- set up interaction and playback controls in the interactive multimedia product
- save an interactive multimedia product in the format appropriate to the software being used
- export an interactive multimedia product so that it is appropriate for its original use and purpose
- use version control throughout the production of an interactive multimedia product.

For LO4

Learners need to:

- review the interactive multimedia product demonstrating an understanding of what worked well and what did not in relation to the client brief
- review the interactive multimedia product identifying further areas for improvement and development; this can be in terms of meeting the specific brief.

LO1 Understand the uses and properties of interactive multimedia products

There are many industry sectors that use interactive multimedia products, such as websites, information kiosks, mobile applications and e-learning products.

Getting started

Working individually or in small groups, list the different ways that you think interactive multimedia products are used in the entertainment industry, such as music, film, television and gaming. Give an example for each.

Websites

All websites are interactive multimedia products. Most organisation have a website to promote their products and services; these may feature digital video, audio, animation, hyperlinks, rollovers and a carousel of images to engage the audience. Interactive e-commerce websites, such as eBay, use images and audio-visual content to promote the items they sell. Some websites, like hoddereducation.co.uk, feature a carousel of images that allow the user to scroll through recommended content that they can buy.

Figure 7.1 Screenshot of Hodder Education homepage showing multimedia features

Key term

Navigation: this is the term used for the way in which an interactive multimedia product directs a user to content through a series of structured buttons and links.

Websites created by the entertainment industry, such as film and television, feature pop up adverts, digital video and forums that allow audiences to **navigate** through content. Playback controls on sites such as YouTube allow the user to play, pause and link to further content so they can choose what they want to watch. Similarly, news websites such as BBC News and public information websites use multimedia to inform and educate audiences. Modern websites are created so they can be accessed on desktops, smartphones and tablet devices.

Classroom discussion

Your teacher will identify a website for this exercise. Look at the different types of media content on the website, why it is used and how it is interactive. For each of these three areas, discuss: 'what is its purpose and how is it interactive?'

● Audio-visual content
● Images
● Buttons and hyperlinks

Information kiosks

Information kiosks are often located in museums, galleries, airports, train stations, supermarkets and town centres. For example, a train station may use an information kiosk to inform customers of train times, and tourist information centres may use them to inform people about services and attractions. Some kiosks link to external websites, others are simple, standalone products. Kiosk interfaces must be easy to use. They are usually touch screen.

Figure 7.2 An information kiosk in a shop

Mobile applications

Other than websites, mobile applications (apps) are the most widely used interactive multimedia products. Apps can be standalone or create links to the features of a company's larger website. The most popular apps – that can be downloaded from services such as Apple's App Store or Google Play – include games, photo editing, television channel services and social media.

Figure 7.3 Apps for tablet and mobile devices

Apps feature enhanced navigation capabilities. Users are able to control when they want to use audio-visual content, communication, messaging functions or make in-app purchases. Many industry sectors and businesses – such as banks and retailers – have a mobile app.

e-learning products

Interactive e-learning products have been available since the 1990s to enhance content and to teach people new skills. Originally, these were distributed on DVD or CD-ROMs; users would navigate through the content and video using buttons, links and controls. These days, e-learning products can be found on websites – often for free – or can be downloaded as a free or paid app. They are often embedded quizzes and games – you may have used them yourself, such as BBC Bitesize, to help you with homework and revision.

Key elements to consider when designing interactive multimedia products

In this section we will investigate the key design features and elements that you need to consider when planning a new product.

Colour scheme

Think carefully about the colour scheme in relation to the brief.

Think about the purpose and target audience. For example, if you are designing an interactive multimedia product for children, then bright primary colours might attract their attention. Or, if the brief is to promote a local nature and animal park, you could use colours found in nature, such as green, brown and blue.

Big companies in the UK, such as British Airways, often use the colours of the recognised flag of the United Kingdom to show where they are based. They use this colour scheme across their websites, apps and the design of their staff uniforms.

Figure 7.4 British Airways colour scheme

House style

House style used is the consistent use of colour schemes, fonts, logos, text, and so on, across all multimedia products. The style of text can say a lot about a company and their services. For example, a modern company may use a sans-serif font, whereas a company aimed at an older audience is more likely to use a serif font.

Layout

This is important because the audience need to be able to understand the navigation in order to access the content. It should also be appealing and eye-catching to the target audience, and be suitable for their age group.

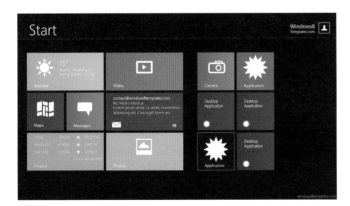

Figure 7.5 GUI for Windows 8 Surface Tablet

Key term

Graphical User Interface (GUI): a term used for the layout and display of the display screen, which forms the basis of the way that the user interacts with the product. An effective GUI will be intuitive and easy to use.

Graphical User Interface (GUI)

The GUI is the interface between a screen and users to access the content. Many devices, such as smartphones and tablets, have a touch screen; users interact with them through icons, menus graphics and images. On a PC and laptop, a GUI will feature the same features to access content and software but these will be accessed using a mouse or trackpad.

Accessibility

Accessibility means how usable a site is by people with disabilities, such as vision or hearing impairments. One way to do this would be by using features such as <alt> tags with images – this is when (invisible) descriptions of images are added to products which can be read aloud to blind users on a screen reader.

Hardware, software and peripherals required to create and view interactive multimedia products

It is important that you understand the range of equipment and resources that you can use to help you create an interactive multimedia product. You also need to make sure that you know what platforms you can use to view (or operate) interactive multimedia products. This is the target platform.

Hardware

Creating a product

You need a computer that is powerful enough to run software that can import multimedia assets, and has enough storage space. The computer should enable you to create some of your own content, such as banners and logos, if you want to. Your school will be able to provide you access to PCs or iMacs for this purpose.

Viewing a product

You will need access to hardware devices to check that your interactive multimedia product works. Examples of hardware that you might need access to include:

- PC/iMac
- laptop/MacBook
- tablet device
- smartphone
- other target platform or emulator.

Where necessary, you may need access to the internet so you can check that an interactive multimedia product works online.

Peripherals to create and view

Peripherals are the add-ons that you may need to view or engage with an interactive multimedia product. These include a smartphone or digital camera that allows you to take photographs and record video footage, or a microphone if recording audio. You will need the display screen and speakers to view the final product.

Software

You need to know what software applications can be used to create an interactive multimedia product. Refer to *Resources for this unit* at the start of the chapter.

Classroom discussion

Your teacher will lead a discussion on what software is available in your school to create interactive multimedia. Make notes on the capabilities and limitations of the options available.

Limitations caused by connections, bandwidth and data transfer

If an interactive multimedia product can be accessed online via devices that connect to the internet, then there may be problems, or limitations, for audiences using the product. In this section we will investigate these.

Connections

The main three ways people connect to the internet are:

1 **Ethernet:** a computer or laptop connected to the internet by a wired (Ethernet) cable. A cable from a computer is plugged straight into the router, which is connected to the internet via a telephone socket. The connection is fast, but not portable.

2 **Wi-Fi:** a device connects to a wireless internet signal at home, in a public place or at work. The interactive multimedia product can be viewed anywhere, but there may be a problem with the signal and the connection may be lost if you are sat too far away.

3 **3G, 4G and 5G:** a device, usually a smartphone or tablet, uses mobile communication technology to connect to the internet. This is a popular option for people when a Wi-Fi signal is not available. As with Wi-Fi the mobile signal may not be strong enough in some places. This means content such as video and audio might be slow or inaccessible.

Bandwidth and data transfer

Bandwidth or 'broadband speed' is the speed data can be transferred over a connection at one time. If a service provider says they have the 'fastest' broadband or highest bandwidth, it means that users can download large amounts of data at once, which will allow them to stream content, such as films, music and television programmes, quickly and without any lags or glitches.

Data transfer refers to how much data can be transferred over a certain period of time, and is often referred to in broadband packages as 'limited data'. So, even though the broadband is fast, there is a monthly limit on how much can be downloaded. Similarly, website hosting services normally limit how much data can be transferred from your website over a period of time.

A popular website could exceed the data transfer specified by the hosting service.

File formats supported by different platforms

Many interactive multimedia products can be accessed online. However, some, such as kiosk and museum interactive products, are still run from a server that stores the media content used in the interactive multimedia product. Many Apple device platforms do not support .swf files, and .flv is being phased out. In this section, we will look at the main file formats that interactive multimedia products are saved in.

MP4 audio-visual file format

A file with the MP4 file extension (.mp4) is a compressed file format. The format is used when audio-visual multimedia files need to be embedded into an interactive media product that is viewed on the web or saved onto a personal computer. An MP4 has a small file size, but is relatively high quality. This makes it suitable for embedding into websites and packages that are built using HTML5 code or software such as Microsoft PowerPoint.

MP3 audio file format

A file with the MP3 file extension (.mp3) is a compressed file format for sound or music. The format is used when audio files need to be embedded into an interactive media product that is viewed on the web or saved onto a personal computer. An MP3 has a small file size, and keeps some quality when it is saved.

PNG image file format

A file with the PNG file extension (.png) is a compressed yet high quality format used when images are transferred over the internet or saved in multimedia projects. A PNG has a small file size, but it keeps quality when it is saved at a web resolution of 72 dpi. This makes it suitable for embedding into websites and presentation packages.

HTML and PPSX

It is likely that you will use web-based or online software to build your project, or a package such as Microsoft PowerPoint. You should, therefore, ensure that you think about the most appropriate way to save and export your files so they can be viewed on the intended device.

Online will need to be exported as HTML so that they can be opened in, and be compatible with, a variety of web browsers. Interactive multimedia products designed for a kiosk or computer which have been created using PowerPoint, for example, should be exported as a .pps or .ppsx file. This is a PowerPoint Show file, and can be opened as a standalone product.

Stretch activity

1 Explain the term *data transfer* in relation to an internet connection.
2 State the file formats that could be used when creating an interactive multimedia product that needs to be accessed online. Explain your choice(s).

Know it!

1 Write down four uses and purposes of interactive multimedia products.
2 Explain the difference between a *connection* and *bandwidth*.
3 Justify why you would embed MP4s and MP3s into software when creating an interactive multimedia product.

Assessment preparation

Think about the individual performance you need to undertake. Make sure you:

- know about the different uses and purposes of interactive multimedia products
- know the different hardware, software and peripherals used to create and view interactive multimedia products
- explain the limitations caused by different connections and bandwidth and data transfer speeds when accessing interactive multimedia products
- are able to identify the file formats used to create and export your interactive multimedia product and the suitability of using different file formats to view on varied platforms.

LO1: Understand the uses and properties of interactive multimedia products		
Mark band 1	Mark band 2	Mark band 3
Identifies a limited range of products and where they are used. Produces a limited identification of design principles.	Identifies a range of products, includes some details of purpose and where they are used and with some identification of design principles.	Identifies a wide range of products, includes most details of purpose and where they are used and with detailed identification of design principles.
Mark band 1	Mark band 2	Mark band 3
Identifies a limited range of hardware, software and peripherals required to create and view interactive multimedia products, demonstrating a basic understanding of their use and purpose.	Identifies a range of hardware, software and peripherals required to create and view interactive multimedia products, demonstrating a sound understanding of their use and purpose.	Identifies a wide range of hardware, software and peripherals required to create and view interactive multimedia products, demonstrating a thorough understanding of their use and purpose.
Demonstrates a basic understanding of the limitations caused by connections, bandwidth and data transfer speeds when accessing interactive multimedia products.	Demonstrates a sound understanding of the limitations caused by connections, bandwidth and data transfer speeds when accessing interactive multimedia products.	Demonstrates a thorough understanding of the limitations caused by connections, bandwidth and data transfer speeds when accessing interactive multimedia products.
Identifies file formats and their suitability for different platforms with limited accuracy.	Identification of file formats and their suitability for different platforms is mostly accurate.	Identification of file formats and their suitability for different platforms is accurate.

Assessment guidance

The OCR set assignment

When completing your work for the OCR set assignment, you will need to:

- investigate the purpose of different interactive multimedia products together with the design principles that were used
- describe a range of hardware, software and peripherals that are used to create interactive products and also to test/view/use the products
- discuss the limitations of connection methods for transferring interactive media product content in terms of bandwidth and data transfer speeds
- identify file formats used within multimedia products and their suitability for different target platforms.

What do the command words mean?

Detailed [design principles]: can be demonstrated by considering the use of screen layout, colour, consistency of design across screens and ease of navigation.

Thorough understanding [purpose of hardware/software]: should be evidenced by discussing the equipment needed to create multimedia products together with any differences for people that would view/use the product.

Thorough understanding [connections]: should be discussed by applying your knowledge of connection methods in terms of bandwidth and data transfer speed to different products and content in order to demonstrate your understanding.

Accurate [file formats]: means that you understand the suitability of different file formats when used/viewed on different target platforms.

LO2 Be able to plan an interactive multimedia product

Getting started

Working individually or in small groups, think of the planning you might need to do if you were asked to make an interactive multimedia e-learning resource aimed at 6 to 12 year-old children.

Interpret client requirements for an interactive multimedia product

Client requirements are based on the purpose of the product (in other words, what do they want it for?). It might be to advertise and promote, inform and educate, or entertain. The interpretation of client requirements is the starting point for your planning.

The first step is to break down the client requirements. It is important that you document that you have understood and broken down the client requirements as part of your initial planning of your interactive multimedia product.

Here are three ways to present this.

1 Summarise the client requirements by creating a mind map (see R081). This will allow you to organise ideas into sub-sections. For the production of an interactive multimedia product, sub-sections in a mind map may include ideas about:
- colour scheme
- house style
- navigation
- audio-visual/animation content
- music
- user controls
- access and devices.

2 Link the client requirements to product ideas by creating a mood board. Mood board content could include examples of:
- colours and house style, such as fonts, that would appeal to your audience

- similar images you might use to appeal to your audience
- screenshots of similar audio-visual content you might use to meet the brief
- buttons or images that you might use to create your navigation signs.

3 Document your understanding of the client requirements by writing the key aspects of the in a short report. Headings might include:
- Form
- Purpose and use
- Target audience
- Multimedia content needed
- Navigation required
- Deadline date
- Devices that the audience can access the product on

Links to other units

You can find further information on this topic in LO2 of **units R081, R082** and **R085**.

Understand target audience requirements for an interactive multimedia product

Once you have identified the main client requirements, it is important that you document, in detail, your target audience for the interactive multimedia product.

Here are two ways that you can present this.

1 Create an audience profile. This is a piece of creative writing where you write about the interests of the type of person who would be part of your target audience for the product. This will allow you to really think about who your audience is and the content they could access in your product to engage them. In the profile, you could discuss:
- age
- gender
- hobbies and interests
- type of consumer products they like
- type of media content they like.

2 Interests and requirements of the target audience can now be added. This can include:

- the devices they would use to access the product (such as PC, smartphone)
- any similar interactive multimedia products they might consume
- content, video, audio, images, buttons, diagrams, maps and sound needed in the interactive multimedia product that would appeal to the audience
- content that should be avoided, such as video with violent content, based on the age of the target audience.

Links to other units

You can find further information on this topic in LO2 of **unit R081**.

Creating a work plan for an interactive multimedia product

You will need to produce a work plan before you produce your product. This should include a list of:

- **tasks and associated activities:** what you will do to create and source content and produce the interactive multimedia product
- **resources:** the equipment you require to create your interactive multimedia product
- **workflow:** the order that your activities and specific tasks need to be completed in
- **timescales:** the deadlines you need to meet
- **milestones:** key aspects of the production that have to be completed before you move on; for example, sourcing and creating the assets
- **contingencies:** there are specific contingencies you might need to think about when creating interactive multimedia products; for example, this can include having backups of your assets and product in secure cloud storage.

Tasks and activities – creating and testing an interactive multimedia product

You need to break down the different tasks into a sequence of activities that you have to do as part of the production process.

These main tasks will be for:

- pre-production and planning
- production
- reviewing your interactive multimedia product.

The activities within the tasks include:

- organising the equipment you need to create original assets and the product
- collecting assets e.g. images, video and audio
- secure storage of assets; for example, SD card or cloud storage system (Dropbox or Google Drive)
- repurposing of assets
- creating the navigation and control structure in your chosen software
- testing your navigation and assets to ensure they work as planned
- making changes and re-testing
- exporting in the appropriate format so that the product works for your client and the intended target audience.

Planning the structure and features of your interactive multimedia product

It is important to structure your interactive multimedia project so it is easy to follow and use, and the correct information appears as the audience expects.

Screen size

You need to know what size screen your product will be viewed on; this affects how much information can be displayed. Think in more detail about screen size when producing visualisation diagrams in the next section.

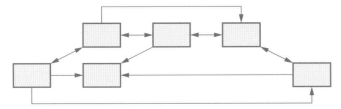

Figure 7.6 Examples of a structure for a product with non-linear navigation

Non-linear navigation

A non-linear navigation system within an interactive media product means that the user doesn't have to access content in a straight line or pre-defined sequence. The user is free to choose and click on content in any order they want to. This is how all websites and apps work; it allows users to select the material most relevant to them. Whether you want to build your interactive multimedia product in web design software or presentation software, you will need to clearly identify how the user will navigate between pages/screens.

Interaction

A typical feature of interactive multimedia products, such as websites, apps and games,

Figure 7.7 Popular icons and buttons that act as hyperlinks in interactive media products

are the links that enable the user to navigate the product. Buttons, icons, controls, images and text can be used to link to other content within the product. Links can also be used to access content on other websites. You can use web design software to create an interactive multimedia product. However, packages such as Microsoft PowerPoint have a method that does this without the need for coding.

Rollovers

A rollover or 'mouse over' is a feature used to provide interactivity between the user and a page in an interactive multimedia product. Rollovers can be created by using images, text or buttons. Creating a rollover is usually quite easy – you select the first image that will be displayed on the page, and a second image that will be displayed when the mouse rolls over the first image. Set the mouse action to either 'on click' or 'mouse over' to activate the rollover. This feature makes content and hyperlinks more engaging.

Using visualisation diagrams to plan the layout and style

Create a visualisation diagram for every page of your interactive multimedia media product before you create them. These can be annotated to add more detail about the type of content, colour scheme, house style and navigation you intend to create. This shows that you have completed careful planning. There are two main areas.

1   **Screen design:** the visualisation diagrams should show screen design and layout for each page of your interactive multimedia product. This will clearly show the position and size of:

   ● logos and titles
   ● space for media content
   ● sub headings
   ● key button text
   ● copytext that you have already written.

The colour scheme should also be shown through annotations – or you can colour it in – so that the visualisation diagrams are clear.

2 **Navigation features:** the position of navigation buttons, icons or links should be clear on your visualisation diagrams. Features include:

- style and shape of buttons (such as blocks or circles)
- where the buttons or navigation bars appear
- annotations of what content the buttons and links can access
- colour scheme of the navigation
- how the navigation works with the GUI; for example, if it is touchscreen, what navigation can be pressed by the user?

Assets

The size and position of **assets** on a page/screen should be decided at this planning stage. Think about what assets will be accessed when a certain link is pressed and how this will impact on your screen design. Include:

- images and background graphics
- animation, video or sound that plays on loading
- space and size, in pixels, for any videos, animation or images.

> ### Links to other units
>
> You can find further information on this topic in LO2 of **units R081**, **R082** and **R085**.

Identifying the assets and resources needed

Content assets

You need numerous assets to make sure your multimedia product engages the audience.

You will need:

- menus and buttons
- images and graphics
- video and/or animation
- sound effects and/or music.

> ### Key terms
>
> **Assets:** the content collected or created for the final product, such as images, sound and video.
>
> **Resources:** hardware, software and peripherals to create the assets and product.

If you have more than one type of asset, then the product is multimedia. If you have all four types of asset, then the final product will be engaging and interesting.

Resources

You need different **resources** to produce your interactive multimedia product.

You need:

- PC, laptop, iMac or MacBook
- software package to create your interactive multimedia product; such as Microsoft PowerPoint, Serif WebPlus, Adobe Dreamweaver or Google Web Designer
- suitable graphics and video software to design titles and repurpose image assets, such as Adobe Photoshop, GIMP, Movie Maker or iMovie
- a digital camera (optional) to take photographs and/or record video and audio; a smartphone could also be used.

Creating a test plan

You must test that the navigation works for each link and button, and that all content launches as planned. So, you need to create a test plan that tests all the key interactive functions, lists evidence/results of each test, and explains how to fix any problems found. This could be a table or list; you could even have one for each page or asset.

The table on the next page shows an example of a test plan that tests the opening of a browser.

Test	User requirement addressed	Expected result	Actual result	Pass/fail	Date	Corrective action
Logo displayed	The website uses the company's house style	CompuTech logo is displayed	As expected	Pass	01/12/17	None
Navigation bar appears	Website is easy to navigate	Navigation bar appears	As expected	Pass	01/12/17	None
Navigation bar drop downs work	Website is easy to navigate	When mouse goes over labels, menus drop down	As expected	Pass	01/12/17	None
Navigation bar hyperlinks work	Website is easy to navigate	When mouse goes over, link turns to red and can click on it to take you to correct page	As expected	Pass	01/12/17	None

Legislation

You need to source assets for your interactive multimedia product. Depending on your client requirements these assets might include:

- images and background graphics
- digital video footage
- sound effects
- background music.

Remember that your assets may be subject to copyright. However, there are many places to get copyright-free assets.

YouTube is a good resource for videos, because they have embedded codes that allow the video to be placed directly into your software. There will be information under the titles of many of these videos that state whether they are copyright free or not.

For images and graphics, you can use websites such as www.freeimages.co.uk, and for music, websites such as www.freesound.org.

These allow you to download material that is not under any copyright. However, legislation around music is a little more complicated than for other assets – a good source of information on this is the Performing Rights Society website: www.prsformusic.com/licences/releasing-music-products/limited-manufacture

Remember, any assets you find should be credited to the source you downloaded them from. For each asset you should:

- write down why you need this to create your interactive multimedia product
- have evidence that you have thought about copyright law.

Links to other units

You can find further information on this topic in LO2 of **unit R081**.

Know it!

1 Explain why you need to break down the client requirements before producing an interactive multimedia product.
2 Justify why you need annotated visualisation diagrams that show the navigation of your assets and content before you start to create your product.

Assessment preparation

Think about the individual performance you will need to undertake. Make sure you:

- are able to interpret the client requirements and understand the requirements of your target audience
- understand the different assets and resources that you will need to create an interactive multimedia product
- are able to explain how legislation relates to the assets you will use to create your interactive multimedia product.

LO2: Be able to plan an interactive multimedia product		
Mark band 1	Mark band 2	Mark band 3
Produces an interpretation from the client brief for an interactive multimedia product which meets few of the client requirements.	Produces an interpretation from the client brief for an interactive multimedia product which meets most of the client requirements.	Produces an interpretation from the client brief for an interactive multimedia product which fully meets the client requirements.
Produces a limited identification of target audience requirements.	Produces a clear identification of target audience requirements.	Produces a clear and detailed identification of target audience requirements.
Produces a work plan for the creation of the interactive multimedia product which has some capability in producing the intended final product.	Produces a work plan for the creation of the interactive multimedia product which is mostly capable of producing the intended final product.	Produces a clear and detailed work plan for the creation of the interactive multimedia product which is fully capable of producing the intended final product.
Draws upon limited skills/knowledge/understanding from other units in the specification.	Draws upon some relevant skills/knowledge/understanding from other units in the specification	Clearly draws upon relevant skills/knowledge/understanding from other units in the specification.
Mark band 1	Mark band 2	Mark band 3
Uses basic planning techniques to show what the product will look like with limited consideration of design principles.	Uses sound planning techniques to show what the product will look like with some consideration of design principles.	Uses complex planning techniques to show what the product will look like with full consideration of design principles.
Identifies a limited range of assets and resources to be used as part of these plans, some of which are not appropriate.	Identifies a range of assets and resources to be used as part of these plans, which are mostly appropriate.	Identifies a wide range of assets and resources to be used as part of these plans, which are wholly appropriate.
Produces simple visualisation diagrams for the intended final product.	Produces sound visualisation diagrams for the intended final product.	Produces clear and detailed visualisation diagrams for the intended final product.
Creates a test plan for the interactive multimedia product which tests some of the functionality.	Creates a test plan for the interactive multimedia product which tests most of the functionality, identifying expected outcomes.	Creates a clear and detailed test plan for the interactive multimedia product which fully tests the functionality, listing tests, expected and actual outcomes and identifying re-tests.
Demonstrates a limited understanding of legislation in relation to the use of assets in interactive multimedia products.	Demonstrates a sound understanding of legislation in relation to the use of assets in interactive multimedia products.	Demonstrates a thorough understanding of legislation in relation to the use of assets in interactive multimedia products.

Assessment guidance

The OCR set assignment

When completing your work for the OCR set assignment, you will need to:

- produce your own interpretation of the client brief
- identify the target audience and what they will want from the product
- produce a work plan to create the product

- use knowledge and skills from other units such as R081
- plan the product in terms of both the content and navigation that applies your understanding of design principles
- identify the assets and resources that will be needed
- produce visualisation diagrams for the interactive product
- develop a test plan for the functionality of the product that you intend to create
- describe the legal issues of using assets in your product.

What do the command words mean?

Fully [interpretation of the brief]: needs to be your own individual ideas and thoughts on what is required that expands on what is given in the scenario and brief.

Clear and detailed [target audience]: should be a clear definition of who the target audience is and what they will want from the interactive multimedia product.

Clear and detailed [work plan]: should cover all the tasks and activities for planning, creating, testing and reviewing the interactive product.

Clearly draws on [knowledge, skills and understanding]: must be from other units and not something that is already in R087.

Complex [planning techniques]: should include a product structure with content and navigational features that apply good design principles.

Wide range [assets and resources]: generally accepted as five or more.

Clear and detailed [visualisation diagrams]: should clearly show the content, colours and navigational features for each page/screen of the product.

Clear and detailed [test plan]: should check the functionality of the content display and navigation throughout the product.

Thorough [understanding of legislation]: should be applied to the actual assets that you intend to use in the product. Their use should also be in a commercial context and not just education.

LO3 Be able to create an interactive multimedia product

Getting started

Working individually or in small groups, make a list of three of the main benefits of using interactive multimedia when trying to sell a product.

Creating, repurposing and storing assets

You need to make sure your assets are in the correct file format to use in your interactive multimedia product. The best way to do this is to use software that allows you to change or repurpose format. You can also create assets such as buttons and shapes in your digital imaging software.

Links to other units

You can find further information on this topic in LO3 of **units R081**, **R082** and **R089**.

Creating an interactive multimedia product structure

Your interactive multimedia product requires a clear structure. The best way of doing this is by ensuring that you set up a folder and organise it to show you keep all your pages, images, video, buttons, sound in separate folders.

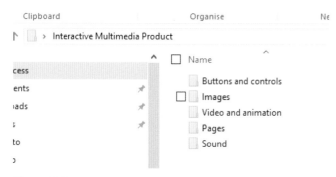

Figure 7.8 A basic organised file structure

You should then begin to create a structure by ensuring that there is a standard navigation system that appears in the same place on each page. In Microsoft PowerPoint, you can do this by creating a Master Slide and a Navigation Menu. Any new page you create will include the menu. You can create a master slide or page in PowerPoint by going to View > Slide Master.

Figure 7.9 Creating a Master Slide in Microsoft PowerPoint

Setting up interaction and playback controls

Once you have your folder structure, you can start adding the menu, content and controls.

Navigation

You will create a Navigation menu using buttons, icons or graphics that you can insert in a navigation bar structure on a website or in a table format in presentation software. In Microsoft PowerPoint, you can insert a table bar into the Master Slide and insert the icons or buttons into the bar.

Once you have created your basic menu, each icon or image can be hyperlinked to the correct page or content. On a website, you can hyperlink using the <a> anchor tag. In Microsoft PowerPoint, you simply click on the icon, image or text and use the hyperlink command.

Figure 7.10 Creating a navigation menu in Microsoft PowerPoint

You can also create action buttons in Microsoft PowerPoint without having to use icons. If you click Shapes > Action Buttons, you can choose a design and link to a page or content. You can then edit it to match your chosen colour scheme.

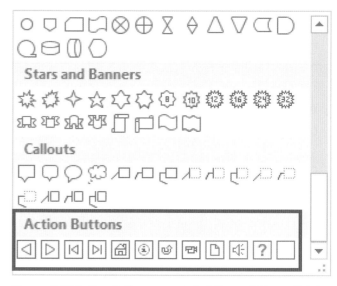

Figure 7.11 Action Button controls in Microsoft PowerPoint

Rollovers

Rollovers (or mouse overs) and triggers allow for interactivity and further information to be accessed by the user. The rollover command in HTML and presentation software allows for a change in content. This can be a replacement image or additional text. The easy way to create a rollover is to use two images with a link between them.

Triggers

These 'trigger' content to appear using a command called 'On Mouse Click'. In presentation software, the effect can be applied to buttons and content with the command 'Start Effect on Click' or 'On Click'. Content will then appear. Figure 7.12 shows this command in the animation controls in Microsoft PowerPoint. So, the appearance of the additional content can be further controlled to fit your design or house style.

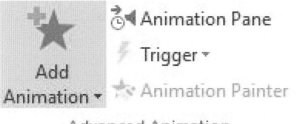

Figure 7.12 Creating a trigger action in Microsoft PowerPoint

Saving and exporting the interactive multimedia product

If you do not finish your interactive multimedia product in one session, you will need to save your work so you can go back and edit it. To make this possible, you must save it in the software project format. For example, an unfinished web project that you have created in Serif WebPlus should be saved as .wpp. Similarly, a PowerPoint should be saved as .pptx (or .ppt on older versions).

As discussed in LO1, one of the most popular ways to access interactive multimedia products is via the web. This is because multimedia content embedded within a project will retain its quality when compressed, so it can be viewed on smartphone and tablet devices when accessed on websites. If a project required a product that can be exported so it can be viewed on a tablet or smartphone, the pages may need to be exported as HTML files.

All presentation packages will have the option to export as a standalone interactive product to view on hardware and GUIs similar to kiosks. Microsoft PowerPoint, for example, needs the linear navigation disabled and the final product exported as a .ppsx (or .pps). To disable the linear navigation, make sure it is set up as a 'Show' document before saving it as a .pps. You can do this by Set Up Slideshow > Browsed at a Kiosk, as shown in Figure 7.13.

Version control

When creating your interactive multimedia product, always use version control. This means that you save versions of work as you progress. The best way is to name your work V0.1, V0.2, and so on (refer to R081 for more information).

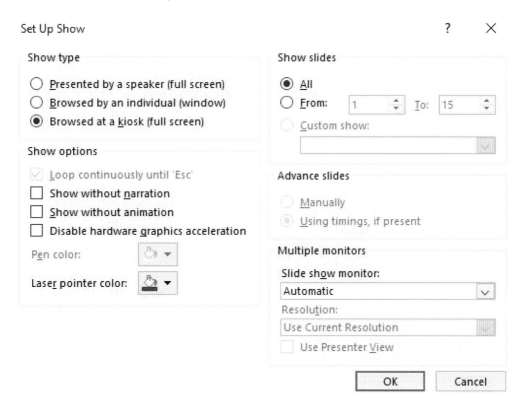

Figure 7.13 Setting up a show type in Microsoft PowerPoint

Links to other units

You can find further information on this topic in LO3 of **unit R085**.

Know it!

1 Identify the purpose of a navigation system.
2 Explain why it is important to use your test plan throughout production.
3 Explain how accessibility features can help improve the effectiveness of an interactive multimedia product.

Assessment preparation

Think about the individual performance you will need to undertake. Make sure you:

- are able to source and create assets for your interactive multimedia product
- use different types of interactive functions and controls in your interactive multimedia product
- create a working and clear navigation system
- are able to save and export your interactive multimedia product.

LO3: Be able to create interactive multimedia products		
Mark band 1	Mark band 2	Mark band 3
Sources and creates the assets to be used in the interactive multimedia product occasionally using methods that are appropriate.	Sources, creates and repurposes the assets to be used in the interactive multimedia product mostly using methods that are appropriate.	Sources, creates and re-purposes the assets to be used in the interactive multimedia product consistently using methods that are appropriate.
Prepares the structure for the interactive multimedia product in a way which is sometimes consistent or does not reflect the designs.	Prepares the structure for the interactive multimedia product in a way which is mostly consistent and reflects the designs.	Prepares the structure for the interactive multimedia product in a way which is wholly consistent and fully reflects the designs.
Mark band 1	Mark band 2	Mark band 3
Combines a limited range of different planned asset types with a basic navigation system to create a working interactive multimedia product. Some elements do not work as intended.	Combines a range of different planned asset types with a clear navigation system to create a working interactive multimedia product. Most elements work as intended.	Combines a wide range of different planned asset types with a clear and coherent navigation system to create a working interactive multimedia product. All elements work as intended.
Saves and exports the multimedia product in a file format that sometimes retains interactivity but has limited appropriateness to the client brief.	Saves and exports the multimedia product in a file format that retains interactivity and is mostly appropriate to the client brief.	Saves and exports the multimedia product in a file format that retains interactivity and is wholly appropriate to the client brief.
Occasionally saves electronic files using appropriate file and folder names and structures.	Mostly saves electronic files using file and folder names and structures which are consistent and appropriate.	Consistently saves electronic files using file and folder names and structures which are consistent and appropriate.

Assessment guidance

The OCR set assignment

When completing your work for the OCR set assignment, you will need to:

- source some assets and create some assets for use in the product
- repurpose the assets to make them suitable for use in the product
- prepare the structure for the product, implementing the content and navigation from your designs
- create the interactive multimedia product by combining the assets, features and navigation within your authoring software
- save and export the product in a suitable file format that retains the interactive features for the user
- use appropriate file and folder naming conventions.

What do the command words mean?

Consistently [source/create/re-purpose]: relates to storing the assets in suitable formats and with optimum properties for use in the product (display and speed of operation/loading).

Wholly [consistent with designs]: means that the product must clearly be the implementation of the intended design.

Wide range [assets with navigation]: generally means five or more.

All [work as intended]: will be a result of the testing to ensure that the functionality is correct (with correct display, layout and navigation).

Wholly appropriate [save and export]: means exporting in a format that is compatible with the target platform and retains the interactive features that were produced.

Consistently appropriate [export]: means that the development of the product should be organised using descriptive file names and folders for the different parts together with using different version numbers for the product during its development.

LO4 Be able to review an interactive multimedia product

You must be able to reflect on your work and review whether your final interactive multimedia product met the client and target audience requirements. You should think about improvements that you could make. Reviewing your work is useful because it will help you develop your skills when you create your next project.

Getting started

Choose a website or smartphone app that has poor reviews. Work through it yourself making a list of what works and what doesn't. From this, summarise what is needed to make it better. You might find this website a useful starting point: www.theworldsworstwebsiteever.com

Reviewing your interactive multimedia product against the brief

Try to critically review the product as if you were the user. Assess your interactive multimedia product against the set brief. Use the following prompts to help.

- Forget that you know how it should work, and navigate the product in a random manner. Ask yourself:
  - can you read the text information and instructions easily?
  - would it be intuitive for a first-time user?
  - are the colours clear and suitable for the intended purpose?
  - does it provide all the information that you need?
- Does the product meet its purpose? For example, if the product is advertising a sports park, does it follow the conventions of adverts, such as including exciting videos, clear images and details of activities, to promote the sports park?
- Does the final product meet the target audience requirements? For example, if it is a web resource to help 14 to 19 year olds investigate careers in the digital media industries, does it feature audio-visual interviews with professionals in the industry, and does it have an interactive form to ask questions, or a playable show reel of work?
- Was the interactive multimedia product exported in the correct format from the software so that the target audience can access it?

Making improvements to your interactive multimedia product

You need to assess your interactive multimedia product and think about improvements that you could make to the final piece. Use the following prompts to help you think about how you could write about improvements to your work.

- Has the final interactive multimedia product shown that you can use a variety of multimedia to meet the brief? If not, how could you develop your skills when you want to use ways to engage the target audience that would be useful to include next time?

- Has the final interactive multimedia product shown that you can create a working navigation system in your chosen software so that the audience can use the product? If not, how could you develop your skills in your chosen software so that you could improve the navigation and usability of content?

Read about it

PowerPoint Basics In 30 Minutes: How to Make Effective PowerPoint Presentations Using a PC, Mac, PowerPoint Online, or the PowerPoint App, by Angela Rose (In 30 Minutes Guides, 2017).

Know it!

1 From the client requirements identified in LO2 for the interactive multimedia product, make a list of anything that you did not meet.

2 Explain how you could change your product to ensure all the client requirements were met.

Assessment preparation

Think about the individual performance you will need to undertake. Make sure you:

- are able to review how your final interactive multimedia product met the client target audience requirements
- are able to review how you could improve and develop your work.

LO4: Be able to review interactive multimedia products		
Mark band 1	Mark band 2	Mark band 3
Produces a review of the interactive multimedia product which demonstrates a limited understanding of what worked and what did not, making few references back to the brief.	Produces a review of the interactive multimedia product which demonstrates a reasonable understanding of what worked and what did not, mostly referencing back to the brief.	Produces a review of the interactive multimedia product which demonstrates a thorough understanding of what worked and what did not, fully referencing back to the brief.
Review identifies areas for improvement and further development of the interactive multimedia product, some of which are appropriate and sometimes explained.	Review identifies areas for improvement and further development of the interactive multimedia product, which are mostly appropriate and explained well.	Review identifies areas for improvement and further development of the interactive multimedia product, which are wholly appropriate and justified.

Assessment guidance

The OCR set assignment

When completing your work for the OCR set assignment, you will need to:

- produce your own review of the interactive multimedia product that you have created
- comment on the final interactive multimedia product and how this relates to the brief
- following on from the review, identify what could be improved further.

What do the command words mean?

Thorough [review]: means commenting on all the features, content, pages/screens and navigation of the interactive media product (not the process through the unit).

Appropriate and justified [areas for improvement]: areas for improvement should be relevant and supported by your reasons why.

R088 Creating a digital sound sequence

About this unit

As one of the less popular units, this chapter covers only the key points.

R088 is about digital sound sequences. You will investigate the uses and properties of sound before planning, recording, mixing and reviewing a digital sound sequence to meet a client brief.

Note that this unit cannot be combined with R089.

Resources for this unit

Hardware: Computer system, audio recorder, microphone(s).

Software: Sound editing application, such as Audacity® or Apple GarageBand.

Learning outcomes

LO1 Understand the uses and properties of digital sound

LO2 Be able to plan a digital sound sequence

LO3 Be able to create a digital sound sequence

LO4 Be able to review a digital sound sequence

LO1 Understand the uses and properties of digital sound

Getting started

A good way to start this unit would be to create a mind map of different audio products that you hear on a regular basis. Think about the radio, television, telephones and websites. Where possible, identify the different types of products such as news broadcasts and radio dramas.

Sectors and uses of digital audio products

The areas that you will need to investigate are:

- commercial contexts (such as voiceovers and advertising)
- entertainment (such as broadcast radio and computer games)
- business (such as information)
- education (such as podcasts and tutorials)

Sound may take the form of voiceovers, background music, event/actions or voxpop. These can be used in radio, television, broadcasting, websites, games or computer sounds for events such as at start-up. Examples of where they are used include:

- **broadcasting:** radio and television, voiceovers, jingles, adverts
- **internet:** some websites incorporate sounds such as background music, voiceovers, page clicks or podcasts
- **multimedia:** any type of multimedia product or presentation can also use sounds to enhance the experience; may also include ring tones on mobile devices
- **games:** used as background music, environment sounds (such as water or animals) or actions/events
- **computer sounds:** start-up, shutdown, error messages, alerts and alarms.

Audio file formats

File format	Description	Compressed format?
.mp3	MPEG-1 audio layer 3; an audio format that can be compressed using different bit rates, providing a range of options for the sound quality/file size	Yes
.wav	Windows Wave format; widely supported by computer systems and web browsers	No
.wma	Windows Media Audio format developed by Microsoft	Yes
.aiff	Audio Interchange File Format; the default audio format used on Apple Mac computers	No
Ogg Vorbis	Alternative to MP3 with similar file sizes	Yes

Note: Newer formats that can be used for audio include .mp4 (a multimedia format for audio and video) and .m4a, which is for audio only. These are relevant but not currently listed in the specification.

Properties of digital audio

Bit depth: most sound files are stored in either 12 bit or 16 bit data. Higher bit depth produces more detailed sound quality. Audio CDs have sound stored using 16 bits which has 65 536 levels.

Sample rate: this is the frequency that analogue sounds are sampled when creating a digital file. Audio CDs contain sound that has been sampled at 44.1 kHz, which means there are 44 100 samples every second.

Note: 1 Hz = 1 hertz = 1 sample per second.

1 kHz = 1 kilohertz = 1000 hertz.

1 kHz = 1000 samples per second.

Pitch: this is how high or low a note sounds; pitch is sometimes referred to as the 'frequency' of the note.

Tone or tonal range: tone refers to the balance of frequencies of notes that are present; for instance, a violin plays higher notes than a cello, and so a violin would be described as having a 'treble' tone, and a cello a 'bass' tone. Different pieces of music, or genres, can also have different tones, displaying more treble or bass.

Timbre: the 'quality' or 'character' of the sound that distinguishes it from something similar. When a key is struck on a piano, a complex serious of vibrations of the entire instrument causes different notes to be heard along with the original note. These are called overtones or harmonics. Different instruments create different harmonics from the same basic note, and this is why different instruments have a different sound, sometimes referred to as the tonal colour.

Clarity: how pure or clear the sound is. When listening to a person's voice – how easy is it to make out what they are saying?

Volume: as volume increases, the sound will increase in loudness. However, the human ear does not have the same sensitivity to all audio frequencies; some sounds can appear louder even though they are at the same volume level. The loudness must allow the listener to hear the sounds clearly.

Considerations when recording audio

Environmental considerations: include background noise, echo, weather, wind, rain.

Limitations: relating to audio recording include the audio volume levels, signal to noise ratio and distance from audio source.

Distance: set for the best sound signal to noise ratio (but not too close so as to get distortion). The recording levels should be checked before recording the actual sounds needed.

Microphone handling and wind noise: use shock mount holders and/or a furry windshield (also known as a dead cat).

If you are recording a voice interview, maintain a constant distance between the mouth and the microphone to keep the recording volume at a constant level. Try to avoid the idea that you can fix it in the sound editor later – it will take a lot longer and the results are unlikely to be as good as a first-class recording. Use the pointing of the microphone as a cue for who should be speaking.

Background noise: can be from traffic or other people's conversations. The choice of microphone will be important so that the directionality minimises unwanted sounds.

Characteristics of microphones

Directionality refers to the direction where the microphone is sensitive to sounds. All microphones will pick up sounds from directly in front, but some are not as sensitive to sounds from the sides. This property is usually illustrated using a polar pattern diagram (Figure 8.1).

Omni-directional: picks up sound from all directions (equally in front of the microphone and behind).

Cardioid: a word that usually refers to the heart – and in microphone terms this means a heart shaped polar pattern. The strongest signal comes from sounds that are directly in front of the microphone with almost nothing from behind.

Super-cardioid: a narrow directional microphone useful for picking up sounds with a specific source or at a longer distance, such as wildlife or from a stage.

Shotgun: has a very narrow forward pointing response although it may also have a significant sensitivity to sounds directly behind it as well.

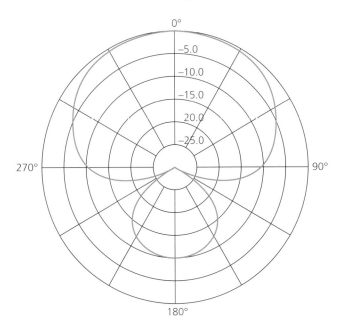

Figure 8.1 Microphone directional sensitivity in a polar pattern

Note: a directional microphone (especially shotgun types) should be pointed at the mouth of the person, not just the body. Moving 'off target' with this type of microphone can affect the recording volume. Refer to the polar diagram of the microphone to see where the sensitivity starts to drop away.

Assessment preparation

LO1: Understand the uses and properties of digital sound		
Mark band 1	**Mark band 2**	**Mark band 3**
Produces a summary of the uses and properties of digital sound, identifying a few sectors in which digital sound is used which demonstrates a limited understanding.	Produces a reasoned summary of the uses and properties of digital sound, identifying a range of sectors in which digital sound is used which demonstrates a sound understanding.	Produces a detailed and thorough summary of the uses and properties of digital sound, identifying a wide range of sectors in which digital sound is used which demonstrates a thorough understanding.
Describes with limited accuracy different audio file formats and the properties of digital sound.	Describes with reasonable accuracy different audio file formats and the properties of digital sound.	Describes accurately different audio file formats and the properties of digital sound.
Demonstrates a basic understanding of environmental considerations and limitations relating to audio recording.	Demonstrates a sound understanding of environmental considerations and limitations relating to audio recording.	Demonstrates a thorough understanding of environmental considerations and limitations relating to audio recording.

Assessment guidance

The OCR set assignment

When completing your work for the OCR set assignment, you will need to:

- discuss the uses and properties of digital sound
- describe a wide range of sectors where sounds are used
- describe the different audio file formats and their characteristics
- discuss the environmental considerations and limitations of recording sound.

Links to other units

You can find information on the command words in **unit R082**.

LO2 Be able to plan a digital sound sequence

Before planning the recording of your sounds, you need to know what is required for the audio project. This will be described in a client brief or specification. Read this document carefully and think about how to satisfy the needs of the client using your own creative talents and ideas.

Note down some ideas on how to complete the sound recording, and what equipment will be needed. Discuss your ideas with the client before going out to record the sounds.

A script, depending on the content, is likely to be an ideal way to plan your work for this subject.

You will need an equipment list and a concept of what will be created, to show your client. If you are developing initial ideas, try a spider diagram. This is described in more detail in R081.

Links to other units

You can find further information on planning and pre-production techniques in **unit R081**.

Creating the work plan

A key aspect in the work plan is to include tasks for both recording and editing sounds. In general, the work plan should include:

- sound recording tasks
- post-production (editing) tasks
- activities for the tasks
- timescales and milestones
- contingencies (especially for recording)
- workflow (sound recording through to editing and export).

Resources required

These include the appropriate equipment and software to be used in the creation of a digital sound sequence. It must cover the different stages, which are:

- recording audio clips
- transfer and storage of audio files
- mixing audio files within sound editing software.

You can use either a PC or Mac with a sound card for sound projects. Connections are usually colour coded 3.5 mm sockets:

- **Blue:** line in (from external sources such as audio playback devices).
- **Green:** speakers.
- **Pink:** microphone.

Some audio devices can also plug into a USB port on the computer.

Sound and audio device properties

You will find the sounds and audio devices in Windows Control panel. These settings may be used to control the recording and playback volume when recording sound directly into Microsoft Office applications, for example. However, in this unit, you will be using dedicated recording software to capture the sounds, which has its own recording controls.

Storage

Digital sound files can be saved and stored on the computer hard disk, CD, DVD, MP3 player, flash memory devices, external hard disks or even

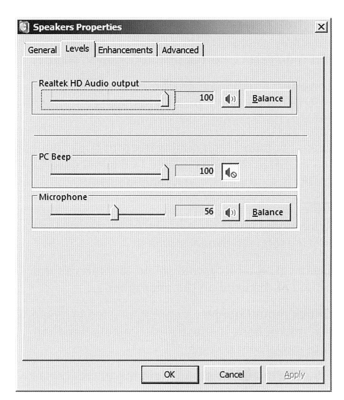

Figure 8.2 Windows sound and audio properties

mobile phones. They can also be easily transmitted over the internet. The size of the digital file will depend on the format used.

Microphones

Microphones convert sound into electrical signals that can be digitised on the sound card by the computer. There are several different types.

Dynamic: range from economical general purpose microphones through to professional vocal types (recognised by their lower impedance). They do not have the same flat frequency response of condenser types and don't need power since they do not have an internal amplifier. They also tend to be more rugged.

Condenser: uses a capacitor (condenser) to respond to the sound level and convert this to electrical signals. Unlike a dynamic microphone, it needs power to operate either from an internal battery or external 'phantom' power source. Many external video microphones are condenser types and may have XLR type connectors instead of the smaller 3.5 mm jack. Condenser microphones are often used for high quality music recordings but are more sensitive.

Electret: type of condenser microphone with built in supply voltage for the capacitor, hence does not require an external phantom power source.

Lavalier: small lapel or tie clip condenser microphone used to pick up the speech from one person (for example, for an interview).

Some, popular, high quality microphones connect via a USB port. The analogue to digital conversion (ADC) is built into the microphone itself.

Other equipment

Line amps: boost the signal from a microphone, often used with dynamic types.

Dead cat: is a furry wind shield to minimise the sound of the wind on the microphone.

Shock mount holder: sometimes used to suspend the microphone in elastic to eliminate handling and movement sounds.

Boom arm and/or stand: hold the microphone steady and in the correct position for the recording.

Phantom power supplies: for use with condenser microphones when other power sources are not available.

Hand held recorders and other devices

As well as microphone and computer systems, there is a range of other recording equipment which can be used.

- Dictation machines (analogue tape or digital)
- Mini disk
- Mobile phone (using voice memo feature)
- Video camera (can leave the lens cap on and just record the audio onto tape using a suitable microphone)

Speakers

These are the opposite of microphones, but have similar construction. Speakers convert electrical signals into sound that can be heard. There are three types that you could choose from when working on this unit.

1 **Standard computer speakers (or built into laptop):** usually quite low quality.
2 **External amplifier and speakers:** connected via the headphone socket.

3 **Headphones:** for testing the sounds that you have produced.

Software options

The most commonly used applications for this unit:

Name	Provider	Description
Audacity	Soundforge	Widely-used Open Source sound editor with a good range of tools and features
GarageBand	Apple	Well-featured sound editing application for the Apple Mac

You may also have access to Adobe Audition®, SoundBooth, Steinberg Cubase or Apple Logic Pro, which are professional level audio mixing applications. Basic sound editing can also be completed in many video editing software applications.

Planning the content and sequence for a digital sound

A good approach to planning the content of the sound sequence is to write a script. This can identify the sequence of sounds and the voiceover or narration. Refer back to R081 for typical formatting and layout conventions.

Creating and maintaining a test plan

The only element not covered by R081 is the test plan. For this, the concept of testing should be based around technical checks that the audio sequence is fit for purpose and meets the brief. Some aspects that could be checked would be:

- **Audio quality:** check for distortion and clarity of sounds, especially voices.
- **Audio levels (volume):** check that it is loud enough to be heard.
- **Audio levels (consistency):** check that the loudness is at the same level throughout the sequence.
- **Duration:** check that the sequence is the right length and is within an acceptable tolerance.

Legislation

This should be in an applied context for the sounds, whether sourced or recorded.

Assessment preparation

LO2: Be able to plan a digital sound sequence		
Mark band 1	Mark band 2	Mark band 3
Produces an interpretation from the client brief for a digital sound sequence which meets few of the client requirements.	Produces an interpretation from the client brief for a digital sound sequence which meets most of the client requirements.	Produces an interpretation from the client brief for a digital sound sequence which fully meets the client requirements.
Produces a limited identification of target audience requirements.	Produces a clear identification of target audience requirements.	Produces a clear and detailed identification of target audience requirements.
Produces a work plan for the creation of the digital sound sequence, which identifies a limited range of content and a partly appropriate sequence for the digital sound.	Produces a work plan for the creation of the digital sound sequence, which identifies a range of content and an appropriate sequence for the digital sound.	Produces a clear and detailed work plan for the creation of the digital sound sequence, which identifies a wide range of content and a sequence for the digital sound which is fully appropriate and has some complexity.
Produces a list of equipment and software to be used in creating the digital sound sequence and gives basic reasons for selection in relation to the identified success criteria.	Produces a list of equipment and software to be used in the creation of a digital sound sequence and gives sound reasons for selection in relation to the identified success criteria.	Produces a comprehensive list of equipment and software to be used in the creation of the digital sound sequence, thoroughly justifying selection in relation to the identified success criteria.
Demonstrates a limited understanding of legislation in relation to the use of sounds in digital sound sequences.	Demonstrates a sound understanding of legislation in relation to the use of sounds in digital sound sequences.	Demonstrates a thorough understanding of legislation in relation to the use of sounds in digital sound sequences.
Draws upon limited skills/knowledge/understanding from other units in the specification.	Draws upon some relevant skills/knowledge/understanding from other units in the specification.	Clearly draws upon relevant skills/knowledge/understanding from other units in the specification.

Assessment guidance

The OCR set assignment

When completing your work for the OCR set assignment, you will need to:

- produce your own interpretation of the client brief
- identify the target audience and what they will want from the sound sequence
- produce a work plan for the sound sequence
- identify the range of audio content and how these will be mixed
- identify success criteria for the digital sound sequence
- identify the equipment and software needed, justifying your choices in relation to the success criteria
- describe the legal restrictions regarding the use of any sounds
- use knowledge and skills from other units such as R081 or R082.

Links to other units

You can find information on the command words in **unit R082**.

LO3 Be able to create a digital sound sequence

Sourcing sounds

In addition to recording sounds, you may be able to source these from pre-recorded locations although you must check any copyright issues.

- **Web:** often in .mp3 format
- **CD/DVD:** music and sounds can be 'ripped' from the discs but you must be aware of any copyright restrictions. Look for CDs created by artists which specifically state that they are copyright free for use in video projects or 'music on hold' telephone systems.
- **Sound library:** licensing fees and usage rights must be checked and observed when sourcing sounds from these commercial libraries.

Digital sound files may be obtained in a range of file formats. Many of these should be supported by your sound editing software although you need to be aware of the sound quality that can be achieved when using compressed formats.

Recording sounds

To make a new sound recording directly into Audacity:

1 Set the audio I/O preferences for the number of channels you will be recording (in other words, when recording in stereo with two microphones use a value of '2').

2 Plug a microphone into the 'Mic' socket.

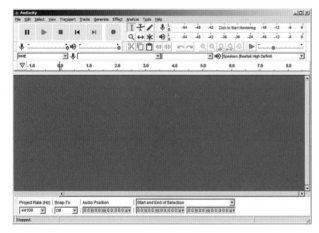

Figure 8.3 Audacity user interface

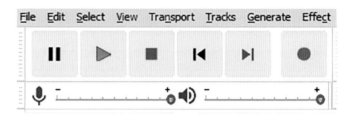

Figure 8.4 Audacity record/playback controls

3 Perform a sound check to make sure the volume levels are suitable and adjust the recording volume level as needed (click on the level meter to monitor this before starting to record); the sound levels should stay within and use most of the meter window.

4 Make sure there will be no background distractions during the recording.

5 Click the red Record button to start.

You can pause or stop the recording at any time by clicking on the appropriate button. Note that mono recordings will only have a single audio waveform and volume level, which will be labelled as the Left channel.

Import assets into sound editing software

Pre-recorded or sourced sounds can be imported into Audacity or other sound editing software. The editing and mixing are then applied to the sounds that are placed on audio tracks.

Edit and enhance assets

Once imported, the first step is generally to clean up the recording(s). Typical actions as part of your initial workflow include:

- trim, cut and copy selections from tracks
- volume/gain adjust
- noise removal
- use the envelope tool
- save as new files in an uncompressed file format.

Trim and cut tools

In Audacity, you use the selection tool to click and drag on the section that you want from the track waveform display. In the track shown in Figure 8.5, a selection has been made between 02:775 and 05:433 on the timeline.

Once selections have been made, a range of editing effects can be applied.

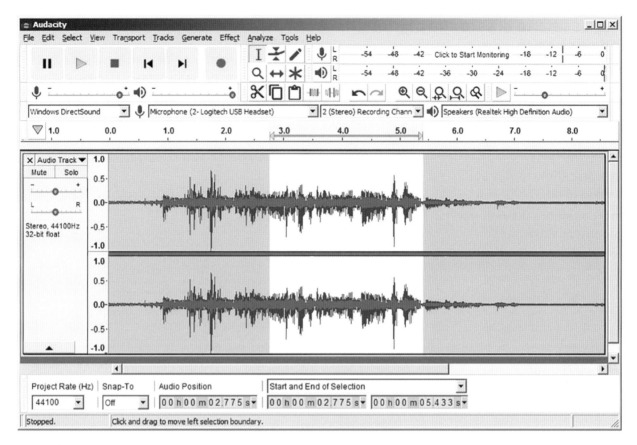

Figure 8.5 Selection in Audacity

Available trim tools are:

- cut selection
- trim outside selection
- trim inside selection.

The track control panel is displayed alongside each track. It shows the track name, properties and provides the track pop down menu. The top slider is the gain control (volume) and the bottom slider is the left/right balance on stereo tracks.

Enhancement of assets

This can include one or more of several techniques. The ones you should know about are:

- fade
- gain
- filter
- noise removal
- pitch
- invert.

In Audacity, effects can only be applied to current selections. Commonly used basic effects are:

- **Amplify:** changes the volume (amplitude) of the current selection; this is also known as 'gain'
- **Fade in:** fades in the current selection from silence to full volume
- **Fade out:** fades out the current selection from full volume to silence
- **Noise removal**: sometimes this is needed to clean up the sound recordings; the procedure in Audacity is:
  - make a selection of a section of the track that is meant to be silent (it only has background noise)
  - select Noise Removal from the Effects menu and then Get Noise Profile (this stores information about the noise profile which is used in the next step)
  - make a new selection of the whole track that has the noise which needs to be removed
  - select Noise Removal from the Effects menu again and click Remove Noise.

Mixing assets to create the digital sound sequence

Some key tools and techniques include:

- equalisation
- audio compression
- looping
- generating silence.

A typical workflow to mix audio tracks and add effects would be:

- import audio tracks required for project or assignment work

- mix ambient sound tracks with vocals or other content
- align sound tracks or synchronise with video
- add effects for fade in/out, reverb, mono/stereo conversion
- audio level compression
- export and save in suitable formats.

Using Audacity, two separate sound files can be mixed as follows:

1 Open the first file (for example, background music)

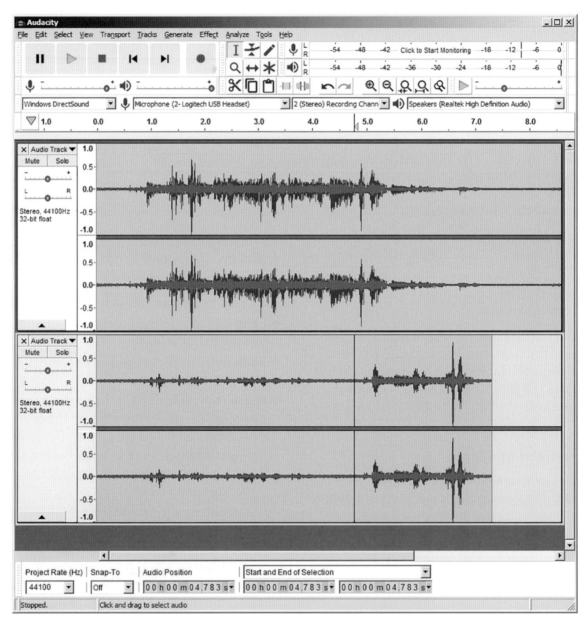

Figure 8.6 Mixing tracks in Audacity

2 Open the second file (for example, voiceover) using 'import audio'
3 Play the combined sound to check for timing, clarity, volume and any clipping
4 Adjust the gain controls for each track to balance the sounds as required
5 Use the time shift tool to change the timing or synchronisation of the two tracks
6 Export as a new file in a suitable format.

Audio level compression

This type of compression reduces the dynamic range of the sound so that high volume levels are not quite as high as originally recorded. This helps to maintain a more consistent volume level between normal sound levels and the loudest parts. First make a selection of the waveform. From the Effects menu choose Compressor. The amount of compression and the point where it is applied can be chosen although the default values are a good starting point.

Save and export a digital sound sequence

From Audacity, you can export the sound into one of several different formats depending on how you want to use the file.

Format	Properties
.aup	Audacity Project file; can only be used for further editing and is not a generic format for export or playing on other equipment
.mp3	Requires a LAME encoder to be installed separately for use by the Audacity software (due to mp3 licensing restrictions)
.mp4	Alternative to mp3 but not as popular for purely audio files; requires FFmpeg library
.wav	Windows Wave format (uncompressed); files will be larger than mp3 but there is no reduction in sound quality
Ogg Vorbis	An effective format similar to mp3 but slightly better performance in terms of file size/sound quality

Considerations when exporting different file formats

There are several factors to be considered.

● **Compression:** whether as a compressed or uncompressed file format (note, this is different to audio compression).

● **Optimisation:** this means choosing the most appropriate file size and quality depending on what it is being used for (for example, website podcast or CD audio quality).

● **Codecs:** a computer program that encodes an analog audio or video signal into digital – it stands for coder – decoder.

● **Bit rate:** affects the quality of audio.

● **Compatibility:** with different playback devices.

This table shows a comparison of file sizes in different formats.

Track information	Duration: 1 minute, 16 bit, 44.1 kHz
.wav (uncompressed)	5500 kB (5.5 MB)
.mp3	1000 kB (1 MB)
Ogg Vorbis	660 kB (0.66 MB)

After you have exported the sound files, play them back using the target player or equipment. This is necessary to make sure the file format is correct and the volume level is suitable for the intended use.

Links to other units

You can find information on how to use version control in **unit R081**.

Using Apple GarageBand

If using an Apple Mac, GarageBand is a good alternative.

Figure 8.7 GarageBand allows you to create, record and edit digital sound on a Mac computer.

Assessment preparation

LO3: Be able to create a digital sound sequence		
Mark band 1	Mark band 2	Mark band 3
Records or sources a few sounds to create assets for the digital sound sequence. Imports a range of basic assets into the chosen software that are appropriate in some cases. Uses a limited range of sound editing, mixing and enhancement tools and techniques in ways that are appropriate in some cases.	Records and sources a range of mostly appropriate sounds to create assets for the digital sound sequence. Imports a range of assets into the chosen software that are mostly appropriate. Uses a range of sound editing, mixing and enhancement tools and techniques in ways that are mostly appropriate.	Records and sources consistently appropriate sounds from a wide range of sources to create assets for the digital sound sequence. Imports a range of assets into the chosen software that are wholly appropriate. Uses a wide range of sound editing, mixing and enhancement tools and techniques in ways that are appropriate.
Mark band 1	Mark band 2	Mark band 3
Saves and exports the digital sound sequence occasionally using a format which is appropriate. Demonstrates limited awareness of the limitations imposed by different file formats and sizes. Produces a digital sound sequence with few simple parts to the sequence which partially reflects the planning and meets some of the client requirements. Occasionally saves electronic files using appropriate file and folder names and structures.	Saves and exports the digital sound sequence mostly using a format which is appropriate. Demonstrates some awareness of the limitations imposed by different file formats and sizes. Produces a digital sound sequence with some complexity which reflects the planning and meets most of the client requirements. Mostly saves electronic files using file and folder names and structures which are consistent and appropriate.	Saves and exports the digital sound sequence consistently using a format which is appropriate. Demonstrates clear awareness of the limitations imposed by different file formats and sizes. Produces a complex digital sound sequence which clearly reflects planning and fully meets the client requirements. Consistently saves electronic files using file and folder names and structures which are consistent and appropriate.

Assessment guidance

The OCR set assignment

When completing your work for the OCR set assignment, you will need to:

- record original audio sounds for use as assets
- source and store a range of sounds
- import the sounds into the audio editing software applying editing techniques
- enhance the sounds using a range of tools and techniques
- mix the sounds to create the sound sequence as planned
- save and export the sound sequence in suitable formats to meet the client requirements
- describe the limitations of different file formats for export
- use appropriate file and folder naming conventions to organise your work.

Links to other units

You can find information on the command words in **unit R082**.

LO4 Be able to review a digital sound sequence

Reviewing a digital sound sequence

When reviewing your digital sound sequence, there will be a number of questions to ask.

1 Does the sound meet the needs of the client?

2 Is the sound file size and format suitable for the client?

3 Is the quality of the sound suitable in terms of clarity and tone

4 Is the sound editing and mixing effective?

5 Are the volume levels suitable and consistent across the sequence?

6 What improvements could be made; for example, re-recording, different equipment, microphones, mixing and editing?

Assessment preparation

LO4: Be able to review a digital sound sequence		
Mark band 1	Mark band 2	Mark band 3
Produces a review of the digital sound sequence which demonstrates a limited understanding of what worked and what did not, making few references back to the brief.	Produces a review of the digital sound sequence which demonstrates a reasonable understanding of what worked and what did not, mostly referencing back to the brief.	Produces a review of the digital sound sequence which demonstrates a thorough understanding of what worked and what did not, fully referencing back to the brief.
Review identifies areas for improvement and further development of the digital sound sequence, some of which are appropriate and sometimes are explained.	Review identifies areas for improvement and further development of the digital sound sequence, which are mostly appropriate and explained well.	Review identifies areas for improvement and further development of the digital sound sequence, which are wholly appropriate and justified.

Assessment guidance

The OCR set assignment

When completing your work for the OCR set assignment, you will need to:

● produce your own review of the digital sound sequence that you have created

● comment on the final sound sequence and how this relates to the brief

● identify what could be improved further.

Links to other units

You can find information on the command words in **unit R082**.

R089 Creating a digital video sequence

About this unit

Modern films and television programmes are mostly produced using digital video technology. However, other media – such as online advertising campaigns, interactive media, apps, websites and gaming technologies – also use digital video to enhance their content and engage their audiences.

This unit helps understand where digital video is used in digital media industries. You will understand the purpose of digital video products and where they are used. You will be able to plan a digital video sequence, and then create and edit it to produce a digital video to a specific brief. You will then learn how to review the final sequence, reviewing how you met the client brief and how you could improve your digital video.

Note that this unit cannot be combined with R088.

Resources for this unit

To produce a digital video sequence, you will need access to, and be able to use different types of hardware and software.

The hardware that you will require access to are:

- a device, such as a digital video camera, to record footage; examples include:
  - handheld digital video camcorders
  - DSLR cameras with video recording capability
  - smartphone that can record video
- a computer system to import and edit digital video footage
- video editing software, such as Serif MoviePlus, Apple iMovie, Windows Movie Maker, Windows 10 Photos app, Adobe Premiere® Pro or Elements.

Learning outcomes

LO1 Understand the uses and properties of digital video

LO2 Be able to plan a digital video sequence

LO3 Be able to create a digital video sequence

LO4 Be able to review a digital video sequence

How will I be assessed?

You will be assessed through an OCR model assignment, marked by your tutor and externally moderated by OCR. It is worth 25% of the overall mark when working towards a Certificate in Creative iMedia.

For LO1

Learners need to:

- investigate the uses of digital video products across different industry sectors
- describe the different file formats and properties of digital video products.

For LO2

Learners need to:

- plan a digital video sequence to meet a client brief
- produce an identification of the target audience for the digital video sequence
- produce a workplan, script and storyboard that are capable of meeting the client and target audience requirements
- discuss the legislation in relation to the use of digital video assets in the chosen industry sector.

For LO3

Learners need to:

- use a range of camera techniques to record original footage
- source any additional footage and assets to complete the digital video sequence
- save and organise all assets in a file structure that the chosen software can access
- import both original and sourced assets into the chosen video editing software to begin to edit the digital video sequence
- use video editing production and enhancement techniques to produce a digital video sequence that meets the requirements of the client brief
- save and export the digital video work so that it is appropriate for its original use and purpose
- produce a final export that shows understanding of editing techniques, special effects and use of titles and graphics.

For LO4

Learners need to:

- review the digital video sequence demonstrating an understanding of what worked well and what did not
- review the digital video sequence identifying further areas for improvement and development.

LO1 Understand the uses and properties of digital video

The content covered here will help you understand the different sectors that produce digital video and the uses of digital video products. In this section, we will investigate digital video products that are produced for:

- **commercial contexts:** this includes companies that use digital video to advertise consumer goods on television and the internet, promoting a film by film trailers, promoting a new song by music video and enhancing content in multimedia products to sell goods and services
- **entertainment industries:** including films, television programmes, and computer games
- **business and marketing:** including digital video promotions for services, and company information
- **education and information:** including online tutorials, news reports and public information films.

You will investigate different video file formats, the purpose and uses of each, and the different devices used to access video.

Here are the export extensions of the file formats you will be learn about:

- .avi
- .mp4
- .wmv
- .flv
- .mov

Before producing a digital video sequence, you should understand the properties of formats to use when filming and editing video. You will learn about how display resolution and aspect ratio have an impact on the video that you film, and how to edit and export it.

Getting started

Working individually or in small groups, make a list of the different ways that you think digital video is used by businesses and the general public, giving a real example of each if you can. You should try to list at least five different uses.

The sectors and uses of digital video products

There are many industry sectors that use digital video products, and there are different purposes that digital videos are used for. However, the uses of digital video can be grouped into four main contexts and purposes.

Commercial contexts

Different industry sectors use digital videos to sell their products to audiences. Digital video is engaging and can be used to catch the attention of the intended target audience. In the following, you can see contexts where digital video is used to help sell **commercial** and **consumer goods** and services.

Television advertising
One of the most successful ways that digital video is used to advertise products is by television advertising. This is where companies create digital video advertisements of around 30 seconds long to show in the commercial break of a television programme. Television adverts feature the product or service, a catchy slogan and music. Many also incorporate interactive features and social media links – made possible by smart televisions – to involve the audience.

Multimedia products
Multimedia products use digital video to engage the audience to market their products and services. Interactive e-commerce websites use digital video to enhance explanations and information. For example, the Amazon.co.uk homepage features personalised recommended trailers for their Amazon Prime shows. Controls on such sites, as with adverts on YouTube, allow the user to play and pause content. Similarly, smartphone and tablet apps feature short digital

Key terms

Commercial: this is when a company or individual produces products to make a profit.

Consumer goods: these items include cars, clothing, music, food, jewellery, toiletries, DVDs, downloads that people, or consumers, buy every day.

video sequences to market their service and encourage users to download.

Music videos

Music videos are the most watched digital video products on YouTube; they are produced to promote the release of new songs. Music videos show the artist performing their work, sometimes with a storyline, and often use special effects and transitions to make them engaging and entertaining. Some music videos have gained billions of views on YouTube; 'Despacito' by Luis Fonsi and Daddy Yankee has had more than 5 billion, and 'The Shape of You' by Ed Sheeran has had more than 3 billion. Specialist music digital television channels, such as Kerrang! TV, still play music videos all day.

Entertainment

The different sectors of the entertainment industry create digital video content as their core products to sell to audiences. Digital video is filmed and produced using professional hardware and software to sell to global audiences.

Films and television programmes

Large Hollywood film companies invest millions of pounds in every production using advanced computer-generated images to ensure that they create successful feature films that target all age groups. Similarly, most television programmes are highly advanced digital video products. Trailers and teasers for film and television programmes are released on social media and feature interactive content before the main product is released.

Computer games and virtual reality

Computer games have become complex 3D digital video sequences that are created using specialist software packages such as Unity and Unreal. Computer games, such as the Halo and Oblivion sagas, often have complex storylines with extended sequences explaining character background.

Vlogging

Vlogging has become popular through online video sites such as YouTube. Although they started out mainly for entertainment, vlogs can span the education and business categories too.

Business and marketing

Promotional videos

Digital video is used so that companies can share their unique selling points of their specific services with audiences. This is done through digital video sequences that feature interviews with people that work at the company or testimonies from previous clients. Such videos are used to build a connection with potential customers.

Education and information

Tutorials

Digital video is used by companies and individuals to create tutorials so that others can learn from them. Tutorials can be downloaded as a package or streamed from services such as YouTube. Tutorials are created on many topics from make-up vlogs and gaming walkthroughs to foreign language courses and software skill development. Some of the most popular online tutorials over the past decade have been those that teach people how to fold laundry correctly and how to make the perfect Yorkshire pudding! Tutorials are easy to make, edit and upload to the internet which is why they are so popular for both their producers and audiences.

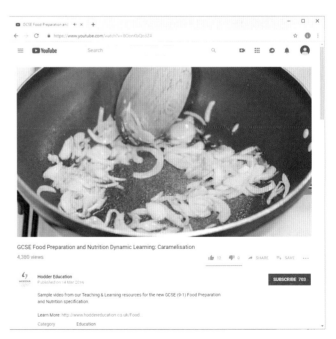

Figure 9.1 A cooking tutorial on YouTube

News articles

News services, such as the BBC and Sky News, increasingly use digital video to enhance and report their online news stories. Breaking news videos are accessible via smartphone apps and websites at any time of day.

Public information films

Public information films are produced to help the public in some way. Many of these films target children and cover topics such as crossing the road safely. The types of companies that produce public information films are charities, such as the NSPCC, and are often found on YouTube.

Figure 9.2 The National Archives Public Information Film archive

Video file formats

Digital video products are distributed across different platforms and accessed across a variety of devices. In this section, we will discuss the main file formats and the advantages and disadvantages of each.

AVI file format

AVI stands for Audio Video Interleaved (.avi). It is a file format developed by Microsoft. It is one of the most well-known digital video formats. You can easily play an AVI file in a player such as Windows Media Player and you can use some services, such as Google Drive, to play AVI files stored on the servers.

Advantages of AVI

AVI files are high quality, meaning digital video intended for professional use can be exported in this format. Playable DVDs and disks can be created using AVI file format in order to store the digital and audio information at a high quality.

Disadvantages of AVI

AVI files can be very large if they are not compressed when exported. Therefore, they would not be suitable for sharing online, download or stream. If AVI files are too compressed, however, they lose quality, which is noticeable on HD and 4K screens. Playback can be problematic on Apple Mac computers so additional software may be needed.

WMV file format

Windows Media Video (.wmv) format was developed by Microsoft to work with Windows Media Player. It is one of the most commonly used and oldest formats available for digital video. The WMV format allows you to create good quality video files that are small in size.

Advantages of WMV

WMV files are small considering the amount of video information they preserve. WMV files can, therefore, be used to upload video products, such as company promotional and information videos, to websites quite quickly.

Disadvantages of WMV

WMV is not widely compatible with non-Windows operating systems. Older Apple and Linux players are not always capable of playing WMV files. For this reason, WMV has not become a standard web format, despite its small size.

MOV file format

The MOV format is a QuickTime file (.mov) and was developed by Apple in the 1990s to work with the QuickTime Player. The technical structure of the format is a lot simpler than the AVI, so it is a popular choice for digital video editors when exporting their work.

Advantages of MOV

Like AVI files, video editors choose to export their work as a MOV file when they want to produce a high-quality video product. This makes it suitable for DVD creation. MOV files can support multichannel audio while others, such as MP4 files, can only be played in stereo.

Disadvantages of MOV

MOV files are not a recommended format for uploading to YouTube to watch on a smartphone or tablet. This is because it is too large to upload to the internet. MOV files can only be played on a computer with a Windows Operating System if QuickTime or VLC is downloaded.

MP4 file format

A file with the MP4 file extension (.mp4) is an abbreviation for an MPEG-4 Video file, which is a compressed file format based on Apple's MOV format. As with AVIs, WMVs and MOVs, the format can contain video, audio and titles and graphics. The format is extremely popular for use when sharing video content. Its popularity is mainly down to the Apple iTunes Store, since the format is used for most of the video that people download from the store and play on their smartphone and tablet devices.

Advantages of MP4

MP4s are a compressed format, and are the standard format for use on the internet, smartphone and tablet platforms. Most videos you watch on YouTube will have been uploaded as an MP4. They provide good quality video in a small package.

Disadvantages of MP4

MP4s are so compressed that they are not recommended for use in projects that require further compression after you have exported your work.

FLV file format

FLV stands for Flash Video file (.flv). It uses Adobe Flash Player to contain digital video for streaming over the internet. Flash Video was the standard format used by websites such as YouTube and Vimeo. However, most streaming services do not use Flash Video anymore because the HTML5 <video> tag allows the video to be embedded into the webpage.

Advantages of FLV

FLVs provide good quality video and animation content in a small package. This made them popular before HTML5 owing to their limited storage space and a good file format for sharing video on social media.

Key terms

Compression: this is when a digital video sequence is saved in such a way that its file size is reduced. The quality of the video may or may not be reduced depending on the codec used to reduce the size of the video.

Codec: stands for 'coder-decoder'. Media is 'encoded', or read by the software. It is then 'decoded' so that media, such as digital video, can be played back. Most codecs compress the original media, reducing the size of the original file. This is important for video files, since they often have large file sizes. Compressed files take up less disk space and can be uploaded and downloaded more quickly.

Disadvantages of FLV

Some devices do not support FLV and require a converter such as CloudConvert to change the file into a format, such as MP4, that can be played across a range of smartphone, tablet and laptop devices. FLV as a video format will no longer be supported by Apple from 2020. So, do not use FLV if you want your digital video to have longevity.

The properties of digital video

When you record your footage and set up an editing project, your editing software will provide the option of choosing different settings. You must choose the correct settings because they will affect how your digital video sequence will be viewed on a range of devices.

Resolution

Resolution is the size of the digital video image. Every digital video file has dimensions, measured in the number of pixels. When you see a measurement, such as 1920 × 1080 or 1080p, it means the size of the image.

In current digital video production for television, online video, feature films and DVD/Blu-ray there are five recognised display resolutions:

- **480p:** 720 pixels across the screen and 480 pixels from top to bottom of the screen; total number of pixels displayed on the screen = 345 600.

Figure 9.3 Image of the different resolutions of digital video

- **720p:** 1280 pixels across the screen and 720 pixels from top to bottom of the screen; total number of pixels displayed on the screen = 921 600.
- **1080i/p:** 1920 pixels across the screen and 1080 pixels from top to bottom of the screen; total number of pixels displayed on the screen = 2 073 600.
- **4k/2160 p:** 4026 pixels across the screen and 2160 pixels from top to bottom of the screen; known widely as 4k, although services such as YouTube list 2160 p as a standard video **resolution**.

The larger the resolution, the higher the quality or definition of the digital video. This is where terms such as standard definition (SD) and high definition (HD) come from.

Format

The term 'format' is also linked to the ways that broadcast technologies distribute video content differently in some areas of the world.

PAL

The Phase Alternating Line (PAL) is a display system and technology for broadcast television that is used in the UK from the 1960s. The frame rate for video sent by PAL is 25 frames per second (fps). Using analogue systems, the way in which television was broadcast meant that there would be a problem if we tried to watch a PAL broadcast on a screen set to play NTSC video. Now that we have digital video that is broadcast and distributed globally in HD formats, most countries follow the Digital Video Broadcast (DVB) international standards. There are minimal differences in frame rates and colour of the footage on screen.

NTSC

The National Television System Committee (NTSC) is a colour coding and display system and technology for broadcast television. The **frame rate** for video sent by NTSC is 30 fps. Countries, such as the USA, used this system from the 1960s onwards.

Aspect ratio

Aspect ratio is the relationship between the height and width of a digital video. Aspect ratio is linked to both format and resolution, and the clarity, size and quality of the final digital video we see is linked to all three properties.

Key terms

Display resolution: this is the size of the digital video image. Display resolution is measured in pixels. The device that we watch our digital video on determines the size and density of the pixels.

Frame rate: the frequency that film footage, animation and title and graphics sequences appear on screen when a digital video is watched by the audience.

Aspect ratio: this is the height and width that a digital video can be created, exported and viewed in. Depending on the screen that you are watching a digital video on a process known as letterboxing and pillar-boxing, where two black bars appear either horizontally or vertically at the edges of the video.

4:3

This was the ratio of SD videos, and it allowed viewers to see a full-screen, almost square-like picture. Old television and computer monitors were square shaped. 4:3 aspect ratio video content still exists but the majority of displays cater for the 16:9 HD standard. The quality of a digital video can be kept, if a video has a 4:3 aspect ratio, by pillar-boxing the display. Many amateur producers find that their YouTube videos are displayed like this because their video was automatically set up with a 4:3 aspect ratio and they hadn't intended it to look like that.

16:9

Most television programmes and online content is now distributed with 16:9 aspect ratio. This is also known as widescreen. It is called 16:9 because the ratio of pixels (1920:1080, for example) is equivalent to 16:9.

Before HD, the 16:9 ratio could not exist. The good news is that any video you make can be edited to the 16:9 aspect ratio because of the easy access to HD camcorders. You must remember to ensure your editing project is set up with a 16:9 aspect ratio.

Stretch activity

1 Explain the advantages of using digital video for each industry sector you have studied to show you have a thorough understanding of the uses of digital video.

2 Explain the difference between 4:3 and 16:9 aspect ratio to show that you can accurately describe the properties of digital video. Give an example of how this difference might affect you if you had been commissioned to make a music video for distribution on YouTube.

Know it!

1 Write down four uses for digital video products.

2 Explain the difference between a resolution and aspect ratio.

3 Justify why you would use digital video as part of a campaign to launch a new band.

Assessment preparation

Think about the individual performance you will need to undertake. Make sure you:

- know about the different uses of digital video
- understand the different file formats in which digital video can be exported
- are able to explain the properties of a digital video product for a specific purpose.

LO1: Understand the uses and properties of digital video		
Mark band 1	Mark band 2	Mark band 3
Produces a summary on the uses of digital video products, identifying some of the sectors in which digital video is used which demonstrates a limited understanding.	Produces a summary of the uses and properties of digital video, identifying a range of sectors in which digital video is used which demonstrates a sound understanding.	Produces a summary of the uses and properties of digital video, identifying a wide range of sectors in which digital video is used which demonstrates a thorough understanding.
Describes with limited accuracy different video file formats and the properties of digital video.	Describes with reasonable accuracy different video file formats and the properties of digital video.	Describes accurately different video file formats and the properties of digital video.

LO2 Be able to plan a digital video sequence

LO2 will help you understand how to plan a digital video sequence for a specific client brief and target audience. We will investigate the ways you can interpret the client brief and requirements of your digital video sequence, and how you can plan your digital video sequence using industry standard methods.

Getting started

Working individually or in small groups, think about the planning you might need to do if you were to film a video in an outdoor location, such as a public park.

Interpret client requirements for a digital video sequence

There are different reasons that clients require the production of a digital video. As we have investigated in LO1, the requirements of the client are based on the purpose. This can be to advertise and promote, inform and educate, or entertain.

Breaking down the client requirements

Within these broader purposes, the digital video that you will be required to create will be of a particular **genre** or style. Each type of video production has its own styles and **conventions**.

 Key terms

Genre: a term to describe the way that digital video producers categorise a specific type of digital video. For example, horror and action are different film genres.

Conventions: a term used to describe the different ingredients or elements that help audiences understand the genre of a digital video product. For example, a music video for a pop artist may feature the conventions of bright colours, special effects and dance routines.

For example, the types of camera, editing techniques, special effects and music needed to create a horror film trailer are different to those for a short, local news piece.

Group activity

In pairs or small groups, identify the elements that you will need to plan to meet a client brief that requires you to:

- make a film trailer for a new horror film
- produce a tutorial that teaches the baking skills to make a cake or biscuit of your choice.

Interpret and document the client requirements

You must document that you have understood and broken down the client requirements as part of your initial planning of your digital video sequence.

Here are two ways that you can present this.

1 Document your understanding of the client requirements by writing the key aspects in a short report. You could include these headings:
   - genre and form
   - purpose and use
   - target audience
   - product or storyline
   - deadline date.

2 Present your understanding of the client requirements by creating a mind map. This will allow you to organise ideas into sub-sections. For the production of a digital video sequence, sub-sections in a mind map may include ideas about:
   - filming locations
   - props
   - actors
   - camera shots and techniques
   - special effects
   - editing techniques
   - music and sound effects
   - distribution
   - devices the product must play on.

Understand target audience requirements

Once you have identified the main client requirements, it is important that you document in detail who your target audience is. Here are two ways that you can present this.

1 Create an audience profile. This is a piece of creative writing where you write about the interests of the type of person who would be part of your target audience for the video sequence. In the profile you could discuss:
   - age
   - gender

   - hobbies and interests
   - type of consumer products they like
   - type of films, television programmes or games they like.

2 Document your understanding of the audience requirements by writing the key aspects in a short report. You could include these headings:
   - age and gender
   - how they access the product
   - any similar digital video products they might consume
   - content, such as actors, needed in the digital video product that would appeal to the audience
   - content that should not be included, such as music with offensive lyrics, based on their age.

Links to other units

You can find further information on this topic in LO2 of **units R081** and **R082**.

Creating a work plan

You will need to produce a work plan before you produce your digital video sequence. This should include a list of:

- **activities:** the specific tasks you need to film and edit the digital video sequence
- **workflow:** the order that your activities and specific tasks need to be completed in
- **timescales:** the deadlines you need to meet
- **milestones:** key aspects of the production that have to be completed before you move on (such as filming)
- **contingencies:** there are specific contingencies you might need to think about when filming video
- **resources:** the equipment you require to film your digital video sequence but might be separate to the work plan document.

Activities and tasks – filming and editing

For your activities you will need to break this down and think about each task you will have to do when as part of the production and filming process:

These tasks will include:

- organising the digital video equipment you need to film
- organising the actors and locations for your production and checking you have permission to film people and film in your chosen places
- collecting any assets you need to create your production.

You will also need to break down and think about each task you will have to do when as part of the video editing process:

These tasks will include making sure you:

- can use the tools in your chosen editing software
- have access to your footage and assets on an SD card, wired transfer or via a cloud storage system.

Contingencies: filming and editing

The tasks you need to complete don't always go to plan. So, you need to make sure you have contingency planning in your work plan. Here are two examples of contingencies.

1 If filming outside, there is a chance that the weather might be poor, so you should always prepare for an alternative, indoor location in case it rains.

2 If you have arranged actors for your digital video sequence, some may unexpectedly be unable to film, so you should have a reliable understudy.

Links to other units

You can find further information on this topic in LO2 of **unit R081**.

Producing a shooting script

A shooting script is a planning document for you to plan the content of each shot of your digital video sequence in detail. The shooting script gives further breakdown of each shot for the actors, camera operator and production team. You write the specific actors involved in the shot and their dialogue, the locations the action is set in and any key editing transition and sound you intend you use. Note that the shooting script(s) do not have to be in the same sequence as the final video. They are organised for ease of recording the video footage for the different scenes, such as using the same locations, people and props. Shooting scripts can be used in conjunction with the production schedule (see R081). Below is an example of what a shooting script looks like.

Shot	Camera/Action	Time	Audio
1	Close up on bottom of legs, sunset going down next to the river.	3 seconds	Voice over "Around six months ago"
2	Long shot of Bailey sitting down on the wall and looking out over the water moving her head a little.	3 seconds	Voice over "I stood here"
3	Side mid shot of Bailey smiling	3 seconds	"Ready to throw myself off"
4	Point of view shot (little more de-saturated) head looks to side	3 seconds	"and say goodbye"
5	Extreme long/low angle shot	4 seconds	"you may be questioning why"
6	Camera tilts up to face the sky	2 seconds	"but this is my story"

Producing a storyboard

A storyboard is a planning document for you to plan each of the camera shots you intend to include in your digital video sequence, and the editing techniques that you think you will use. It should be clear enough so that it can be followed when you are editing your video, even if it can't be followed *exactly*. Figures 9.4 and 9.5 show examples of a blank storyboard and a drawn sequence. Note: You could think of the shooting script as a planning document for the recording of video footage and the storyboard is the planning document for the editing.

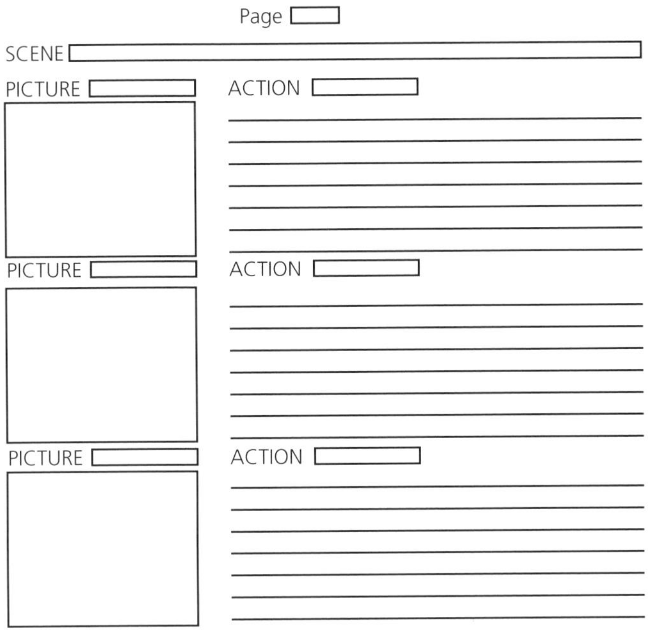

Page ☐

SCENE ☐

PICTURE ☐   ACTION ☐

PICTURE ☐   ACTION ☐

PICTURE ☐   ACTION ☐

Figure 9.4 Blank storyboard (or you can use an OCR supplied template)

Camera techniques and their annotations

There are two main elements to camera work. You should draw and annotate these on your storyboard so it is clear what – and how – you need to film.

1 Shot types
2 Camera movements

In the LO3 section, we will look at this in more detail so that you understand the different shot types, angles and how you can annotate your intended camera movement.

Planning the order, sequence and content of your video

When drawing your storyboard, remember that it should be in order from the content that is at the start of the digital video sequence to the content at the end. Even if you do not film in this order, it is important that the storyboard shows each shot. When you film and you are confident that you have got a shot that you planned in your storyboard, you can then tick it off. Most storyboard templates have room for you to write what is happening next to each shot. This helps you get the right type of shot if the storyboard hasn't been fully annotated.

Timings for each shot

Note how long each shot is intended to last on your storyboard – you need to make sure that you have enough footage to complete your digital video sequence to meet the client requirements.

Write the length of each shot in timecode format. This is measured in seconds, and tenths of seconds. For example, a two and a half seconds long shot would be written 00.02.30.

Links to other units

You can find further information on this topic in LO3 of **unit R081**.

Understanding the equipment you need to film your digital video sequence

In the section *Resources for this unit*, there is a list of the equipment that you will need to create your digital video sequence.

It includes:

- digital camcorders, DSLR or other video camera
- accessories
- computer
- digital video editing software.

Group activity

In pairs or small groups, identify the main hardware and software that you have available using the *Resources for this unit* section that you will need to create your video.

Create a table, mind map or short report for each resource that discusses:

- why you need the piece of equipment or resource to film a digital video
- how and why each piece of equipment will enable you to meet the brief.

Legislation

You are required to source assets to create your digital video sequence. Depending on your client requirements these assets might include:

- existing digital video footage
- sound effects
- background music
- title sequences.

You should understand that assets may be subject to copyright (refer to R081 for more information). You may have to ask for permission and arrange a fee to use the asset. However, there are many places that you can get copyright free resources from.

For video production, websites such as https://videos.pexels.com allow you to download video assets for use in your assignment work.

For music and sound effects, websites such as www.freesound.org allow you to download material at no cost and that is not under any copyright.

Remember, any assets you find should be credited to the source you downloaded them from. For each asset you should:

- identify why you need this for your video production
- document the copyright restrictions.

Know it!

1 Explain why you need to break down the client requirements before producing a digital video.
2 Explain why you need an annotated storyboard and shooting script before you start filming.

Figure 9.5 Storyboard with camera shot types and camera movement annotations for a Bollywood digital video sequence

Assessment preparation

Think about the individual performance you will need to undertake. Make sure you:
- are able to interpret the client and target audience requirements
- are able to understand the elements of storyboards and shooting scripts so you can produce them to plan your digital video sequence
- understand the different equipment, resources and assets that you will need to create and edit a digital video and identify why it is needed
- are able to explain how legislation relates to the assets you will use to create your digital video.

LO2: Be able to plan a digital video sequence		
Mark band 1	Mark band 2	Mark band 3
Produces an interpretation from the client brief for a digital video sequence which meets few of the client requirements.	Produces an interpretation from the client brief for a digital video sequence which meets most of the client requirements.	Produces an interpretation from the client brief for a digital video sequence which fully meets the client requirements.
Produces a limited identification of target audience requirements.	Produces a clear identification of target audience requirements.	Produces a clear and detailed identification of target audience requirements.
Produces a work plan, shooting script and storyboard which have some capability in creating the intended digital video sequence.	Produces a work plan, shooting script and storyboard which is mostly capable of creating the intended digital video sequence.	Produces a clear and detailed work plan, shooting script and storyboard which is fully capable of creating the intended digital video sequence.
Produces a list of equipment and software to be used in creating the digital video sequence and gives brief reasons for selection in relation to the identified success criteria.	Produces a list of equipment and software to be used in the creation of a digital video sequence and gives sound reasons for selection in relation to the identified success criteria.	Produces a comprehensive list of equipment and software to be used in the creation of the digital video sequence, thoroughly justifying selection in relation to the identified success criteria.
Demonstrates a limited understanding of legislation in relation to the use of video footage (sourced and recorded).	Demonstrates a sound understanding of legislation in relation to the use of video footage (sourced and recorded).	Demonstrates a thorough understanding of legislation in relation to the use of video footage (sourced and recorded).
Draws upon limited skills/knowledge/understanding from other units in the specification.	Draws upon some relevant skills/knowledge/understanding from other units in the specification.	Clearly draws upon relevant skills/knowledge/understanding from other units in the specification.

Assessment guidance

The OCR set assignment

When completing your work for the OCR set assignment, you will need to:
- produce your own interpretation of the client brief for the digital video
- identify the target audience and what they will want from the digital video
- produce a work plan and shooting script
- produce a storyboard
- define the success criteria for the digital video
- identify the resources needed and justify these against the success criteria
- describe the legal issues of using assets in your digital video.

What do the command words mean?

Fully [interpretation of the brief]: needs to be your own individual ideas and thoughts on what is required that expands on what is given in the scenario and brief.

Clear and detailed [target audience]: should be a clear definition of who the target audience is and what they will want to gain from the digital video.

Clear and detailed [work plan/shooting script/storyboard]: the work plan should break down the tasks and activities into small steps that must be completed in order to create the digital video (note: not for the entire assignment/unit). Shooting script and storyboard should be sufficiently detailed for somebody else to follow them.

Comprehensive [list of equipment]: should identify everything that will be needed.

Thorough [understanding of legislation]: should be applied to the actual video footage that you intend to use. Their use should also be in a commercial context and not just education.

Draws on [knowledge, skills and understanding]: must be from other units and not something that is already in R089. For example, this could use a mind map and mood board.

LO3 Be able to create a digital video sequence

LO3 is about creating the digital video sequence. You will investigate the different camera techniques that you can use when you are filming, how you import footage into your digital video project, and the types of transitions that you can use. Finally, you will investigate how to save your digital video work and export it so that it meets the client requirements.

Getting started

Working individually or in small groups, make a list of three camera techniques that you saw in a film or television programme that you watched recently. Write down why you think the producer used it.

Camera techniques used in video recording

You will have seen many camera techniques when watching films, television programmes, news reports and video games. The way that a digital video is filmed is not random; camerawork is carefully planned based on the client requirements. We will look at a range of camera techniques and investigate why each are used.

Camera shot types

Extreme long shots or wide shots

These shots mainly establish a setting. They are sometimes called 'establishing shots' to show the audience where the digital video is set.

Long shots

Show people from head to toe. These are good for showing action.

Mid/medium shots

Shows people from their hips to head. This is a good shot to use when viewing a moving character in action.

Medium close-up

Shows the head and shoulders. It is often used in conversation sequences so you can see the reactions of characters talking to each other.

Close-up shot

Shows the main features of a character's face so that the audience can see their emotion.

Extreme close-up shot

Show part of somebody's face, such as the eyes or the mouth, or a part of a prop or object that a character is using to tell the audience information.

Camera movements

Panning

When a camera on a steady tripod is controlled to move the camera head left and right. This technique shows the location and establishes distances between characters.

Tilting

When a camera on a steady tripod is controlled to move the camera head up and down. This technique shows the scale or height of something.

Tracking and dolly movement

When a camera is mounted and moved along a track with wheels (to prevent up and down movement from walking). This means the camera is able to follow the action of characters and vehicles easily.

Extreme long shot XLS

Long Shot LS

Mid Shot MS

Medium Closeup MCU

Closeup CU

Extreme Closeup ECU

Figure 9.6 Image of the different camera shot types

Stretch activity

In LO2, you have to produce a storyboard. This should be annotated with the movement. The main signs are:

- **panning annotation:** a curved arrow sign in the specific direction of the pan movement; if a pan is to be filmed from left to right, the curved arrow will point right
- **tilt annotation:** a curved arrow sign in the specific direction of the tilt movement; if a tilt is to be filmed from bottom to top, the curved arrow will point up
- **tracking annotation:** a straight arrow sign in the specific direction of the tracking movement; if the tracking movement is to be filmed from right to left, the straight arrow will point left.

Sourcing additional footage and other assets

You can source assets to help you create your digital video sequence. These include:

- **static frames and graphic:** still images that you can add to your digital video to explain something; often, in history documentaries, still images of paintings or artefacts are used to break up the footage of an interview with an expert

- **title and motion graphics:** required for all digital video sequences; moving title graphics catch the attention of the audience
- **background music and sound effects:** used to enhance content; in a film trailer, for example, music is used to indicate genre and enhance key parts of the action.
- **additional footage:** sometimes you might need to include footage filmed by someone else – this is often the case in documentaries. You can find royalty free footage on a number of websites such as https://videos.pexels.com.

Classroom discussion

In small groups, watch two digital videos of your choice, preferably with different purposes, such as a promotional video on a company website and a music video.

- For each video, make a list of all the assets used.
- Write down what each asset is and the reason you think it was used.

Identifying appropriate original footage

When you film people in different locations, you often make technical mistakes; some of the content might not be appropriate. When you look at your footage, you might think it is too light or too dark to be used in the final video sequence, for example. Your task is to assess the suitability of the digital video footage you have filmed.

One way to do this is to create a table, like this:

Shot/Footage name	Content	Appropriate for use? (Y/N)	Reason(s)

Import footage and assets into the digital editing software

Once you have decided that your footage and assets are appropriate for use, you need to import them into your software. Create folders for the video, images and sound before you import these into a new project.

Once the footage is imported, you can move it onto the editing timelines.

Figure 9.7 Importing footage into Windows Photos video editor

As Figure 9.8 shows, digital editing software includes multiple tracks so you can layer your assets.

Use digital editing software features to produce, edit and enhance a video sequence

Cutting and splitting footage and audio

You can use your editing software tools to edit your video and audio. Each software will have a particular tool to split or cut footage and audio when it is in track or timeline. Most will refer to it as the 'razor tool' or 'blade tool'.

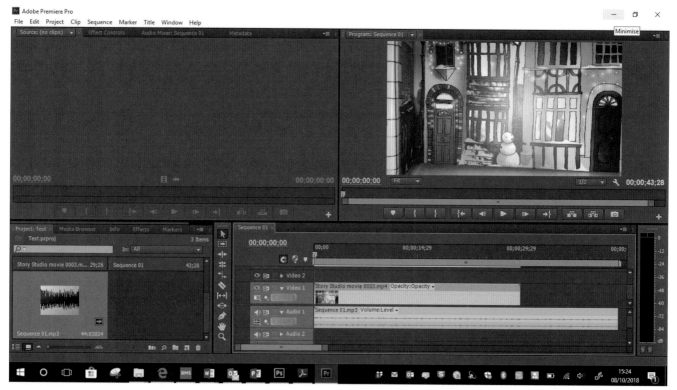

Figure 9.8 Adobe Premiere Pro video and audio tracks

Figure 9.9 Template for the title of an action film

Transitions
Different editing software will have the same standard transitions, such as:

- cross dissolve
- wipe
- fade in/out
- fade to black/white.

These transitions feature in nearly all video; they are used to show the passage of time, or a change in location. Your software will have the transitions in a specific palette or tab in the software.

Titles and graphics and special effects
All digital video sequences feature titles and enhancements. It is relatively easy to create moving titles and motion graphics. Editing software, such as iMovie, has templates that you can use to design a title graphic. In the 'video effects' bucket or bin the title tools, lighting tools and colour tools are available for you to drag and drop onto the footage in the tracks and timelines.

Saving and exporting the digital video

If you do not finish your digital video sequence in one session, you will be able to save your work so you can go back and edit it. If your video is not finished and it still requires editing, then you must save it in the software project format. For example, an unfinished video project that has started to be edited in Premiere Pro will have the file extension .prpoj. This means that, when it is opened again, further changes can be made to it before it is exported.

As discussed in LO1, one of the most popular file formats for saving digital video is .mp4. This is because it can retain its quality when compressed so it can be viewed clearly on websites. Most of your assignment briefs will require you to create a sequence that can be exported, for example, for use on a website, smartphone or tablet.

All digital editing software will have the option to export your digital video sequence as MPEG 4. However, the industry standard for exporting a digital video to be viewed online is to select the H.264 codec. This format is a type of .mp4 file that is capable of retaining high quality output. When you choose this option, the file exported will have the extension of .mp4 and can be viewed on a variety of different devices. You may still want to export your digital video work as an .avi or .mov file if you know your final video will be used, for example, to create a DVD or showreel.

Version control

While creating your digital video sequence, you must use version control. This means that you will save versions of work as you progress.

Know it!

1 Identify the types of camera shots and techniques you could use when creating your video.
2 Explain why you need to use a variety of transitions and effects when editing your video.
3 Justify why it is important that you understand why you need to compress your digital video sequence.

Assessment preparation

Think about the individual performance you will need to undertake. Make sure you:

- are able to interpret the client and audience requirements
- are able to understand the elements of storyboards and shooting scripts so you can produce them to plan your video
- understand the different equipment, resources and assets that you will need to create and edit your video sequence
- are able to explain how legislation relates to the assets you will use to create your video.

LO3:Be able to create a digital video sequence		
Mark band 1	**Mark band 2**	**Mark band 3**
Uses a limited range of camera techniques to record original video footage. Identification of original footage for use in the digital video sequence is partly appropriate.	Uses a range of camera techniques to record original video footage. Identification of original footage for use in the digital video sequence is mostly appropriate.	Uses a wide range of camera techniques to record original video footage. Identification of original footage for use in the digital video sequence is wholly appropriate.
Sources additional video footage to create assets which are appropriate in some cases for the digital video sequence.	Sources additional video footage to create assets which are mostly appropriate for the digital video sequence.	Sources additional video footage to create assets which are wholly appropriate for the digital video sequence.
Imports a limited range of assets into video editing software, demonstrating a basic understanding of the limitations imposed by the software.	Imports a range of assets into video editing software, demonstrating a sound understanding of the limitations imposed by the software.	Imports a wide range of assets into video editing software, demonstrating a thorough understanding of the limitations imposed by the software.
Mark band 1	**Mark band 2**	**Mark band 3**
Uses a limited range of video editing, production and enhancement tools and techniques, in ways that are occasionally appropriate.	Uses a range of video editing, production and enhancement tools and techniques, in ways that are mostly appropriate.	Uses a wide range of video editing, production and enhancement tools and techniques, in ways that are consistently appropriate.
Saves and exports the digital video sequence occasionally using a format which is appropriate. Demonstrates limited awareness of the limitations imposed by different file formats and sizes.	Saves and exports the digital video sequence mostly using a format which is appropriate. Demonstrates sound awareness of the limitations imposed by different file formats and sizes.	Saves and exports the digital video sequence consistently using a format which is appropriate. Demonstrates thorough awareness of the limitations imposed by different file formats and sizes.
Occasionally saves electronic files using appropriate file and folder names and structures.	Mostly saves electronic files using file and folder names and structures which are consistent and appropriate.	Consistently saves electronic files using file and folder names and structures which are consistent and appropriate.
Produces a digital video sequence with few simple parts which partially reflects the planning and meets some of the client requirements.	Produces a digital video sequence with some complexity which reflects the planning and meets most of the client requirements.	Produces a complex digital video sequence which clearly reflects planning and fully meets the client requirements.

Assessment guidance

The OCR set assignment

When completing your work for the OCR set assignment, you will need to:

- use a video camera to record your own footage with a range of camera shots and techniques
- source additional footage to use in your final video
- import the footage into video editing software, identifying limitations of the software
- use a range of editing and enhancement tools and techniques to create a complex video sequence that meets the client brief
- save and export the video in suitable format to meet the brief, identifying limitations of the file format
- use appropriate file and folder naming conventions.

LO4 Be able to review a digital video sequence

You need to reflect on and review your work to check that your final video sequence meets the client and target audience requirements. You should think about ways you could improve your digital video.

Getting started

Working individually, make a list of at least five planning or production techniques that you need to revise. When you create and review your digital video, you can think about what you missed out.

Reviewing your digital video sequence against the brief

You need to assess your digital video against the set brief. Use these guidelines to review your work.

- Does the final video meet its purpose? For example, if it is a film trailer does it follow the conventions of film trailers, such as titles, production details and duration?

- Does the final video meet the target audience requirements? For example, if it is a promotional video for a school recruiting 14 to 19 year olds, does it include interviews with students and staff?

- Was the video exported in the correct format so that the target audience can access it?

Making improvements to your digital video sequence

Once you have assessed your digital video, you need to think about ways you could improve it. Use these guidelines to help you think about relevant improvements.

- Has the final video footage shown that you can use a range of camera techniques? If not, how and where could this be better?

- Has the final video shown that you can edit video and audio together in a way that makes sense to the audience and meets the client brief? If not, how could the content and synchronisation be improved?

- Did you use titles and graphics and special effects? If not, what would you need to include if you were to edit the video further?

Know it!

1 Identify the key client requirements when producing your digital video sequence. List any that you did not meet.

2 Explain how you could change your digital video work to ensure all the client requirements were met.

Assessment preparation

Think about the individual performance you will need to undertake. Make sure you are able to review how:

- your final video met the client target audience requirements
- you could improve and develop your work.

LO4: Be able to review a digital video sequence		
Mark band 1	**Mark band 2**	**Mark band 3**
Produces a review of the digital video sequence which demonstrates a limited understanding of what worked and what did not, making few references back to the brief.	Produces a review of the digital video sequence which demonstrates a reasonable understanding of what worked and what did not, mostly referencing back to the brief.	Produces a review of the digital video sequence which demonstrates a thorough understanding of what worked and what did not, fully referencing back to the brief.
Review identifies areas for improvement and further development of the digital video sequence, some of which are appropriate and sometimes are explained.	Review identifies areas for improvement and further development of the digital video sequence, which are mostly appropriate and explained well.	Review identifies areas for improvement and further development of the digital video sequence, which are wholly appropriate and justified.

Assessment guidance

The OCR set assignment

When completing your work for the OCR set assignment, you will need to:

- produce your own review of the digital video that you have created
- comment on the final video and how this relates to the brief
- identify what could be improved further.

What do the command words mean?

Thorough [review]: means commenting on all the aspects and elements of the digital video (not the process through the unit).

Appropriate and justified [areas for improvement]: areas for improvement should be relevant and supported by your reasons why.

Read about it

My iMovie, by Craig James Johnston and Cheryl Brumbaugh-Duncan (Que, 2014).

R090 Digital photography

About this unit

Smartphones are now frequently used instead of a dedicated digital camera. Their quality and proliferation mean that most people can take excellent photographs. However, professional photographers can apply different techniques and use advanced settings, and control the subject, scene and lighting to produce something extra special. This unit introduces the key concepts and techniques of professional digital photography.

Resources for this unit

Hardware: Digital cameras, such as DSLR, mirrorless and compact (using a smartphone will limit your access to higher mark bands, and is not recommended).

Software: Image editing applications, such as Adobe Photoshop, Lightroom®, Serif PhotoPlus, Affinity Photo or Apple Photos, for basic digital photographs processing.

Learning outcomes

LO1 Understand the features and settings of digital photographic equipment

LO2 Be able to plan a photoshoot

LO3 Be able to take and display digital photographs

LO4 Be able to review digital photographs

How will I be assessed?

You will be assessed through an OCR model assignment, marked by your tutor and externally moderated by OCR. It is worth 25% of the overall mark when working towards a Certificate in Creative iMedia.

For LO1

Learners need to:

- know about the capabilities and limitations of different digital cameras
- know about the features that are found on digital photographic equipment
- understand the settings used to take digital photographs
- understand the suitability of digital cameras for different situations
- know about the rules of photography and composition.

For LO2

Learners need to:

- be able to interpret the client requirements for a photoshoot
- understand the target audience for a photoshoot
- produce a work plan for a photoshoot

- identify the equipment and resources needed to create a photographic portfolio
- understand how legislation applies to taking photographs and producing portfolios of images.

For LO3

Learners need to:

- organise a photographic subject and scene
- use a range of digital camera features
- use a range of digital camera settings
- take a wide range of photographs with different compositions
- store their digital photographs
- create a digital photographic portfolio to meet client requirements
- display their digital photographic portfolio in a suitable medium.

For LO4

Learners need to:

- review their portfolio of photographs
- justify their selection of photographs from those taken on the photoshoot
- identify areas for improvement and further development of the photographic portfolio.

Links to other units

Completing **units R081** (LO2 and LO4) and **R082** (LO3 and LO4) provides knowledge and skills that can be applied in this unit.

LO1 Understand the features and settings of digital photographic equipment

Getting started

Make a list of what cameras you have access to. Think about any you have plus those from family, friends and school. Include comments on what you know about the cameras and what features they have.

Capabilities and limitations of different digital cameras

In this section, you will learn more about dedicated digital cameras. There are several different types of digital camera, each with its own capabilities and limitations. Mirrorless cameras are included in this section; these have made rapid advances over the last few years.

Figure 10.1 DSLR and compact digital cameras

Digital single lens reflex (DSLR)

This is the most common camera for professional (and keen amateur) use. It is the digital development from a film-based SLR. Note: the history of cameras and film-based techniques is not required in this unit.

Capabilities/advantages of DSLR	Limitations/disadvantages of DSLR
● Interchangeable lenses, with range of options for wide angle, telephoto, macro using both zoom and fixed focal length primes ● Wide range of automatic and manual controls, plus full access to the range of settings ● Good clear viewfinder ● Excellent battery life	● Size ● Weight ● Can be seen as complex until features and settings are understood ● Cost (both camera body and lenses) ● Depreciation – can drop in value as newer models are brought out

When researching DSLR cameras, it is useful to investigate typical lenses, since these form part of the overall system to capture photographs.

DSLR lenses

Standard zoom: such as 18–55 mm on a crop sensor camera body or 28–85 mm on a full frame camera body. Both have the same field of view (a feature of the sensor in the camera rather than the focal length of the lens).

Wide angle: gives a much wider angle of view than the standard zoom range.

Telephoto: gives a very narrow field of view so it appears that you have 'zoomed in' to magnify something in the scene.

Compact cameras

A large part of this market has been taken over by smartphone cameras. However, for those wanting more features, a compact camera is the next logical step.

Capabilities/advantages of compact cameras	Limitations/disadvantages of compact cameras
● Range of automatic modes for good results as a point and shoot camera ● Easily carried, small and light ● Wide depth of field (a feature of smaller sensors) ● Close focussing ability	● Basic models are a point and shoot camera but are more bulky than smartphones ● Fixed lens (most likely with some sort of zoom range) ● Small image sensor so difficult to isolate a subject from the background using small depth of field ● Noise at high ISO

Advanced compact cameras have more features and settings that can be changed, including exposure mode, exposure settings and other manual controls. Regularly used settings such as ISO, white balance and exposure compensation may have direct access dials or buttons. Action cameras, such as GoPro, are included in this list – but keep in mind that the unit is about taking photographs and not recording video.

Mirrorless compact system cameras (CSC)

Compact system cameras are more often called mirrorless cameras. Most manufacturers now produce this type of camera, which many believe will be the future of photography.

Capabilities/advantages of mirrorless cameras	Limitations/disadvantages of mirrorless cameras
● Smaller and lighter than a DSLR ● Interchangeable lenses (similar to DSLR) ● Have an electronic viewfinder (EVF) ● Silent shutter release (all electronic with no moving parts inside the camera) ● Fast and accurate focus	● Larger than most compact cameras and not small enough to carry in a pocket ● Battery life (and hence number of photos that can be taken) ● Cost can be quite high ● Limited range of lenses currently available

The different camera models and their capabilities, which are available from several manufacturers, is expanding rapidly. The next few years will be interesting for both professionals and keen amateurs with this type of camera system.

Bridge cameras

So-called because they are halfway between an advanced compact and a DSLR. At first glance, it may look like a small DSLR, but the lens will not be detachable. These are sometimes referred to as *prosumer* cameras.

Capabilities/advantages of bridge camera	Limitations/disadvantages of bridge camera
• Typically has a very wide zoom range on the lens • Easy access to more camera settings through dials and buttons (not just in the menu)	• Fixed lens • Size and bulk • Limited battery life

Capabilities and limitations of other devices for taking digital photographs

The most widely used of these is a smartphone with its built-in digital camera. Tablet devices are also used.

Smartphones and other mobile phones

These have become very popular approaches to everyday photography but have minimal settings that can be adjusted unless using a more advanced app.

Figure 10.2 Smartphone being used to take photographs

Capabilities/advantages of phone cameras	Limitations/disadvantages of phone cameras
• Small and light • Nearly always carried • Connectivity for social media sharing or sending via the internet	• Fixed lens (excluding adaptors) • Battery power (since used for a wide range of applications) • Apps needed for more control

Tablets

Examples include iPad and Android devices.

Capabilities/advantages of tablet cameras	Limitations/disadvantages of tablet cameras
• Portable and light • Connectivity for social media sharing or sending via the internet	• Slightly large for carrying in a pocket • Fixed lens (excluding adaptors) • Battery power (since used for a wide range of applications) • Apps needed for more control

Features and settings of digital photographic equipment

In this section, you will start to learn about photographic concepts and how to get the best results from a digital camera. This does not mean leaving it on a fully automatic mode and using it as a point and shoot camera. By developing your understanding of camera features, you will know which would work well for different situations. By investigating the settings available, you will start to develop an understanding of what to use in different lighting situations.

Pixel count

This is typically expressed as a number of megapixels (Mp). Common examples are 8 Mp, 12 Mp, 16 Mp, 24 Mp, 36 Mp, 48 Mp; higher quality cameras have higher pixel count. Using the example of a 24 Mp camera, this may have an image sensor that is around 6000 pixels wide by 4000 pixels high.

Zoom range

Optical zoom: where the magnification or 'zooming in' is produced optically using the lens.

Figure 10.3 Angle of view using different focal length

Digital zoom: a software feature that simulates zooming in by cropping out the edges – with a reduced digital resolution of the image that is produced.

The focal length of the lens determines the angle of view (how much of the scene is in the photograph). Figure 10.3 shows some examples from lens focal lengths on a full frame DSLR.

Exposure modes

Digital cameras have built-in light meters to measure how much light is in the scene. The light meter calculates what **exposure** is needed (exposure value or EV). The exposure mode affects the balance between shutter speed and aperture, sometimes setting one of these as the priority. Anything other than a very basic camera will have exposure modes as follows:

- P, S, A, M (used on Nikon cameras and others)
- Av, TV (used on Canon cameras)
- Auto, scene

🔑 Key term

Exposure: a key aspect of photography. This is basically a 'quantity' of light, which is determined by how long the shutter is open plus how large the aperture (hole) is in the lens to let the light through. Shutter speed and aperture are the core concepts, but the camera's ISO setting can shift these up or down.

Mode	Type	Description
P or Auto	Fully automatic	This a programmed automatic mode where the camera selects both shutter speed and aperture. Generally ok for point and shoot photography.
S or Tv	Semi-automatic	Shutter priority mode. The photographer decides what shutter speed to use and the camera's metering system selects a suitable aperture. Nikon use 'S' and Canon use 'Tv'.
A or Av	Semi-automatic	Aperture priority mode. The photographer decides what aperture to use and the camera's metering system selects a suitable shutter speed. Nikon use 'A' and Canon use 'Av'.
M	Manual	This is where you set both the shutter speed and aperture. Not often used in everyday photography but more practical in special situations such as creative lighting, night scenes or special effects.
Various symbols	Scene	These are a set of programmed automatic modes that optimise the settings for the type of photograph. Examples would be sports, portraits, landscape and night.

Photographic image file format

Many digital cameras offer two types of image file – RAW and .jpg (some might have a third option which is .tiff). Basic cameras save photographs as .jpg files that offer good quality and relatively small file sizes. RAW is popular for keen photographers and professionals who want more control over the processing of the images, but the file sizes are much larger and more specialised software is needed. With RAW files, the image information is stored straight from the sensor without any in-camera processing.

Photographic image quality settings

Image quality can be affected by two main parameters – pixel dimensions and file format.

The menu in a digital camera might provide options to change the image size, with a default setting at the maximum Mp for the sensor. If very high resolution images are not needed, this can be changed from, say, 24 Mp to 12 Mp or possibly 6 Mp. This means more photographic images can be stored on the memory card, but you are not capturing the same detail. Most photographers leave this at the highest setting.

The second parameter is related to the image file type. If storing images as .jpg, the menu might provide options for 'fine', 'normal' and 'basic'. This refers to the amount of compression used when saving the file.

Fine: uses the least compression, creating high quality images and large files.

Normal: uses some compression, for a practical balance of image quality and file size.

Basic: uses a lot of compression, for images that are reasonably good but with a much smaller file size.

Photographic subjects and the suitability of digital cameras (plus other equipment and resources)

Some would use a DSLR for just about every photographic purpose. If working as a professional photographer, a DSLR (or possibly a mirrorless system) is likely to always be the preferred option.

Many people take photographs for personal use. But we need to look at commercial requirements as the vocational nature of the qualification. For this, you may be working in the photographic industry and be getting paid for what is produced as a portfolio.

We will consider a few categories and the options available depending on what the photographs are for.

Figure 10.4 Wedding shoot: 1/125s, f8, ISO 200, twin flash

Weddings

A professional photographer covering a wedding is likely to use a DSLR or possibly a high-quality mirrorless system such as those from Sony, Nikon, Canon or Fuji.

Both of these camera systems provide interchangeable lenses and perform well in different lighting situations. Focus accuracy and image sharpness are important, as are a range of lenses and high ISO performance for dimly lit environments. A DSLR is a traditional, reliable choice. A great range of lenses and flash accessories are available. Professional models can be rugged and weather sealed. Mirrorless are lighter for all day shooting and silent shutters can be useful.

Figure 10.5 Action photography, 1/2000 s at f8, ISO 400

Sporting events and action

This category is not limited to sports; it can include any fast-moving subjects such as cars, boats, horses, dogs and wildlife. If the subject is moving within the scene to be photographed, you will need to use a faster shutter speed to 'freeze' the movement.

DSLRs (or possibly mirrorless systems) are usually used for professional sports photography. However, consumer photography with action or movement could use any type of camera with some control over shutter speed.

Figure 10.6 Night photography – Media City, Salford 1/20 s, f5.6, ISO 3200

Low light

Low light situations may be indoors or outside during dawn, dusk or night time. This often needs slow shutter speeds so the camera can be mounted on a tripod. Those cameras with good performance (low noise at high ISO settings) are the most useful. So, usually, DSLR are used since they typically have larger sensors.

Portraits

Photographs of people are referred to as portraits. These can be taken in natural light and environments, or in a studio where the lighting can be set up for a particular style. Portraits can be full length or half length (not long shot and mid shot, which is terminology used in video work for R089). Photographic terminology includes 'close ups', but beyond that they become macro shots and not 'extreme close ups'. Portraits can be taken with any type of camera.

Figure 10.7 Portrait photography, 1/160s, f5.6

Figure 10.8 Landscape photography, 1/160s, f11, ISO 200

Landscapes

These are photographs taken of an outdoor scene, from lakes to mountains to urban environments. Many are taken with wide angle lenses. Image composition plays a large part. Using the rule of thirds, together with some foreground interest, is a popular approach. Often, a small aperture is used to get a wide depth of field so that, potentially, everything is in focus.

Cameras can be DSLR or mirrorless for the highest quality images. Compact cameras are more often used if travelling light.

Figure 10.9 Studio photography

Studio work

Subjects for studio work can be people (portraits) or products/still life. Some type of studio background and lighting will be required, depending on whether you are photographing people or table-top objects. A professional studio will have paper, cloth or vinyl backgrounds in different colours and textures. They will also most likely have studio flash systems with two, three or more lights. Cameras can be either DSLR or mirrorless in a professional studio.

Rules of photography and composition

There are some established compositions that work. Here is a selection of the basic guidelines, concepts and ideas.

Rule of thirds

This is where you imagine the photograph to be divided by vertical and horizontal lines, which are at one-third and two-thirds distance apart, to create a grid with nine separate areas. The main points of interest can then be placed on the intersection of these lines inside the frame. A horizon can also be placed on the horizontal line that is one-third from the top (or bottom) of the frame rather than straight across the middle. This is the most well-known 'rule' of photography – but you can be a rebel and break the rule! The challenge is knowing when you can, or should.

Leading lines

When composing the photograph, look for natural lines that draw the viewer into the frame. Ideally, start at the lower left or right corner of the frame. These can be from a road, river, fence, path or similar object. Perspective is where lines converge, such as a road or by standing underneath a bridge. A wide angle lens often works well with this type of photograph.

Figure 10.11 Leading lines and perspective, 1/400 s at F11

Frames

This compositional technique is a way to focus the attention of the viewer so that there is less reason to think about the overall scene and where the photograph was taken. The impact is to make the viewer look at what is within the frame, rather than wonder what is outside.

Figure 10.10 Using the rule of thirds

Figure 10.12 Using natural frames, 1/320s, f8

High Angle | Low Angle

Figure 10.13 Viewpoint – high/low

Figure 10.14 Landscape and portrait orientation

Viewpoint

The viewpoint is where you take the photograph from. Most people take photos while being stood up. Try getting low down to the floor or higher up than everybody else. This gives a different perspective that can make your photographs more eye catching and interesting.

Orientation

There are two main orientations: portrait and landscape. Depending on who might use the photograph, try taking a photo in both orientations if possible. In-between these is something called a dutch angle or tilt, where the camera is held at an angle.

Within a portfolio of images, try not to overdo the dutch angle as a compositional approach – it can soon start to lose its appeal.

Classroom discussion

Discuss the photograph in Figure 10.15; what is the photographic category and what compositional rules have been used?

Figure 10.15 Discuss the composition and subject, 1/2000s at f8, ISO 200

Know it!

1 You have been asked to take some photographs as a spectator at a sporting event that will be used in a local newspaper. What camera and lens would you choose and why?

2 You want to take some discreet photographs inside a quiet building without disturbing anybody. What camera might you use and why?

Assessment preparation

LO1: Understand the features and settings of digital photographic equipment		
Mark band 1	Mark band 2	Mark band 3
Gives a basic description of some features and settings of digital photographic equipment.	Gives a sound description of most features and settings of digital photographic equipment.	Gives a thorough description of most features and settings of digital photographic equipment.
Describes some capabilities and limitations of different types of digital camera and other methods of taking digital photographs.	Describes many capabilities and limitations of different types of digital camera and other methods of taking digital photographs.	Describes most capabilities and limitations of different types of digital camera and other methods of taking digital photographs.
Mark band 1	Mark band 2	Mark band 3
Describes the suitability of digital cameras, with limited accuracy, for a limited range of scenarios.	Describes the suitability of digital cameras, with some accuracy, for a range of scenarios.	Describes accurately the suitability of digital cameras, for a wide range of scenarios.
Describes a few rules of photography and composition with limited accuracy.	Describes some rules of photography and composition with some accuracy.	Describes many rules of photography and composition accurately.

Assessment guidance

The OCR set assignment

When completing your work for the OCR set assignment, you will need to describe the:

- features of different digital photographic equipment
- settings available on digital photographic equipment
- capabilities and limitations of different types of camera
- suitability of digital cameras for different situations
- rules of photography and composition.

What do the command words mean?

Thorough [description]: should cover a wide range of features of digital cameras together with a wide range of settings (features are what you can see on the camera whereas settings are what can be adjusted).

Most [capabilities and limitations]: means describing the key areas such as those included in the section above.

Accurately: what you describe must be correct.

Wide range [of scenarios]: generally means five or more.

Many [rules]: since there are few 'rules' this means that you should describe a wide range of compositional approaches to photographic subjects.

LO2 Be able to plan a photoshoot

Client requirements and the target audience for a photoshoot

Photography can be subjective, so that it means different things to different people. What you consider a good photograph might not be what somebody wants from your work. You might take a great 'head and shoulders' portrait photo of somebody at a wedding, party or holiday, but if they want it for a passport it won't be any use. Therefore, you must know *who* wants the photograph and understand *what* it will be used for. The skill is to take a photograph that meets those requirements. Some examples that are part of this unit are:

● exhibition
● display
● promotion
● historical record.

Planning considerations

After reading the brief, before venturing straight out with your camera, you will need to plan what you are going to do. Write a summary in your own words of what is needed for the photoshoot so that you are clear about the purpose, content and range of photographs needed.

Subject or theme of the photoshoot: this should be straightforward – for example, is it a wedding, landscape shoot, sport, nature, wildlife, portrait or urban architecture? Use a planning sheet or mind map and write it down as the starting point.

'Must get' and 'would like' photos: a wedding will likely have a clear list of 'must get' shots. Other events will certainly have a list of ideal shots – such as the winner crossing the finishing line or a natural smile in a portrait.

Opportunities during the photoshoot: You may have a list of what you want to photograph but the majority of shots might be based on what you actually see and have the opportunity to capture.

Where the photos will be taken: Think about where you will stand and what viewpoint; for example, high up, low down and camera orientation.

Equipment required: what type of camera? You could add lenses, flash, tripod, and filters.

Expected camera settings: such as shutter speed, aperture, ISO, WB, use of flash.

Time required: will the photoshoot take an hour, all day or until the event finishes? Think about what clothing to wear if outside.

Image processing workflow: this will depend on the photograph file format (RAW or jpeg) and what software you will use to process the images.

Produce a work plan for the photoshoot

As part of your planning, you will need a work plan. For this unit, the work plan should also include:

- photographic location
- time of day or night
- photographic subjects.

Links to other units

You can find further information on how to create a work plan or project plan in **unit R081**. If an outdoor location for the photoshoot, you might also consider a recce and risk assessment (also in **unit R081**).

Identify the equipment and resources

This should be a list of equipment needed for the photoshoot, and to create the digital photographic portfolio. Using a smartphone camera for the photographs introduces limitations in LO3 because you will need to show that you have used a range of camera features and settings. Equipment for the photoshoot is more than just 'camera' – think about what sort of camera and why. What features does it have? What lens(es) will you use? Also consider accessories, such as a tripod, flash or filters. The resources to create the portfolio will include any software for processing the images and their display, as well as the computer system.

Legislation

This applies to the initial taking of photographs and the production of a digital photographic portfolio. In addition to the general considerations for legal and ethical issues covered in R081, here are the main areas specific to photography.

Model releases

A model release is a permission form that is signed by each person (or model) that is recognisable in the photograph. It gives the photographer the right to use their image for commercial reasons. Any photograph of a young person under the age of 18 should be supported by a consent form which is signed by a parent or guardian. This is part of child protection legislation.

Property releases

A property release is a permission form that is needed when the photograph is taken on private property. If taken from a public place, this is not needed.

Welfare considerations

This is closely related to health and safety considerations, which you learn about as part of R081. Think about whether your model will be comfortable; for example, are they cold and wet on an outdoor photoshoot? If so, you need to look after them as well.

Privacy

This is more about any people that might be in the photograph that are not signing a model release. Think about whether they might complain about an invasion of privacy, depending on where they are, what they are doing and where you might be publishing the photographs that they are in.

Copyright and trademarks

These are covered in R081. You might need to consider whether your photographs show anything that is protected by copyright or a trademark. If so, there could be restrictions on its use in a commercial context.

Know it!

1 You want to take photographs of a friend to use on a website to promote your photographic services. What document is needed to gain permission for this?

2 Make a list of what could go wrong if you are going to a wedding as the main photographer without any preparation or planning.

Assessment preparation

LO2: Be able to plan a photoshoot		
Mark band 1	Mark band 2	Mark band 3
Produces an interpretation from the client brief for a photoshoot which meets few of the client requirements.	Produces an interpretation from the client brief for a photoshoot which meets most of the client requirements.	Produces an interpretation from the client brief for a photoshoot which fully meets the client requirements.
Produces a limited identification of target audience requirements.	Produces a clear identification of target audience requirements.	Produces a clear and detailed identification of target audience requirements.
Draws upon limited skills/knowledge/understanding from other units in the specification.	Draws upon some relevant skills/knowledge/understanding from other units in the specification.	Clearly draws upon relevant skills/knowledge/understanding from other units in the specification.
Mark band 1	Mark band 2	Mark band 3
Produces a work plan for the photo-shoot, which has some capability in producing the intended final photo-shoot.	Produces a work plan for the photo-shoot, which is mostly capable of producing the intended final photo-shoot.	Produces a clear and detailed work plan for the photoshoot, which is fully capable of producing the intended photoshoot.
Lists some of the equipment and software to be used in creating the digital photographic portfolio and gives basic reasons for selection in relation to the identified success criteria.	Lists most of the equipment and software to be used in creating the digital photographic portfolio and gives sound justification for selection in relation to the identified success criteria.	Lists all of the equipment and software to be used in creating the digital photographic portfolio, thoroughly justifying selection in relation to the identified success criteria.
Demonstrates a limited understanding of legislation in relation to the taking of photographs and the production of a digital photographic portfolio.	Demonstrates a sound understanding of legislation in relation to the taking of photographs and the production of a digital photographic portfolio.	Demonstrates a thorough understanding of legislation in relation to the taking of photographs and the production of a digital photographic portfolio.

Assessment guidance

The OCR set assignment

When completing your work for the OCR set assignment, you will need to:

- produce your own interpretation of the client brief
- identify the target audience and what they will want from the portfolio
- use knowledge and skills from other units such as R081 or R082
- produce a work plan to create the photoshoot
- identify the equipment and software to be used in the photoshoot and portfolio creation
- identify the success criteria for the photoshoot
- justify equipment and software choices in relation to the success criteria
- describe the legal restrictions on the photoshoot and use of images in a photographic portfolio.

What do the command words mean?

Fully [meets the brief]: needs to be a comprehensive description of your own individual ideas and thoughts on what is required from the photographs.

Clear and detailed [target audience]: should be a clear definition of who the target audience is and what they will want to gain from the photographic portfolio.

Relevant [knowledge, skills and understanding]: must be from other units and not something that is already in R090, such as a work plan.

Clear and detailed [work plan]: should break down the tasks and activities into small steps that must be completed in order to complete the photoshoot (not LO1).

All [equipment] and thoroughly [justifying selection]: should identify all the photographic equipment that will be taken and used on the photoshoot. The justification must be made in relation to success criteria (what is needed from the photoshoot to make it successful and for example, may refer to the capabilities and features of the camera selected).

Thorough [understanding of legislation]: should be applied to the photoshoot, creation and publication of the photographic portfolio in a commercial context.

LO3 Be able to take and display digital photographs

Organise the photographic subject and scene choosing a suitable viewpoint

This section is about setting up the scene and camera before you start taking the photographs.

Use appropriate features and settings of a digital camera

Keep in mind from your investigation in LO1 that features relate to the camera and settings relate primarily to the exposure settings. You will need to learn about using both. Typical features to be used could be:

- lens focal length (wide angle or telephoto)
- use of flash, which may be part of the camera
- image file format
- image quality settings
- camera battery – check fully charged
- memory card – check size of card and whether formatted.

Exposure settings

Most cameras have different settings that can be adjusted depending on the scene and subject of the photograph.

Shutter speed

Shutter speed is the duration that the shutter is open to record the photograph. A fast shutter speed such as $\frac{1}{1000}$s will 'freeze' most movement. Much slower than $\frac{1}{60}$s becomes difficult to hold steady without camera shake. The following list represents a difference of one exposure 'stop' in between each value. Notice that the time halves.

$$\frac{1}{1000}, \frac{1}{500}, \frac{1}{250}, \frac{1}{125}, \frac{1}{60}, \frac{1}{30}, \frac{1}{15}, \frac{1}{8}, \frac{1}{4}, \frac{1}{2}$$

Aperture

This is the size of the hole in the lens that lets light through. A large **aperture** would be f1.4 and a small aperture f22.

f1.4, f2, f2.8, f4, f5.6, f8, f11, f16, f22

The combination of shutter speed and aperture determines the exposure value. As an example $\frac{1}{250}$s at f8 gives the same exposure as $\frac{1}{125}$s at f11 or $\frac{1}{60}$s at f16.

Key terms

Shutter speed: the duration that the shutter is open for the photograph to be recorded.

Aperture: you can think of aperture as being the size of the hole in the lens to let light through. A larger aperture means a bigger hole so that more light can pass through. Just to keep you on your toes – a larger aperture is actually a smaller 'f' number, such as f2.8 or f1.4 (which tend to be expensive lenses).

Figure 10.16 Camera settings 'info' display

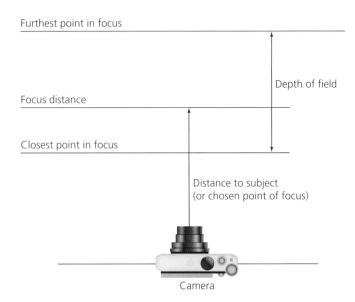

Furthest point in focus

Focus distance

Closest point in focus

Depth of field

Distance to subject
(or chosen point of focus)

Camera

Figure 10.17 Depth of field

 Stretch activity

Depth of field is the range of distances from the camera that are in sharp focus. For example, if you are focussed on your subject at 5 m away, the depth of field will be from 4 m to 6.5 m when using a 50 mm lens and f4. The depth of field is affected by the aperture and lens focal length - experiment with the settings.

Exposure compensation

A camera's built in metering system can be confused by difficult or uneven lighting situations. Most cameras have a dial or menu that allows ±2 stops. After taking a photograph, check the result on the LCD display and decide whether you need to take it again with exposure compensation.

Exposure adjustment	Effect
Increase the exposure; for example, by +1 or +2 stops	The photograph will be brighter
Reduce the exposure; for example, by −1 or −2 stops	The photograph will be darker

ISO

This is a camera setting that determines the sensitivity to different light levels. Higher **ISO**

settings make the camera sensor more sensitive to light levels, which makes it possible to use faster shutter speeds or smaller apertures for greater depth of field. Changing the ISO will have two primary effects.

1 It will change the exposure needed (combination of shutter speed and aperture).

2 At the higher end of the ISO range, the amount of noise in the photograph will increase. This is generally a bad thing and makes the photograph look a bit rough.

White balance (WB)

White balance is a camera setting that compensates for different types of lighting to make sure the colours are correct. Digital cameras have a range of different settings for WB. There will also be an auto mode where the camera will

 Key terms

ISO: a camera setting that determines the sensitivity to light levels.

White balance: a camera setting that compensates for lighting to obtain the correct colours.

set a value, but this is not always accurate. This setting is more important when shooting jpg files, since RAW files are adjusted when processing the images on the computer system. The typical range of options on the camera are:

- incandescent
- fluorescent
- daylight
- cloudy
- flash
- custom
- auto.

Flash mode

Most digital cameras have a built-in flash, the exception being some professional models. External flashguns can often be attached using a 'hot shoe' on top of the camera body. Flash is not just used in darker conditions – it can also be used in bright daylight as 'fill-in' flash. If the faces of people are in the shade (with the Sun behind them), then using flash will brighten their face so you can see it properly.

The other flash mode to know about is 'red eye' reduction. If using flash to take photographs of people, especially at night time, it is not unusual for the eyes to be bright red. This is an effect of the flash, which can be reduced by using the 'red eye' flash setting. This outputs a pre-flash so that the eyes adjust to the bright light before the main flash goes off and the photograph is taken.

Image stabilisation

Nearly all modern digital cameras have some sort of built in system to minimise movement of the camera at slow shutter speeds that would otherwise produce a very blurred image (from camera shake). If your shutter speed is less than $\frac{1}{60}$ s (or faster, when using a telephoto lens) there is a good chance of camera shake creating an image that is not sharp when looked at carefully. There are two main types of system to reduce this: vibration reduction (VR) and image stabilisation (IS). These are internal mechanisms in the camera or lens, and are a useful feature in dimly lit situations.

Group activity

In small groups, share ideas about settings and compositions. Use a digital camera to take digital photographs using:

1 different camera settings (shutter speed, aperture, ISO and WB)
2 different compositions and rules of photography.

Transfer your photographs to a computer and look at the results. Look at the difference the exposure settings make. Discuss this within your group.

Shooting speed (continuous and single)

DSLRs and some advanced compacts have both single frame and continuous shooting modes. In continuous mode, the camera keeps taking photographs for as long as the shutter release button is held down. This can take several frames per second (even into double figures on pro SLRs). In single frame mode, only one photograph is taken each time the shutter release is pressed.

Macro mode

These are photographs that are taken at a very close distance. Typical examples would be flowers and insects. A macro mode is a feature found on compact cameras but not DSLRs, which use a dedicated macro lens. On the camera, it is usually shown with a single flower icon (a mountain icon is usually used for landscapes and general photography). If you are trying to take a photograph of something very close and the camera is struggling to focus, set the macro mode and try again.

Storing digital photographs

The storage of your photographic work has several important areas to consider.

Processing and editing: photographs are transferred from the camera to a computer system and stored in a folder for processing and editing. You might use the standard file management system or dedicated photographic software, such as Adobe Lightroom.

Backups: copies are created using a different medium/location. Examples include portable external drives and web-based storage. Only after this should you consider clearing the memory card from the camera, so you always have two copies somewhere.

Portfolios: final images are made available for clients and display purposes. This could be using cloud or web-based storage, memory stick, or CD/DVD.

Techniques for processing photographic images

Basic image processing is all that is required by this unit since the skills in using a digital camera as part of a planned photographic assignment are the main objectives. In this section, we will review the main image processing techniques that you might want to include to optimise the photographs taken.

Checking image sharpness

This is not a processing technique but something that should be checked before going any further. Keep in mind that, if the image is blurred through camera shake or poor focussing, you will not

be able to fix it in the editing. This is why it is important to take a good photograph in the first place. Zoom in to 100% in the imaging software and check that the photograph is still sharp.

Adjusting colour/white balance

If the colours are not quite true to life, there is a good chance that the white balance was not set correctly when the photograph was taken. This can be adjusted in the image processing. Some image editing/processing software allows you to change the white balance on jpg and RAW files.

Adobe Lightroom allows you to change the white balance on each image using a drop-down menu. Other software applications may have options to adjust the white balance or colour.

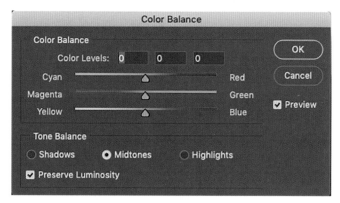

Figure 10.19 Adjusting the colour balance

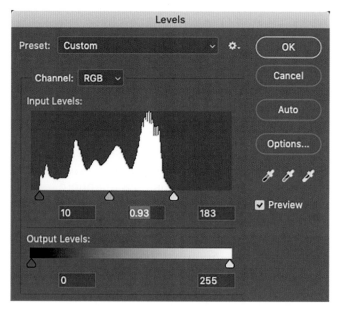

Figure 10.20 Adjusting the levels in Photoshop

Figure 10.18 Checking the image sharpness

Adjusting exposure

Images may benefit from a slight adjustment to the exposure. If using image editing software, the same type of adjustment can be done by changing the brightness and contrast or levels in Photoshop. As long as your monitor displays correctly, you can make changes so that it looks good on the screen.

Cropping

You can improve the framing of the subject by cropping out unwanted parts. Ideally, you would have moved closer to the subject with the camera or used the zoom feature of the lens to effectively get a closer composition. If not, the photographic image can be cropped in the image processing software application.

Creating a digital photographic portfolio to meet client requirements

You should be able to create a portfolio of images that you have taken. It could be a set of photographs from a holiday or day out (although this will not be suitable for your final assignment). Aim to have about 10 to 12 final images that show a wide range of compositions, subjects and settings. The selection of images should take several considerations into account. Record notes on why you have selected them based on:

- suitability of the image content
- composition and visual appeal
- image sharpness
- exposure and colour.

In a photographic assignment, all of these will be important to the client requirement. The content must be what the client wanted, the image should have visual appeal, be sharp (not blurred) and show good exposure and colour. If any one of these is not right, then it shouldn't be included in a final portfolio. It is possible that many photographs are rejected.

Figure 10.21 Cropping a photograph

As a learning activity, produce a table with the headings as shown above. Review a portfolio of images and rate each photograph on a scale of 1 to 5 (except for exposure settings which should have shutter speed, aperture and ISO).

Once you get used to looking at photographs using these criteria, you will be able to decide quickly on an overall rating. Some photographic management software allows you to rate images using 1 to 5 stars. Anything in your final portfolio should have an overall rating of 4 or 5. If it doesn't, go back out and take more photographs.

Image number	Image content	Composition	Sharpness	Exposure and colour	Exposure settings	Overall rating

Display digital photographs using a suitable medium

Depending on what the client wants the photographs for, the options could be

- **print:** a set of large prints such as 12" × 8" (approximately A4), 16" × 12" (approximately A3)
- **digital slide show:** photographs prepared at a specific resolution for display use and a slide show created using the computer system features
- **presentation:** similar to a slide show but possibly with manual advance rather than automatic
- **exhibition:** could be as a set of large framed prints with photo mounts
- **on-screen:** similar to a slide show or presentation.

If exporting your photographs from a software application, the image properties will need to be suitable for the intended use. More information can be found in R082 on this topic.

- **Print:** needs a resolution of 300 dpi so a 12 × 8 inch print will need a total of 3600 × 2400 pixels.
- **Online:** web-ready images should have a resolution of 72 dpi. Website images are rarely more than 800–1024 pixels wide due to the limited display screen size.
- **Interactive media:** similar to online or web use since the images will be viewed on a display screen. Typically 72 dpi but could also be 96 dpi in some cases. Your client might state what this should be.

A photographic portfolio can be used to promote your own services as a photographer. These are likely to be printed although it is also possible to have this as a show reel on a tablet style device.

Know it!

1. Which of these exposures would produce the darker image: $\frac{1}{60}$ s at f11 or $\frac{1}{500}$ s at f8?
2. On a bright day, the photographs all appear dark. What setting should be adjusted?

Assessment preparation

LO3: Be able to take and display digital photographs		
Mark band 1	Mark band 2	Mark band 3
Uses some relevant features and settings of the digital camera, which are not always appropriate to the client brief. The subject and scene are organised with limited appropriateness.	Uses many relevant features and settings of the digital camera, which are mostly appropriate to the client brief. The subject and scene are in the most part appropriately organised.	Uses most relevant features and settings of the digital camera, all of which are appropriate to the client brief. The subject and scene are appropriately organised.
Takes digital photographs using a limited range of the rules of photography and composition.	Takes digital photographs using a range of the rules of photography and composition.	Takes digital photographs using a wide range of the rules of photography and composition.
Mark band 1	Mark band 2	Mark band 3
Stores digital images, occasionally using a medium which is appropriate.	Stores digital images, mostly using a medium which is appropriate.	Stores digital images, consistently using an appropriate medium.
Creates portfolios of stored images that meet some of the client requirements. The selected images are displayed in a medium which has some appropriateness to the brief.	Creates portfolios of stored images that meet most of the client requirements. The selected images are displayed in a medium which is mostly appropriate to the brief.	Creates portfolios of stored images that meet all of the client requirements. The selected images are effectively displayed in a medium which is fully appropriate to the brief.

When completing your work for the OCR set assignment, you will need to:

- organise the photographic subject and scene in readiness to take the photographs
- use a wide range of features and settings when taking photographs to meet the client brief
- use a wide range of photographic rules and compositions when taking the photographs
- store the photographs [safely and securely] in suitable locations and mediums
- create a photographic portfolio of the best images to meet the client requirements, presenting them in a format and medium that is suitable for the client and brief (the photographs as image files plus the final photographic portfolio in a format for display).

What do the command words mean?

Most/all [relevant features]: using a wide range of features that are available on the digital camera (which would not be a smartphone due to the limited features available).

Appropriately organised [subject and scene]: positioning of the subject, positioning of the camera and viewpoint together with consideration of lighting all contribute to meeting this.

Wide range [rules and composition]: generally accepted as five or more. The photographs should demonstrate the effective use of compositional ideas and approaches.

Consistently [store images]: stored securely in a folder with suitable name, backed up where appropriate.

Effectively [displayed] and fully appropriate [to the brief]: combination of digital image files of the final photographs plus a presentation in a suitable format for display use by the client, such as prints or slide show.

LO4 Be able to review digital photographs

Getting started

Hold a photographic competition in your class. Submit the best photograph that you have taken during the course and let the teacher be the competition judge. They may comment on each of the submissions before deciding on the overall winner, explaining the reasons for their choice.

Review the portfolio of photographs

The concept of being able to critically look at your own photographs is an important skill to develop. This does not mean relying on others to tell you what they like about certain photographs. The aim is that you learn how to look at the work you produce. Here you should look at the digital photographic portfolio and comment on the strengths and weaknesses in addition to how well it meets the requirements of the client brief.

Here are some key areas to cover in a review.

- Compare it back to the brief and client's requirements – does the subject and content of the photographs meet what was wanted?
- Are the photographic images technically good – are they sharp and well exposed with good colour?
- Are the photographic images good in terms of their composition?
- Do the photographs demonstrate a conventional or creative style?
- Think about and describe the strengths, positives, advantages and benefits.
- Think about and describe the weaknesses, negatives, disadvantages and drawbacks.
- Use technical language and terminology where possible.

Keep in mind that, for this unit, the key elements are the composition, exposure, lighting and the suitability of content for the client against their specific brief.

Justify the selection of photographs for a portfolio

Your final portfolio should contain around 10–12 photographs. You will probably have rejected many more from the ones you took. In this section, you need to justify *why* you chose the final images and rejected the others. Reasons could be composition, image sharpness, exposure or lighting. You will need to record the decision-making process for this.

Identify areas for improvement and further development of a digital photographic portfolio

Following on from your review and justifications, you may still be able to identify some areas for further improvement. Here are a few common examples.

Image content: could this be different and more relevant to the brief across the portfolio?

Image sharpness: would further editing improve the sharpness where needed or do some photographs need to be retaken?

Lighting: would editing improve the overall brightness or do some photographs need to be retaken in better lighting?

Exposure: can the exposure be improved through further editing?

Different uses: could any of the photographs be used differently? (for example, stock library use, sales to other clients or promotion of your own photographic skills?)

Know it!

1 You have taken a photograph indoors on 'auto' and it looks blurred. What could be wrong and how could it be improved with a second shot?

2 You have taken some photographs of snow outside your school, but they all have a blue colour cast. What is wrong and what setting needs to be adjusted?

Assessment preparation

L04: Be able to review digital photographs		
Mark band 1	**Mark band 2**	**Mark band 3**
Produces a review of the photographic portfolio which demonstrates a limited understanding of what worked and what did not, making few references back to the brief.	Produces a review of the finished portfolio which demonstrates a reasonable understanding of what worked and what did not, mostly referencing back to the brief.	Produces a review of the finished portfolio which demonstrates a thorough understanding of what worked and what did not, fully referencing back to the brief.
Provides a limited justification for the photographs selected.	Provides a reasonable justification for the photographs selected.	Provides a thorough justification for the photographs selected.
Review identifies areas for improvement and further development of the photographic portfolio, some of which are appropriate and sometimes are explained.	Review identifies areas for improvement and further development of the photographic portfolio, which are mostly appropriate and explained well.	Review identifies areas for improvement and further development of the photographic portfolio, which are wholly appropriate and justified.

Assessment guidance

The OCR set assignment

When completing your work for the OCR set assignment, you will need to:

- produce your own review of the photographs that you have taken
- comment on the final photographic portfolio and how this relates to the brief
- following on from the review, identify what individual photographs could be improved and how the overall portfolio could be developed further.

What do the command words mean?

Thorough [review]: means commenting on all the aspects and elements of the photographs (not the process through the unit).

Thorough [justification]: means giving reasons for why each photograph was included in the final portfolio.

Appropriate and justified [areas for improvement]: areas for improvement in either individual photographs or the overall portfolio should be relevant and supported by your reasons why.

Read about it

Digital Photographer's Handbook: 6th Edition of the Best-Selling Photography Manual, by Tom Ang (DK Publishing, 2016).

www.dpreview.com

www.exposureguide.com

R091 Designing a game concept

About this unit

R091 is a creative unit about new ideas for a game design concept. You will investigate the development of games platforms and game genres before generating a new idea for a game. You will create a proposal based on your game idea that could be given to a client based on an outline of what is needed.

Resources for this unit

Hardware: Computer system.

Software: Word processing, desktop publishing and/or presentation.

Learning outcomes

LO1 Understand digital game types and platforms

LO2 Be able to plan a digital game concept

LO3 Be able to design a digital game proposal

LO4 Be able to review a digital game proposal

LO1 Understand digital game types and platforms

Getting started

Working in a small group, create a mind map of games that you have played on a range of different platforms.

The evolution of digital game platforms

Games platforms have evolved rapidly since the early 1970s. Popular platforms are dedicated consoles, PC computers and handheld devices. The evolution is often described as a series of generations that last typically between six and eight years.

Generation 1: 1972–1977. First consoles such as the Magnavox Odyssey. All Pong variants.

Generation 2: 1976–1984. More emphasis on software and no longer limited to Pong style games.

Generation 3: 1983–1992. Consoles powered by 8-bit microprocessors and much improved graphics.

Generation 4: 1987–1996. Consoles powered by 16-bit microprocessors with arcade quality graphics in the home. Introduction of the IBM PC.

Generation 5: 1993–2002. Characterised by the introduction of 32-bit microprocessors and 3D graphics.

Generation 6: 1998–2006. These featured more powerful processors, online gaming options and games supplied on DVD media.

Generation 7: 2004–2011. This includes the Nintendo Wii, PS3 and Xbox 360.

Generation 8: 2012 onwards. This includes the Nintendo Switch, PS4 and Xbox One.

The performance of any platform depends on the electronic hardware. When developing a new game concept, it is not realistic to render detailed and complex 3D scenes with small graphical

displays and low performance processors. Otherwise, the update speed of the display will be too slow and difficult to identify since the resolution would not be high enough. The player would also be very frustrated before long.

For the purposes of this unit as a games designer, you should understand the capabilities of the hardware on your chosen platform before deciding what the game will look like.

Choice of gaming platform

PC: a popular computer platform for both playing and developing digital games. Specifications vary quite considerably and the players' experience of the game could vary from one computer to another.

Games console: these are dedicated platforms for playing digital games which connect to a television screen. The most popular consoles are the Sony PlayStation, Microsoft Xbox and Nintendo Wii. The large display of the game environment gives an immersive experience for the player.

Portable devices: includes Nintendo 2DS, Sony PSP series and Sega portable. These are smaller pocket-sized games consoles that can be carried around easily. The display size is more limited, although many still have a high quality/resolution screen.

Mobile phone/PDA: increased graphics quality and processing power mean they can also now support high quality games as a versatile all in one entertainment and communications device.

The evolution of the characteristics of digital games

Since the early 1970s, the style and genre of games has steadily evolved alongside the platforms. The key changes include:

- early games were 2D arcade-style, such as Pong, Space Invaders and variants
- development of 3D graphics
- 2D maze and racing games into immersive 3D worlds
- introduction of first-person shooter games (FPS)

193

- from single player on one platform to multiplayer online games
- first person role player games (RPG), often in 3D worlds
- strategy and simulation game development, such as Flight simulator, SimCity
- game-based learning to engage the player with practical knowledge
- augmented reality worlds, such as Second life in 2003
- massively-multiplayer online role-playing games (MMORPG), such as World of Warcraft.

Group activity

Make a list of the first games you played when you were younger and how these differ from what you play now. What are the key differences?

Games objectives of digital games

Depending on the type of game and its genre, the game objectives could be:

- quest to find treasure
- racing to get the fastest time
- shooting monsters, aliens, other aircraft
- tactical strategies to win a battle
- escape from somewhere.

Think about your favourite games and write down what you are aiming to achieve in the game – these will be part of the game objectives.

Digital game genres

The evolution of games has enabled a wide range of game genres to be available. The main ones are shown in Figure 11.1.

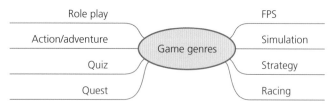

Figure 11.1 Some of the main game genres

Genre: the use of the term 'genre' in game terminology is slightly different to the traditional movie genre. For example, a first-person shooter (FPS) game could be created as a movie genre of the 'wild west' or 'science fiction'.

Genre	Examples (some fall into more than one category)
Action/Adventure	The Legend of Zelda
Arcade	Space Invaders Pac-Man
Educational	Big Brain Academy
First person shooter (FPS)	Star Wars – Jedi Knight
Historical	Age of Empires
Massively Multiplayer Online (MMO)	World of Warcraft
Puzzle	Solitaire Bomberman
Racing	Gran Turismo
Role Playing (RPG)	Dungeons and Dragons
Simulator	FlightGear
Sport	FIFA Wii Sports
Strategy	Sim City Age of Empires

The capabilities and limitations of gaming platforms

The development of platforms for 2D/3D digital games has introduced more powerful processors, higher quality video graphics and game controllers. The capabilities of platforms fall into several key areas.

- Hardware
- Display devices
- Game delivery method
- Networking
- Storage
- Player interface
- Peripherals

Hardware

Hardware includes processor, memory, graphics controller and sound system.

Processor: impacts on the overall game performance and player's experience of gameplay. Low resolution 2D graphics will not need as much processing power as a real time high resolution 3D environment that is rendered for different lighting effects.

Memory: second most important component that will determine the player's experience of the gameplay in terms of performance. In a computer system, memory is used as a temporary storage area which has fast access when compared to a hard disk. If the computer system does not have enough memory installed, it can use the hard disk for temporary storage instead but the speed of access can slow down the overall gameplay.

Graphics controllers: real time 3D graphics can use display technologies that are built into graphics controller cards. The rendering of textures and lighting in a 3D scene is performed by the graphics card instead of the main computer CPU. This enables movie quality visual effects in computer game environments.

Sound cards: standard sound cards only drive two speakers which would normally be placed in front of the player. For improved audio effects during gameplay, a sound card that supports 3D surround sound produces a more realistic experience of the player actually being inside the game.

Display device: screen size and resolution are the main factors for this.

Networking/storage/game delivery method: storage includes hard disk, Blu-ray, DVD, flash memory and even games cartridges (but these have been declining for some time). Networking is usually over the internet, providing downloadable games, additional game components together with online gameplay.

Player interface and peripherals

Keyboard: computer keyboard arrow keys typically used to control movement but can also use other keys such as W-A-S-D for left handed people. Portable devices and mobile phones may have programmable function keys in addition to multi-rockers or jog dials.

Mouse: standard interface device for use with a computer system. Movement could be controlled by pushing the mouse forward or backward. Doors and other objects opened or used by clicking on them with the mouse pointer.

Paddle: controller used on early games platforms with a small wheel or paddle that is manipulated to control the player movement. Buttons are also included for actions in the game such as 'Shoot'.

Keypad/gamepad controller: hand-held game controller used with games consoles. Provides more functions than a simple paddle with movement typically being controlled using the thumbs. For games on mobile phones, the phone itself is a controller and can sense motion through an in-built accelerometer.

Joystick: popular game controller for use with flying, whether flight simulation or air to air combat. Buttons to fire missiles and guns are found using the thumb and forefinger respectively.

Wheel: used in driving or racing games, to navigate a vehicle around a track. This simulates the normal method of vehicle control.

Pedals: used in racing games to control speed or acceleration, in the same way as a car. This is used in conjunction with a wheel for directional control.

Virtual/Augmented Reality headset: More games are being developed for playing in a virtual or augmented reality, which requires a headset or goggles.

Motion detector: a hand-held controller that detects acceleration or movement in several directions, originally gaining popularity with the Nintendo Wii.

Assessment preparation

LO1: Understand digital game types and platforms		
Mark band 1	Mark band 2	Mark band 3
Produces a summary of digital gaming hardware platforms, reviewing a limited range of platforms from different generations which demonstrates a limited understanding. Demonstrates a basic understanding of gaming platform capabilities and limitations.	Produces a summary of digital gaming hardware platforms, reviewing a range of platforms from different generations which demonstrates a sound understanding. Demonstrates a sound understanding of gaming platform capabilities and limitations.	Produces a summary of digital gaming hardware platforms, reviewing a wide range of platforms from different generations which demonstrates a thorough understanding. Demonstrates a thorough understanding of gaming platform capabilities and limitations.
Mark band 1	Mark band 2	Mark band 3
Produces a brief summary of the evolution of digital game characteristics from a limited range of genres. Gives explanations, with limited accuracy, of game objectives from a limited range of digital games.	Produces a clear summary of the evolution of digital game characteristics from a range of genres. Gives mostly accurate explanations of game objectives from a range of digital games.	A detailed analysis of digital games evolution and their characteristics from a wide range of genres. Gives fully accurate explanations of game objectives from a wide range of digital games.

Assessment guidance

The OCR set assignment

When completing your work for the OCR set assignment, you will need to:

- summarise the evolution of gaming platforms in your own words
- describe the capabilities and limitations of a range of platforms
- summarise the evolution of digital games and their characteristics
- describe the game objectives from a range of different games.

What do the command words mean?

Wide range [platforms] and thorough understanding: A wide range is five or more. The thorough understanding can be demonstrated through depth, breadth or a combination. Breadth is the number of different platforms and types, whereas depth would be the detail in the descriptions of selected platform types.

Thorough understanding [platform capabilities/limitations]: This can be demonstrated through depth, breadth or a combination. Breadth would be the number of different platforms that are covered whereas depth would be the descriptive detail in the capabilities and limitations.

Detailed analysis [of games evolution]: This should be a detailed summary of the development of game genres over a period of time and how relatively new genres have evolved. Note a wide range [of genres] is accepted as five or more.

Fully [accurate explanations of objectives]: This should be a fairly comprehensive and correct summary of the game objectives (i.e. what the player must do in a game) using specific examples. A wide range is again accepted as five or more.

LO2 Be able to plan a digital game concept

Links to other units

You can find further information on planning and pre-production techniques in **unit R081**.

Interpreting the client/focus group and target audience requirements

This is a creative unit and client briefs will be open to interpretation using your own imagination. A brief will not say much about the game concept that you are to develop – it sets a theme but the rest will be up to you. Keep in mind that the game concept must be appropriate for the intended target audience so make sure you understand who they are.

Think about what options exist for satisfying the needs of the client and target audience, while designing an interesting and creative new game. The planning for this unit will be the whole design process, since you will be planning the design of a new game without actually creating it. General planning techniques will need to include a range of concepts and visualisation sketches. You may also need to storyboard the narrative or gameplay to illustrate what happens as the player progresses through the levels.

Generating original ideas for a new game

Your ideas should be imaginative, creative and original. A description of a game that is very similar to something that already exists would not be a strong approach. Aim to come up with at least three ideas for any scenario. These should comment on:

- **key game play outlines:** what the player has to do
- **genre:** will probably fall into one or more of the established game genres
- **concept:** what the game is all about, and how it will work
- **narrative:** the story to the game
- **characters:** the player character and other non-player characters (NPC) in the game
- **locations:** where the game world is set.

Assessment preparation

LO2: Be able to plan a digital game concept		
Mark band 1	Mark band 2	Mark band 3
Produces an interpretation from the client/focus group requirements for a digital game concept which meets few of the requirements.	Produces an interpretation from the client/focus group requirements for a digital game concept which meets most of the requirements.	Produces an interpretation from the client/focus group requirements for a digital game concept which fully meets the requirements.
Produces a limited identification of target audience requirements.	Produces a clear identification of target audience requirements.	Produces a clear and detailed identification of target audience requirements.
Generates a few original ideas for a new game, with limited reference to key game play outlines and limited consideration of the success criteria.	Generates some original ideas for a new game, with some reference to key game play outlines and some consideration of the success criteria.	Generates many original ideas for a new game, with extensive and clear reference to key game play outlines and thorough consideration of the success criteria.
Draws upon limited skills/knowledge/understanding from other units in the specification.	Draws upon some relevant skills/knowledge/understanding from other units in the specification.	Clearly draws upon relevant skills/knowledge/understanding from other units in the specification.

Assessment guidance

The OCR set assignment

When completing your work for the OCR set assignment, you will need to:

- produce your own interpretation of the client brief
- identify the target audience and what they will want from the game concept
- describe a set of success criteria for the game concept
- generate a range of ideas for a new and original game
- use knowledge and skills from other units such as R081 or R082.

LO3 Be able to design a digital game proposal

Links to other units

You can find further information on pre-production techniques in LO2 of **unit R081**.

Design constraints and opportunities

The next step before producing your game proposal is to choose one of your ideas from LO2. This will be developed further in LO3. Then identify any design constraints and opportunities for your chosen idea. Items to consider include:

- **availability of assets:** sourced, created and any copyright issues
- **target platform for the game:** PC, console, handheld, smartphone/tablet
- **development timescales:** an estimate of how long it will take to develop the game
- **development costs:** closely linked to the development timescales
- **distribution channels:** how the game would be marketed.

Creating visualisation diagrams

Games are visual products. A lengthy description might be clear to you but a client or games developer would get a much clearer idea of what the game would look like from a set of detailed visualisation diagrams. You can use your skills from R081 and produce a range of visualisations that include:

- **game characters:** main player plus any NPC (non-player characters)

Figure 11.2 Game visualisation created in Photoshop

- **options for character customisation:** such as gender, clothing, car type, colour
- **game start screen (or menu):** but also the end screen and additional setup/configuration screens
- **built-in quizzes:** if applicable
- **battle system:** if applicable; for example, status screens, radar, inventory, options to choose tactics
- **upgrade methodology:** how the player can improve their chances (for example, more equipment or armour); show these upgrades in different diagrams.

The visualisation diagrams should show the game world or environment (what the player sees when playing the game). This is a fundamental part of the game concept and proposal.

Create a game proposal

This will be the main product outcome from the unit. A good approach is to create this as a formal document, with a front cover title, contents page and then multiple pages with subheadings to explain:

- **game outline:** what it is all about
- **game objectives:** what the player must do in the game
- **target audience and PEGI rating:** who the game is aimed at, why it is suitable for them and what age rating (using PEGI guidelines)
- **game structure:** for example, the traditional three parts/acts/chapters to establish the game world, work through the game play and have a main challenge at the end
- **genre:** for example, action, sports, role playing game, quest, strategy
- **narrative structure:** describe the storyline, what actions have taken place, what actions will occur in the game, identify events based on specific actions by the character, write a short script for any dialogue within the game
- **characters:** for both player and non-player
- **visual style:** for example, period, location, game world, environment, theme, whether it is first person or third person, selectable views, realism
- **sounds:** for example, background music, water, vehicles, racing, shooting, explosions, wind, rain, and so on. Make sure you think about the three categories of background sounds, environment sounds and actions/events
- **scoring systems:** if there is one, how it works, whether it is time or points based
- **downloadable content:** explain if any extras can be downloaded within the game to achieve a goal.

Keep in mind that the game objectives are what the player needs to achieve or complete as part of the gameplay. They can be mini-objectives as part of a level or the overall main objective for the whole game. The achievement of mini-objectives helps to engage the player and maintain interest throughout the game. It can form an important part of progression to the next level.

Game play

Narrative (storyline): a game that has a strong narrative is said to have a very definite storyline. There is a clear purpose and reason for the character play. Games with a strong narrative include many role player (RPG), first person shooter (FPS) and action/adventure. Games such as racing or puzzle games generally do not have a strong narrative. As a designer, you will need to consider whether your target audience will like games with a strong narrative. Alternatively, the immediate satisfaction of winning a racing game or solving a puzzle could be more appealing.

Interactions: the gameplay will involve a series of interactions with other characters and items in the game world. This could relate to a discussion or confrontation with another character. Alternatively, the narrative (storyline) may list a series of actions and events that the player must complete in order to complete the level. A simple example would be the opening of a door with a key – but where does the key come from? If the key is originally protected by another character that must be found, then a series of interactions are created that begin to define the gameplay.

By combining a series of levels with increasing difficulty, a larger game can be produced. Each level may still follow the three-act structure and the increasing difficulty will satisfy the need for achievement and success in the game.

Legislation

You need to consider permissions and implications of use for any assets or ideas (the ideas of somebody else are a form of intellectual property). You should also consider the PEGI rating restrictions on content, taking into account your chosen target audience age range.

Links to other units

You can find further information on legislation in LO2 of **unit R082**.

You can find information on using version control in LO3 of **unit R081**.

Assessment preparation

LO3: Be able to design a digital game proposal		
Mark band 1	Mark band 2	Mark band 3
Identifies an idea for a game which makes limited reference to design constraints and lists a few opportunities which have limited appropriateness, given the original idea.	Identifies an idea for a game which makes some reference to design constraints and lists some opportunities, most of which are appropriate, given the original idea.	Identifies an idea for a game which makes full and clear reference to design constraints and lists many opportunities, all of which are appropriate, given the original idea.
Creates a game proposal with a brief explanation of some of the game components.	Creates a game proposal with a sound explanation of many of the game components.	Creates a game proposal with a detailed explanation of most of the game components.
Visualisations of the game are sometimes appropriate and concepts are presented with limited detail.	Visualisations of the game are mostly appropriate and concepts are clearly presented.	Visualisations of the game are consistently appropriate and concepts are clearly and comprehensively presented.
Demonstrates a limited understanding of legislation in relation to the use of assets, ideas and concepts as part of a game design proposal, which is occasionally accurate.	Demonstrates a sound understanding of legislation in relation to the use of assets, ideas and concepts as part of a game design proposal, which is mostly accurate.	Demonstrates a thorough understanding of legislation in relation to the use of assets, ideas and concepts as part of a game design proposal, which is consistently accurate.
Occasionally saves electronic files using appropriate file and folder names.	Mostly saves electronic files using file and folder names and structures which are consistent and appropriate.	Consistently saves electronic files using file and folder names and structures which are consistent and appropriate.

Assessment guidance

The OCR set assignment

When completing your work for the OCR set assignment, you will need to:

- develop your idea for a game that takes into account the design constraints
- create a proposal for a new game concept that makes reference to the game components
- create a series of visualisation diagrams for the game concept
- describe the legal restrictions regarding the use of any assets and ideas in the game concept
- use appropriate file and folder naming conventions to organise your work.

What do the command words mean?

Full and clear [reference to design constraints]: This should be a comprehensive summary of constraints such as assets, platform, timescales, costs and distribution.

Detailed [explanation of most game components]: The proposal should include reference to components such as game characters, objectives, structure, narrative, mechanics, interactions and visual style.

Consistently appropriate and comprehensive [visualisations]: These should have a clear connection to the client brief and intended game proposal, illustrating key features of the game such as game characters, the game environment and what the player will see on the display screen.

Thorough [understanding of legislation]: This should be applied to the actual assets that you intend to use. Their use should also be in a commercial context and not just education.

Consistently appropriate [files and folders]: This means that the development of the game proposal should be documented using different version numbers and with descriptive file names, with assets stored in suitable folders.

LO4 Be able to review a digital game proposal

Review a game proposal

One of the most significant factors is whether the game design could be a commercial success. This means considering whether the needs of the client have been met and whether the game concept will appeal to a large number of people.

Consider these questions when reviewing your work.

- Does the concept of the game design meet the client brief?
- Is the game design suitable for the client's purposes *and* the target audience?
- Is the narrative and genre fit for the client's purposes?
- Does the game design differ from existing games on the market? Are there any unique or innovative ideas which are new? At this level, the main aim is to recognise what has been produced and whether the work represents new and creative thinking.

Identify areas for improvement and further development of a game design concept

Think about what improvements you could make. This may include comments on the game platform, game narrative, environment and terrain, character types/appearance and sounds.

Assessment preparation

LO4: Be able to review a digital game proposal		
Mark band 1	Mark band 2	Mark band 3
Produces a game proposal review with a limited explanation of game components, narrative and game play. Shows limited consideration to the way in which elements integrate to form a playable game.	Produces a game proposal review with a considered explanation of game components, narrative and game play. Shows some consideration to the way in which elements integrate to form a playable game.	Produces a game proposal review with a detailed and thorough explanation of game components, narrative and game play. Shows full consideration to the way in which elements integrate to form a playable game.
Mark band 1	Mark band 2	Mark band 3
Review identifies areas for improvement and further development of the games design concept, some of which are appropriate and sometimes are explained.	Review identifies areas for improvement and further development of the games design concept, which are mostly appropriate and explained well.	Review identifies areas for improvement and further development of the games design concept, which are wholly appropriate and justified.

Assessment guidance

The OCR set assignment

When completing your work for the OCR set assignment, you will need to:

- produce your own review of the game proposal that you have created
- comment on the integration of the game components and how this creates a playable game
- identify what could be improved further.

What do the command words mean?

Detailed and thorough [review of proposal]: This means commenting on all the game components, narrative and game play as stated in the proposal (not related to the process through the unit).

Appropriate and justified [areas for improvement]: The areas for improvement and development of the game concept should be relevant and supported by your reasons why.

R092 Developing digital games

About this unit

R092 is about creating a playable game. You will investigate game engine software and hardware before planning, creating, testing and reviewing a playable game to meet a client brief. It is assumed that the basic game concepts and structure have already been produced by a game designer and it is now necessary to develop those concepts into a playable game.

Resources for this unit

Hardware: Computer system.

Software: Games development applications, such as GameMaker or Clickteam Fusion 2.5.

Learning outcomes

LO1 Understand game creation hardware, software and peripherals

LO2 Be able to plan the creation of a digital game

LO3 Be able to create a digital game

LO4 Be able to review the creation of a digital game

LO1 Understand game creation hardware, software and peripherals

Capabilities and limitations of software applications

There are several popular game engines and editors, each with their own features and capabilities for both 2D and 3D game creation. App development software can also be used to create games for use on smartphones, both Apple iOS and Android.

Games can be coded using computer programming languages such as Visual Basic, C++ or Java. However, it is more likely that you will use a games editor or games engine to create a playable game. These provide a range of high-level functions that simplify the game creation process. The most popular are shown in the table below.

Many commercially available games are supplied with a 'level editor'. This enables you to create new levels and customise the game play. For the purposes of this unit, you will most likely create a new game using a game engine rather than a customised level using an editor.

In general, a level editor will only allow you to modify or customise a game concept that already exists. A game engine will allow you to create a new game from scratch.

Have a look at the game engine software that you have available. Find out some information about the capabilities and features, either from the manufacturer's website, or the built-in help.

The additional options for this unit include app development and software development kits (SDK). Many people create games for a smartphone or tablet using these methods, which would be a great next step after this introductory unit on game development.

Hardware and peripherals required to create and test digital games

The hardware and peripherals needed to create and test digital games will depend on what target platform the game is intended for.

- Computer system for development and possibly a simulator or test bed for the target platform. For example, this could be a simulator for a smartphone, console or a physical tablet device. It is possible that the target platform will also be a computer system, but that doesn't necessarily mean you would use the same computer for both development and functional testing, since the specifications may be different.
- Peripherals, such as speakers, are likely to be needed for testing so that the player can hear any sound effects.
- Interface controls, such as keyboard and mouse for development, and possibly a gaming handset or joystick for testing.

Game Engine	Distributor	Description
GameMaker	YoYo Games	2D game engine with simple user interface
Clickteam Fusion 2.5	Clickteam	Powerful games editor with multi-platform output
Games Factory 2	Clickteam	Drag and drop games development functionality

Assessment preparation

LO1: Understand game creation hardware, software and peripherals		
Mark band 1	Mark band 2	Mark band 3
Produces a summary of the capabilities and limitations of a limited range of 2D and 3D software used for digital game creation which demonstrates limited understanding. Demonstrates a limited understanding of gaming platform hardware and peripherals required to create and test digital games.	Produces a summary of the capabilities and limitations of a range of 2D and 3D software used for digital game creation which demonstrates sound understanding. Demonstrates a sound understanding of gaming platform hardware and peripherals required to create and test digital games.	Produces a summary of the capabilities and limitations of a limited range of 2D and 3D software used for digital game creation which demonstrates thorough understanding. Demonstrates a thorough understanding of gaming platform hardware and peripherals required to create and test digital games.

Assessment guidance

The OCR set assignment

When completing your work for the OCR set assignment, you will need to:

● summarise the capabilities and limitations of a range of both 2D and 3D software that is used to create digital games

● describe a range of hardware and peripherals that are needed to create and test digital games.

What do the command words mean?

Range [2D and 3D software]: This is accepted as three or more, which should cover both 2D and 3D game engines. A thorough understanding can only be evidenced using the candidate's own summaries and commentary (do not copy and paste information for this).

Thorough [understanding platform hardware]: This should be a comprehensive summary of platform hardware and peripherals for both game development and testing.

LO2 Be able to plan the creation of a digital game

Links to other units

You can find further information on planning and pre-production techniques in **unit R081**.

Interpreting client requirements

For the purposes of a digital game, the more specific aspects should identify a number of criteria, such as the:

● target platform that the game will be played on

● genre of the game (or multiple genres)

● visual style of the game

● intended age rating for the game and its content.

These factors must be taken into account while thinking about the target audience and intended PEGI rating.

Key aspects of game creation

As part of the planning, consideration should be given to key information that would normally be identified in the client's requirements specification. These include:

● **game objectives:** these need to be programmed into the game play

● **original concept and narrative:** the effective story that is played out in the game; is there anything to be learned from the game or is it just for entertainment purposes?

● **audio and visual style for the genre:** whether the player's view should be in the first person or third person, and whether audio is consistent with the genre (for example, fast-paced for an action game)

- **assets required in game creation:** includes character objects, obstacles, doors, buildings, textures, game features and objects, together with any sound effects
- **hardware, including peripherals:** for creating and testing the game
- **software:** export formats should be known before creating the game to ensure it can be saved in a suitable format to meet the client requirements.

Creating and maintaining a test plan

Testing a game is a continuous process throughout the development. Items to be tested can be thought of at the start of the planning stage. As the development progresses, it is not unusual to add extra tests. The purpose of testing is to find and debug faults. These should be put right as part of the production, with a full and final test once the game is finished. A formal test plan, in a table, is a good approach for this. Some areas for testing include:

- **movement:** are the game controls (for example, keyboard/mouse or joystick) suitable – do they control speed and direction, or other movements such as jumping or running?
- **scoring:** is the scoring system suitable – does it provide feedback to the player, or bonus points for extra achievement, or a table of high scores?
- **interactions:** are there interactions between the player and game objects, or other game characters?
- **obstacles:** are the obstacles sufficient – would more obstacles give the player a sense of achievement as they develop and use additional skills?
- **characters:** would the game benefit by adding more non-player characters (NPC) to improve player interaction or increase the level of difficulty to the game?

Planning the structure of a game

The structure of a game can be planned using a game flow diagram. This illustrates how the player would move through the game from start to finish. More complex games, such as strategy games, may have numerous pathways through the game.

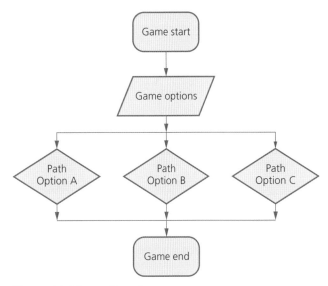

Figure 12.1 Game flow diagram

Character creation

You need to plan the sprites and shapes for the game characters so that they can be imported into the game world. Note, in this unit, this is not about creating visualisation diagrams.

Game play

The style of gameplay should be clear from the client requirements, identification of game genre and the game flow diagram. You could summarise this as part of your planning so that you are clear about what is required.

Scoring systems

This might be defined in the specification from the client. If not, you could ask the client; you may be given a free rein to choose how this should work. There could be points for achieving some game objectives and/or points based on time (for example, a fast route earns bonus points).

Sourcing and storing assets

Before actually starting to create the game, it is a good idea to collect everything that will be needed. This may include:

- component images
- textures
- sprites
- scripting
- sound
- video
- animation.

Store all assets in an assets folder where you can locate them once working in the game development software.

Legislation

This applies to the use of assets within the game. Character names and any resemblance to existing characters (such as from films, comics or other games) is likely to be a problem. Refer back to R081 for further information.

Assessment preparation

LO2: Be able to plan the creation of a digital game		
Mark band 1	**Mark band 2**	**Mark band 3**
Produces an interpretation from the client brief for a digital game which meets few of the client requirements.	Produces an interpretation from the client brief for a digital game which meets most of the client requirements.	Produces an interpretation from the client brief for a digital game which fully meets the client requirements.
Produces a limited identification of target audience requirements.	Produces a clear identification of target audience requirements.	Produces a clear and detailed identification of target audience requirements.
Draws upon limited skills/knowledge/understanding from other units in the specification.	Draws upon some relevant skills/knowledge/understanding from other units in the specification.	Clearly draws upon relevant skills/knowledge/understanding from other units in the specification.
Demonstrates a basic understanding of the key aspects of game creation. The contextualisation of these aspects to the brief is limited.	Demonstrates a sound understanding of the key aspects of game creation. The contextualisation of these aspects to the brief is sound.	Demonstrates a thorough understanding of the key aspects of game creation. The contextualisation of these aspects to the brief is comprehensive.
Creates a test plan for the digital game which tests some of the functionality.	Creates a test plan for the digital game which tests most of the functionality, identifying expected outcomes.	Creates a clear and detailed test plan for the digital game which fully tests the functionality, listing tests, expected and actual outcomes and identifying re-tests.
Applies basic design techniques to the planning of the game structure, including limited reference to pathways, game play and game mechanics and with limited consideration of the success criteria.	Applies sound design techniques to the planning of the game structure, including some reference to pathways, game play and game mechanics and with some consideration of the success criteria.	Applies detailed design techniques to the planning of the game structure, including extensive reference to pathways, game play and game mechanics and with thorough consideration of the success criteria.
Sources and stores the assets to be used in the digital game occasionally using methods that are appropriate.	Sources and stores the assets to be used in the digital game mostly using methods that are appropriate.	Sources and stores the assets to be used in the digital game consistently using methods that are appropriate.
Demonstrates a limited understanding of legislation in relation to the use of assets, ideas and concepts in a digital game.	Demonstrates a sound understanding of legislation in relation to the use of assets, ideas and concepts in a digital game.	Demonstrates a thorough understanding of legislation in relation to the use of assets, ideas and concepts in a digital game.

Assessment guidance

The OCR set assignment

When completing your work for the OCR set assignment, you will need to:

- produce your own interpretation of the client brief
- identify the target audience and what they will want from the digital game
- use knowledge and skills from other units such as R081 or R082
- discuss the key aspects of game creation in relation to the digital game that you have planned
- produce a test plan to check the functionality of the digital game

- identify the success criteria for the digital game
- plan the structure to the game using established design techniques that identify the pathways, game play and game mechanics
- source and store the assets that will be needed for the digital game
- describe the legal restrictions regarding the use of any assets within the digital game.

What do the command words mean?

Fully [interpretation of the brief]: This needs to be your own individual ideas and thoughts on what is required that expands on what is given in the scenario and brief.

Clear and detailed [target audience]: This should be a clear definition of who the target audience is and what they will want from the game.

Draws on [knowledge, skills and understanding]: This must be from other units and not something that is already in R092

Thorough [understanding aspects of game creation]: This should explain the planned approach that will cover the game objectives, narrative, visual style, assets and hardware/software. A **comprehensive** contextualisation will apply all of these aspects to the game that is being created.

Clear and detailed [test plan - functionality]: The tests should be for the functionality of the game and not the visual appeal. Functionality is more about how playable the game is and whether it works or crashes.

Detailed [design techniques, pathways, success criteria]: This should include planning documents for the game flow, pathways (routes through the game), how the game mechanics will work and what the player will do through interactions.

Consistently [appropriate storage of assets]: This should identify how and where the assets will be stored for use within the game, using formats that are compatible, appropriate for the game engine and in a suitable location.

Thorough [understanding of legislation]: This should be applied to the actual assets that you intend to use. Their use should also be in a commercial context and not just education.

LO3 Be able to create a digital game

Software features needed for the creation of a game

The key features that you will need to cover (note some of these will be software specific):

- use of libraries
- drag and drop
- object properties
- event and actions
- triggers
- collisions.

Using geometric parameters

You must consider the geometric parameters to ensure that the game functions and scale is correct. You will learn how to manipulate objects and environments to ensure these are appropriate for a playable game. For example, these may include:

- **conversion:** objects within the game might convert from one shape to another based on an event or trigger; the size and shape must be converted correctly for the game to work with both versions
- **scaling:** an example here would be the inclusion of similar game characters which should be a similar size and hence scale
- **creation:** any objects for use in the game world must be created at the correct size
- **use of grid settings:** these can be set up in the development software so that a suitable size and scale is easily seen
- **spatial relationships:** an example here would be that the player character is a suitable size and scale for the objects in the game world; this means that the character can pass through a doorway when needed.

Setting parameters of objects and environments

When an object is placed in the game world, one of the first activities is to modify its properties. Typical parameters would be:

- **name:** an easily recognisable abbreviation would be typical for this
- **transparency:** are there any parts of the object that are transparent so that the player can see past or through the object?
- **visibility:** similar to transparency, except some objects might be set to be invisible until something happens in the game, such as an event or trigger
- **effects:** anything that is applied to the object
- **colour:** usually a fill colour, which needs to contrast against the background
- **textures:** to make the game objects look more realistic.

Importing assets

Unless these are built into the game library, it might be that the assets that you have stored in a folder should first be imported into the game development software. These can include:

- graphics
- images
- textures
- sounds
- video
- animation
- text.

Interactions

Interactions occur when two objects meet within the game. This can be through one of the following actions:

- **collision:** between the player object and something else in the game
- **triggers:** for example, reaching a particular score within the game
- **activating an object:** for example, from the proximity between two objects such as opening a door when they become close
- **behaviours:** what it does

- **pop-up messages:** triggered by an event or action
- **shake, fades and sounds:** changes that can be applied.

Game-play controls

This is how the player will operate the digital game. It could be from:

- mouse (both mouse movement and mouse click)
- keyboard (the keys used for moving the player object must be clear)
- dialogue activation
- start/pause/exit facilities or menus.

Using algorithms

These can be found in one or more of the:

- scoring systems (the points accumulated through the game play)
- timing systems (the game timer)
- game triggers (starts a process or action)
- speed of movement (for example, high/low).

Using GameMaker

GameMaker is a 2D games engine used to create a variety of computer games. Typical examples include racing, maze and strategy games.

Creating the basics of a new game consists of six steps.

1 Add sprites and set the properties.
2 Add sounds.
3 Add a background (load the background graphics or image for the game).
4 Add objects and set the properties/events (create the events in the game based on the interaction of game objects; examples include movement, collisions, interactions, mouse/keyboard control and scoring).
5 Add a room (define the size and shape of the game room; although it is called a game room, really it is just a place where the game will be played and is not like a physical 3D room).

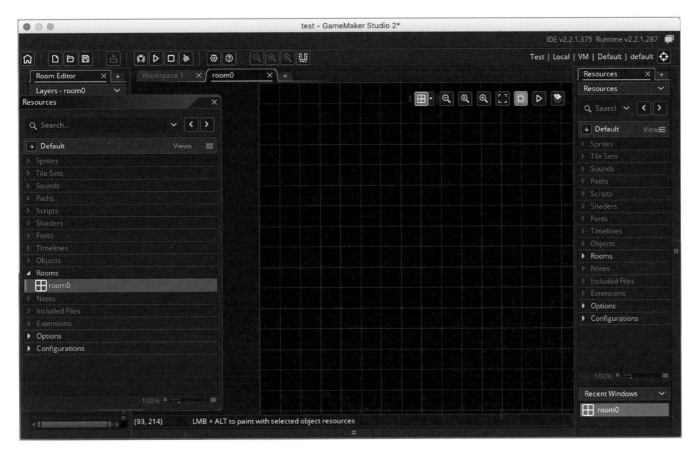

Figure 12.2 GameMaker development software

6 Play and test the game (test the game play using the 'play game' button on the toolbar, which is the green 'play' arrow; GameMaker will build the game and display the game room ready to start play). If something does not work as planned, pressing the 'escape' key will return to the GameMaker development environment. Make any changes required and re-test the game.

Using Fusion 2.5

Fusion 2.5 is the latest game development software (at the time of writing) by Clickteam, which also produced Games Factory 2.

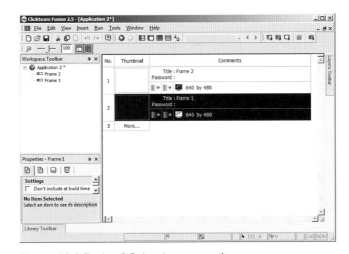

Figure 12.3 Fusion 2.5 development software

Links to other units

You can find further information on using version control when creating a game in LO3 of **unit R081**.

Saving and exporting a digital game

This should always be in a format appropriate to the game development software being used, so that further edits and changes can be made later. The game should also be exported in a format that can be played on a different computer system.

Assessment preparation

LO3: Be able to create a digital game		
Mark band 1	**Mark band 2**	**Mark band 3**
Needs considerable support to select and use appropriate software features to create a digital game.	Needs some support to select and use appropriate software features to create a digital game.	Independently selects and uses appropriate software features to create a digital game.
Occasionally uses basic geometric parameters to manipulate object(s) and environment(s), displaying limited accuracy.	Uses geometric parameters most of the time to manipulate object(s) and environment(s), displaying some accuracy.	Consistently uses geometric parameters to manipulate object(s) and environment(s), displaying excellent accuracy.
Occasionally uses properties to set parameters and manipulate (where appropriate) a limited number of objects and environments.	Mostly uses properties to set parameters most of the time and manipulate (where appropriate) some objects and environments.	Consistently uses properties to set parameters and manipulate (where appropriate) all relevant objects and environments.
Imports assets into the digital game, some of which are not appropriate.	Imports assets and combines components that are mostly appropriate throughout the digital game.	Imports assets and combines components, which are consistently appropriate, effectively throughout the digital game.
Mark band 1	**Mark band 2**	**Mark band 3**
Creates a limited range of basic interactions using the software to aid in game-play experience. The interactions have limited appropriateness to the brief.	Creates a range of appropriate interactions, some advanced, using the software to enhance the game-play experience. The interactions are mostly appropriate to the client brief.	Creates a wide range of appropriate interactions, effectively using the software to enhance the game-play experience. The interactions are consistently appropriate to the client brief.
Creates game-play controls that are sometimes appropriate and partly operational. Uses basic algorithms which are sometimes appropriate. The algorithms work some of the time.	Creates game-play controls that are mostly appropriate and mostly operational. Uses basic algorithms which are mostly appropriate. The algorithms work most of the time.	Creates game-play controls that are consistently appropriate and fully operational. Uses basic algorithms which are consistently appropriate. The algorithms work consistently.
Saves, exports and publishes the digital game with some components and assets working, to form a partially functional game that in part reflects the game design in relation to the client brief.	Saves, exports and publishes the digital game with most components and assets working, to form a fully functional game that generally reflects the game design in relation to the client brief.	Saves, exports and publishes the digital game with all components and assets working, to form a fully functional game that fully reflects the game design in relation to the client brief.
Occasionally saves electronic files using appropriate file and folder names and structures.	Mostly saves electronic files using file and folder names and structures which are consistent and appropriate.	Consistently saves electronic files using file and folder names and structures which are consistent and appropriate.

Assessment guidance

The OCR set assignment

When completing your work for the OCR set assignment, you will need to:

- show how you have used geometric parameters to manipulate objects and the game environment
- set the properties for objects and environments within the game
- import the assets and combine the game components to create a playable game
- create suitable interactions within the game and its objects, applying algorithms where appropriate
- save and export the digital game in suitable formats to meet the client requirements
- use appropriate file and folder naming conventions to organise your work.

Independently [uses software features]: This means you must apply what you have learned without additional assistance from others when completing the assignment.

Consistently [uses geometric parameters]: This means that objects within the game are clearly shown to be appropriate dimensions within the game world.

Consistently [sets properties and parameters]: This means that the properties of the game objects will enable the game interactions to work as expected.

Consistently appropriate [import of assets and combine components]: This means that the game assets and components have been imported for use and combined so that the display and game play work as intended.

Wide range [effective interactions]: A wide range is accepted as five or more. Interactions are between objects and game characters.

Fully operational [game play controls]: This means that the final game can be controlled effectively by the play from start to finish.

Consistently [uses appropriate algorithms]: This means that any algorithms for scoring, timing, triggers and speed control are appropriate for the working game.

Fully [functional game]: This means that a player can complete the game from start to finish without errors or crashes.

Consistently appropriate [files and folders]: This means that the development of the character should be documented using different version numbers and with descriptive file names, with assets stored in suitable folders.

LO4 Be able to review the creation of a digital game

Review a digital game

The most important factors are whether the digital game is playable and fit for purpose. This means considering whether the needs of the client have been met and whether the functionality of the game is as expected.

Consider these questions when reviewing your work.

1 Does the implementation of the game meet the client brief?

2 Is the game suitable for the client's purposes *and* the target audience?

3 Is the narrative and genre fit for the client's purposes?

4 Having tested and played the game several times using different strategies, does the game actually work?

Final testing of the digital game

You should still aim to complete this by yourself. Whatever game engine software you are using, the aims and objectives of testing are the same. At this level, testing is based on playing the game to check the functionality of game play.

There are two approaches to consider.

1 Functional testing to make sure that everything works correctly according to the original brief/specification.

2 General software testing to try and break it or crash the game/computer.

The second approach is just as likely to find problems as the first, since the client brief is not going to cover every possible situation. For example, have a few other software applications running in the background to see if the game or computer system becomes unstable. Try and get the player object out of the game world either by running or jumping at each room boundary. Using this approach, ignore the main objectives of the game play. Instead of shooting the monster, what happens if you try to blast your way through a fixed wall in the game room? This is one area where an imaginative and creative mind-set can identify problems or unforeseen errors that would be missed by conventional approaches.

On the next page is an example of a test plan table. It identifies what is being tested, the criteria for pass or fail, and space to record the test result. When using a test plan and fixing the problems identified, always re-test the game in full to make sure all aspects still work. With any software development, making one change to fix something can cause new problems elsewhere.

Comments may also be put into the Pass/fail results column. The tests shown are general examples and you will need to define your own tests for the game created. This will also depend on what game engine software you used, and the rules/boundaries of the defined game.

Identifying areas for improvement and further development

Think about what improvements could be made. This may include comments on the colours, characters, game environment, interactions, triggers and sounds. Further development might include multiple levels with increasing level of difficulty, rather than just improving the one you have already created.

Test	Criteria for pass/fail	Pass/fail result	Errors/results
Player object shown in the game			
Player object moves left			
Player object moves right			
Graphics are displayed and rendered correctly			
Game and computer system are stable			
Speed of game play suitable			

Assessment preparation

LO4: Be able to review the creation of a digital game		
Mark band 1	**Mark band 2**	**Mark band 3**
Produces a review of the digital game which demonstrates a limited understanding of what worked and what did not, making few references back to the brief.	Produces a review of the digital game which demonstrates a reasonable understanding of what worked and what did not, mostly referencing back to the brief.	Produces a review of the digital game which demonstrates a thorough understanding of what worked and what did not, fully referencing back to the brief.
Partly tests the digital game with limited reference to the brief and to a test plan.	Tests most of the digital game with some reference to the brief and to a test plan.	Fully tests the digital game with clear reference to the brief and to a test plan.
Review identifies areas for improvement and further development of the digital game, some of which are appropriate and sometimes are explained.	Review identifies areas for improvement and further development of the digital game, which are mostly appropriate and explained well.	Review identifies areas for improvement and further development of the digital game, which are wholly appropriate and justified.

Assessment guidance

The OCR set assignment

When completing your work for the OCR set assignment, you will need to:

- produce your own review of the digital game that you have created
- document your testing of the game using a test plan
- following on from the review, identify what could be improved further.

What do the command words mean?

Detailed and thorough [review of proposal]: This means commenting on all the final game in terms of what worked and what didn't (not related to the process through the unit).

Fully [tests the game]: This means that all aspects of the game and gameplay are included in a detailed test plan, which links back to the original brief where necessary.

Appropriate and justified [areas for improvement]: The areas for improvement and development of the digital game should be relevant and supported by your reasons why.

Glossary

Advanced features and techniques: include the use of alt-text, rollovers, forms, tables, rich media (sound and video) and embedded maps.

Aperture: you can think of aperture as being the size of the hole in the lens to let light through. A larger aperture means a bigger hole so that more light can pass through.

Aspect ratio: this is the height and width that a digital video can be created, exported and viewed in. Depending on the screen that you are watching a digital video on a process known as letterboxing and pillar-boxing, where two black bars appear either horizontally or vertically at the edges of the video.

Assets: the content collected or created for the final product, such as images, sound and video.

Bronze age: 1970–1980

Codec: stands for 'coder-decoder'. Media is 'encoded', or read by the software. It is then 'decoded' so that media, such as digital video, can be played back. Most codecs compress the original media, reducing the size of the original file. This is important for video files, since they often have large file sizes. Compressed files take up less disk space and can be uploaded and downloaded more quickly.

Commercial: this is when a company or individual produces products to make a profit.

Compression: this is when a digital video sequence is saved in such a way that its file size is reduced. The quality of the video may or may not be reduced depending on the codec used to reduce the size of the video.

Consumer goods: these items include cars, clothing, music, food, jewellery, toiletries, DVDs, downloads that people, or consumers, buy every day.

Conventions: a term used to describe the different ingredients or elements that help audiences understand the genre of a digital video product. For example, a music video for a pop artist may feature the conventions of bright colours, special effects and dance routines.

Create: you need to actually draw the answer.

Display resolution: this is the size of the digital video image. Display resolution is measured in pixels. The device that we watch our digital video on determines the size and density of the pixels.

DPI resolution: a property of an image that states how many 'dots per inch' to use. Printing requires typically 300 dpi whereas web use only needs 72 dpi. This property is also referred to as PPI or pixels per inch and for the purposes of this qualification, either term can be used.

Export: to change the format of a product that is published for use by the client.

Exposure: a key aspect of photography. This is basically a 'quantity' of light, which is determined by how long the shutter is open plus how large the aperture (hole) is in the lens to let the light through. Shutter speed and aperture are the core concepts but the camera's ISO setting can shift these up or down.

Focal points: the place in a panel where the creator wants the reader's eye to be focused.

Frame rate: the frequency that film footage, animation and title and graphics sequences appear on screen when a digital video is watched by the audience.

FPS: the number of frames per second (fps) that are used to create the effect of movement. Examples would be 6, 12 or 24 fps.

Frames: a single scene, drawing or image that forms an animation when multiple frames are viewed in rapid succession.

Genre: a term to describe the way that digital video producers categorise a specific type of digital video. For example, horror and action are different film genres.

Golden age: 1938–1954

Graphic: a combination of multiple assets and text that forms the final product.

Graphical User Interface (GUI): a term used for the layout and display of the display screen, which forms the basis of the way that the user interacts with the product. An effective GUI will be intuitive and easy to use.

Hardware: the equipment to be used, such as computer, display, tablet.

Illustrate: to add images to support the story or information provided in the product.

Improvements: a description of what is needed to make the product better.

Interpretation: reviewing the information provided and taking the relevant information from the text.

Interpretation of the brief: a key element of your planning as an aspiring graphic designer. It must be individual, fit-for-purpose, and express your creative ideas and understanding of digital graphics.

ISO: a camera setting that determines the sensitivity to light levels.

Items: objects that are on a document.

Late Bronze age: 1980–1984

Legislation: a collection of laws.

Lossy compression: lower quality but a smaller file size.

Modern age: 1985–present day

Narrative: explaining events by speaking or writing them down.

Navigation: this is the term used for the way in which an interactive multimedia product directs a user to content through a series of structured buttons and links.

Onomatopoeia: a word that sounds like the thing it is describing, such as *slurp*.

Origin: where something came from or began (the *origins* of a story or concept).

Panel: a container used to contain one scene in a comic strip.

Pixel dimensions: the combination of how many pixels (px) wide by how many pixels high. For example, 3000 px wide × 2000 px high is 6 million px (6 Mpx).

Primary sources: those where you obtain information 'first hand' from an original source and, therefore, typically more reliable.

Public domain: for the purposes of the research in LO1 of R085, this means available to the public on the internet; this is different to a 'Public Domain' status that applies to a piece of creative work where the copyright has expired (see R081).

Purpose: what is it used for; the reason.

Resources: the hardware, software, peripherals and people used to create the assets or product.

Secondary sources: those where the information is obtained 'second hand', or where somebody else has already put their own interpretation on the original information. The accuracy of information might need to be checked.

Shutter speed: the duration that the shutter is open for the photograph to be recorded.

Silver age: 1956–1969

Site map: a visual method to show how a website is constructed and what pages are linked together in a hierarchy.

Software: what programs or applications can be used to create the pre-production documents, which is different to the software used for reports or web research.

Standard features: include the use of images, text and a simple navigation system since these are the basic building blocks of a website.

Story flow: the path of the story from beginning, to middle, to end.

Strengths: the best parts about something; what works really well.

Weaknesses: the worst parts or those that need to be better.

White balance: a camera setting that compensates for lighting to obtain the correct colours.

Workflow: this is the order that the activities will be completed in but can also be the sequence within a software application between importing assets and exporting the final output.

Index